A GOLDEN

STATE OF MIND

GEOFFREY P. WONG

National Library of Canada Cataloguing in Publication Data

Wong, Geoffrey P.
  A golden state of mind

ISBN 1-55212-635-8

  I. Title.
PS3623.O54G64 2001   813'.6   C2001-910263-1

TRAFFORD

This book was published *on-demand* in cooperation with Trafford Publishing.
On-demand publishing is a unique process and service of making a book available for retail
sale to the public taking advantage of on-demand manufacturing and Internet marketing.
On-demand publishing includes promotions, retail sales, manufacturing, order fulfilment,
accounting and collecting royalties on behalf of the author.

Suite 6E, 2333 Government St., Victoria, B.C. V8T 4P4, CANADA
Phone   250-383-6864   Toll-free   1-888-232-4444 (Canada & US)
Fax   250-383-6804   E-mail   sales@trafford.com
Web site   www.trafford.com   TRAFFORD PUBLISHING IS A DIVISION OF TRAFFORD HOLDINGS LTD.
Trafford Catalogue #01-0037   www.trafford.com/robots/01-0037.html

10   9   8   7   6

APPRECIATION AND THANKS TO:

Marc Laven, Monique Laven, and Brian Wong for research.

Terry Stefani, Patricia Davis, Lynda Welter, Patricia Wong, Kenneth Lum, Alison Picard, and Patty Bonnstetter for shape, texture, color, and tone.

Mary Hanna, Roger Morgan, Kelly Craven, Jean Dent, Jeanne Church, Bob Haas, Roxie Daneri, Jim McGinnis, Bill and Sandy Barton, Candy Caldwell, Bob Bates, Jill Telfer, Ted Grebitus, Gail Forbes, Simon Andrews, Blanche Goldstein, David Goldstein, Jean Runyon, Quincy Brown and Kay O'Laughlin, Don and Dori Organ, Marty and Cathy Majestic, Kay Carter, Tom Fat, Louise Kelly, John Brush, Gwen Beauchamp, Lee Welter, Steve Millich, Ray Gee, Ralph Levy, Jack Wolfe, and Bob Tanenbaum for encouragement, criticism, and comment.

Earl and Ruby Wong for inspiration.

GRATEFUL ACKNOWLEDGMENT IS MADE FOR USE OF THE FOLLOWING:

"All Alone Am I" by Manos Hadjidakis-Jean Ioannidis
(English lyrics-Arthur Altman)

"A Toast To California" by James M. Hunt ('12)

"I've Got You Under My Skin" by Cole Porter

"Louie, Louie" by Richard Berry

"Oh, My Papa" by Paul Burkhard
(English lyrics-John Turner-Geoffrey Parsons)

"Scotch And Soda" by Dave Guard

"Star Spangled Banner" by Francis Scott Key

"That'll Be The Day" by Norman Petty-Buddy Holly- Jerry Allison

"True Love" by Cole Porter

"What Is There To Say" by Vernon Duke-E.Y. Harburg

BLUE AND GOLD APOLOGIES TO:

"Hail to California" by Clinton R. Morse (1896)

"All Hail Blue and Gold" by Harold W. Bingham (1906)

In 1874, a wide-eyed teenager, not unlike Jonathan Aldon, the protagonist of this novel, made a pilgrimage from Canton to San Francisco, seeking adventure and fortune in the land of Gold Mountain. This book is dedicated to that teenager and the four generations of his descendants who have lived the elusive and imperfect dream of California-a golden state of mind-empowered by their education and experiences at Cal, the University of California, Berkeley. Go Bears!

Visiting Berkeley . . I strolled of a Sunday afternoon . . over Strawberry Creek, then past the Campanile, down by the library and back out Sather Gate . . That Sunday, I was over whelmed by the thought that I loved this place, this campus-the paths, the trees, flowers, buildings . . Berkeley more than Paris, more than either Cambridge more certainly than Palo Alto-has now and for decades has been known as the place where things begin."

-John Kenneth Galbraith
(MS'30, PhD'34)

"Berkeley - the University - seems to me more and more to be California's highest, most articulate idea of itself, the most coherent perhaps the only coherent-expression of the California possibility."

-Joan Didion ('56)

1

AULD LANG SYNE

Drifting south along the eastern shore of Lake Superior, the small front inhaled the moisture of the muggy summer day. Wobbling across Minnesota, the expanding pattern ballooned to a storm as it limped southward into Iowa. Black and bloated, the maverick disgorged its sodden rain in a short, sustained downpour on the small, whale-shaped lake, churning its normally placid waters.

Two 18-year-old boys standing at the end of a long, narrow dock ignored the torrent drenching their T-shirts, blue jeans, and black high-top tennies.

"Sure going to miss all this, Ziggy," said Jonathan Aldon, the taller, more muscular of the two, brushing away rivulets of warm rain trickling onto his forehead. He had blond, close-cropped hair and bright blue eyes, looks his mother proudly described as "Tab Hunter handsome."

"Like a big hole in the head, Johnny-boy," said Ziggy Atherton.

With his scrawny build, wavy red hair, and freckled face, Ziggy bore a striking resemblance to Howdy Doody. In grammar school, Jonathan had spent hours counting and recounting the freckles on his buddy's face, and Ziggy had been disappointed when the count was always fifty, two more than the forty-eight adorning the face of TV's famous puppet. But when Hawaii and Alaska were admitted as the forty-ninth and fiftieth states, Ziggy proudly claimed his speckled face was now even "more

1

American" than Howdy Doody's.

The two had been inseparable since that day in 1947 when the Athertons' wheezing Packard sputtered out of gas along the main road to Aldon Farms, and Harry, Sr., a disabled veteran and widower raising his young son, Ziggy, hired on as the bookkeeper for Aldon Farms.

As youngsters, Jonathan and Ziggy shadowed their fathers around the vast acreage of Iowa's largest family-owned hog farm, learning the differences between the major swine breeds: American Landrace and Duroc, Poland China and Chester White, Berkshire, Hampshire, and Yorkshire.

In 1951, at the age of 10, the two learned to play ukuleles and began their careers as Aldon and Atherton, "The Amazing Double A's," plinking and singing for anyone who would listen to their renditions of such Clear Lake favorites as "Ghost Riders in The Sky" and "How Much Is That Doggy in The Window?"

Entering high school in the fall of 1955, the pair graduated to steel guitars, fully embracing rock and roll, the new music that local elders branded as "immoral" and "the wailing of the Devil." Adopting the sound of their musical hero, Buddy Holly, and his band, "The Crickets," The Amazing Double A's enjoyed a devoted teenage following throughout Cerro Gordo County.

Tomorrow, Labor Day, would mark the end of the 8-year career of the Amazing Double A's.

"Think of me sloppin' hogs for Aldon Farms, Johnny-boy, while you're rubbin' elbows with them Beatniks and makin' time with those big-chested California girls," said Ziggy, a tinge of envy in his voice. "You sure as hell ain't gonna miss nothin' 'bout Clear Lake."

Jonathan had confided his fascination with Beatniks, artists, poets, and writers, who thumbed their noses at convention. And while Ziggy had no appreciation for Beatniks, he did favor well-endowed women, showing Jonathan a recent pictorial in the September issue of Playboy entitled "Big Boobs of Berkeley," seven pages of bare-chested college girls living at a university boarding house called "Yearning Arms."

"Wonder when the rain will end?" said Jonathan, avoiding the subject nagging him.

"Don't worry about being homesick, Johnny-boy," said Ziggy, reading Jonathan's mind. You'll be back at Christmas. It'll be like old times for the Amazing Double A's. Nothin's gonna change."

"Yes," said Jonathan, "won't be long. Only 117 days."

Almost an eternity, he thought.

Squinting through the watery blur, Jonathan surveyed the familiar scenes of his life. Across the mile-long lake, the summer boys scurried about Old Man Smith's Boathouse, tying down bucking rowboats. Along Main Street, wooden booths festooned in holiday bunting, American flags swirling red, white, and blue. The shining, bald head of Mr. Vickery at the Corner Drug Store bobbed up and down among new shipments of red licorice and button candy.

"Johnny-boy, let's bomb the buoys for old times sake!"

Selecting small, flat stones from a stack near the end of the dock and carefully gauging the distance to two orange buoys bobbing on the lake surface 30 feet away, each gingerly hefted a stone. Jonathan, a southpaw, sighted the left one emblazoned with an "A" while Ziggy concentrated on the right one bearing an "F." In their younger days, Ziggy was the more accurate, but in recent years, Jonathan had perfected a touch and rhythm that made him proficient in hitting drifting flotsam.

On the count of "three," they pitched the stones underhanded, flipping them with their forefingers and thumbs, the missiles sailing in a high arc, arriving simultaneously, striking the buoys sharply with dull thuds, ricocheting into the turbulent water.

Facing each other, they shouted in unison,

"Shit flies both ways!"

Their exclamation was lost in the crackle and boom of the storm spitting a parade of lightning bolts above Main Street.

Down the shoreline, Jonathan saw the silhouettes of the regulars pressed up against the windows of the Blue Horizon Inn, straining for a view of the heavenly light show.

"Johnny-boy, smell that toe-zone from the lightnin'."

"Ozone, Ziggy," corrected Jonathan softly, closing his eyes, deeply inhaling the pungent scent.

"Yeah, you'll sure miss the toe-zone, too," said Ziggy, gently goosing his friend. "Mother Nature's little farts made special for Clear Lake."

Several patrons of the Blue Horizon, waving long-neck beer bottles, staggered onto the dock behind the inn for a better view of the aerial pyrotechnics. Through the rumble and crackle, the inn's

3

jukebox blared the boys' favorite Buddy Holly tune, "That'll Be The Day."

The Amazing Double A's sang the lyrics, undulating from side-to-side, playing imaginary guitars.

You say you'll never leave me,
but that was a lie,
'Cause that'll be the day
when I die.

Thunder and lightning now exploded directly over Clear Lake in a series of booms and flashes, chasing the beer-drinking gawkers back into the cozy warmth of the Blue Horizon.

"Buddy Holly will always be the greatest, Johnny-boy. We'll always be buddies, too," said Ziggy, smiling, pleased with his pun. "Take good care of Buddy's glasses. They'll bring you a pile of luck someday," he said, referring to Jonathan's prized possession.

"Can't see you off tomorrow, Johnny-boy. Gotta help set up the fireworks show." Shaking Jonathan's hand firmly, Ziggy said, "Take care, kiddo, and cop a feel off those big-titted college girls for old Ziggy, you hear?"

"I'll write soon," said Jonathan, feeling a lump form in his throat. "At Christmas, I'll bring back stories that'll curl your toes."

"Right in the old toe-zone," said Ziggy giving his buddy his best Howdy Doody grin.

"Right smack in the old toe-zone," said Jonathan, tapping Ziggy on the chin with a fist, feeling tears welling up in his eyes.

Whirling, Ziggy skipped the length of the dock, ignoring the slickness of the rain soaked boards. Jonathan watched the skinny frame dodge an approaching beer truck, cross North Shore Drive, and disappear around the corner of Mars Hill Drive.

Above Clear Lake, the black thunder clouds parted, revealing the arcs of twin rainbows in the eastern sky.

Tomorrow will be sunny, thought Jonathan, *perfect weather for the Clear Lake Labor Day Celebration.*

He could smell the rows of plump hotdogs and juicy burgers sizzling on the Kiwanis Club charcoal grills. He could see revelers enjoying the Chamber of Commerce Parade, the water ski show, the Kiddie Pig Races, the lakeside band concert, and the Aldon Farms Fireworks Extravaganza lighting up the night sky.

But tomorrow he would be gone, a freshman bound for the University of California at Berkeley, a stone's throw from San

Francisco, the magical land of the Golden Gate, North Beach, Chinatown, and Fisherman's Wharf.

Jonathan contemplated The Three Promises he had made to his parents, but he quickly dismissed the concern.

No price was too high to pay to attend a university so close to San Francisco.

Or so he thought.

HUAC AND THE GREAT SCOTT

The headwaters of Strawberry Creek swirl leisurely above the University of California's Botanical Garden, snaking down the eastern foothills, disappearing into subterranean crevices, surfacing in meandering, gurgling ecstasy through the majestic groves of the campus, eventually tumbling into San Francisco Bay near the Berkeley marina.

Founded in 1868 in the City of Oakland, the University moved to its hilly site in Berkeley, in part, because of the quiet beauty of Strawberry Creek. The sprawling 800-acre campus was initially a grassy slope filled with more than 500 species of trees, through which Strawberry Creek flows, its water filled with silver salmon, its banks lined with the wild berries that give the creek its name. Later, Coast redwoods, sequoias, and live oaks, Monterey pines, camphor-scented Eucalyptus, Port Orford Cedar, and Italian Stone Pine were introduced, preserving the sylvan heritage of the campus.

From his second-story office in the venerable Tudor style Stephens Hall, Professor Aristotle "Ari" Scott squinted at Strawberry Creek flowing along the northern edge of Faculty Glade, once an ancient settlement of the Huchiun-Ohlone Indians, the bright morning sun filtering through the giant redwoods guarding the creek, revealing the yellow glow of Banana slugs slithering along its banks and the concentric rippling on the creek's surface, the signature of Water Striders feeding on Damsel flies.

Ari hoisted the creaky, bay window and shook the contents of the small, brown paper bag onto the window sill. He meticulously spread the mound of peanuts into a script *Cal*. Soon, his chum, Brutus, the garrulous, brown squirrel from the nearby Buckeye tree would appear in a clatter to claim his daily meal.

Ari Scott was 44-years-old, deeply tanned, with a thin, wiry frame. His once blond, wavy hair was now flecked with silver, but he still enjoyed the admiring glances of coeds attracted to his large, piercing grey eyes. He had returned to campus on Labor Day weekend, putting final touches on outlines for several new philosophy courses he would be teaching this Fall semester of 1959. He was pleased that, despite the national hysteria over the Russian "Sputnik," student signups for humanities courses had increased, a reassuring sign that a new generation of undergraduates would maintain a humane perspective in their pursuit of education.

Ari marveled at how the definition of education had radically changed. In the early 1930's during the Great Depression, as the son of a Cal English professor, he had enjoyed the luxury of a university education reserved for the wealthy and privileged. Today, college students struggled fiercely for grades, a competition unknown to Ari in his halcyon undergraduate days at Cal. Increasingly, the government looked to its colleges for the scientific knowledge to defeat the Soviet Union. Cold War hysteria fueled research grants, scholarships, and student aid.

Catch the Russians! Pass the Russians! Beat the Russians! Education was nothing more than a scientific race into outer space between the Russians and the Americans.

"What the hell are we going to do about HUAC?" A booming voice disrupted Ari's thoughts. "I guess my little letter really stirred up the political pot." The voice belonged to Ari's colleague and friend, Garrick Nelquist.

Professor of Political Science, Garrick Nelquist, had slicked-backed hair and sported a thin manicured mustache. Despite a small town upbringing, Nelquist fancied himself an Anglophile, wearing tweedy jackets with leather elbow patches, argyle socks, and brown and white saddle shoes. He fidgeted with his trademark meerschaum pipe.

A week ago, the <u>New York Times</u> had published Nelquist's Open Letter in its Opinion Page, blasting HUAC and its Chairman,

Clayborn Muck.

HUAC stood for the House Un-American Activities Committee, a Congressional subcommittee investigating subversive or Communist activities in American life. Congressman Clayborn Muck had announced, with great fanfare, that HUAC would be investigating subversive activities among the faculties of the nation's elite colleges and universities, including all the Ivy League Schools, Duke, Northwestern, Michigan, and Wisconsin. At the top of the list was Cal.

Ari closed the window as Brutus scurried off with peanut remnants to the safety of the Buckeye tree.

If only my life were as simple as Brutus's, Ari thought.

"How many of us didn't screw around with some left-wing cause as undergrads?" asked Nelquist, lighting his pipe, drawing deeply and slowly exhaling the smoke from the side of his mouth.

"If it wasn't for the glory of saving the world for the poor and unfortunate, it sure as hell was for satisfying wild hormones," he said. "As I recall," said Nelquist, "the girls who hung out with campus radicals were sure hornier than those stuck up, sorority types."

"Yes, I expect a little love call from HUAC when they hit the Cal campus," sighed Nelquist. "Will you be joining me at the Inquisition, Ari?" Nelquist joked. "After all, you did kick Muck's ass at the '36 Olympics," he said, puffing on the meershcaum.

"Fascinating how things come full circle, Garrick. God, how Muck hated losing to me," said Ari, savoring the old memories of the press headlines heralding "*the Great Scott,*" the "*California Golden Boy*" with the "*luminous grey eyes*" winning the metric mile over his teammate, Clayborn Muck, son of Pennsylvania's governor.

"But losing one foot race to you a quarter of a century ago shouldn't qualify you for the HUAC shit list. Even Muck can't make any political hay from that old story."

"It's more personal than that," said Ari. "We both fell madly in love with the same Italian girl. Muck couldn't take it when Sofia chose me. He swore he'd get even."

"She must have been quite some babe, Ari. I think of her every time I have a cup of that Italian java."

"Quite some babe," echoed Ari, recalling the first love of his life, Sofia Cappuccino, Italian women's breaststroke champion, a voluptuous young woman with smoldering looks, jet-black hair, and dark, silky skin.

It had been love at first sight for both.

After the Olympics, racing ahead of the clouds of the approaching war, the new lovers traveled Italy in what she affectionately referred to as their *toure di amore*. For years, Ari had believed Sofia had died during WW II, until he saw her picture in a 1957 issue of <u>Look</u> magazine, standing next to her husband, the leader of the Italian Communist Party.

"Now that Sofia is Mrs. Pablo Zarzana, Muck will have the opening he'll use for revenge," sighed Ari.

"That peanut-brained little fart. Muck is sinking to a new low if your old romance qualifies as a Commie activity," said Nelquist. "When you two had your big fling, Sofia couldn't have known much about Communism. Probably didn't join the Party until she and Zarzana tied the knot."

"But think about it, Garrick. It's a natural for Muck. The wife of the leader of the Italian Communists was the former sweetheart of a noted left wing Cal Professor of Medieval Philosophy. It'll be great press for Muck and all the other kooks looking for a Commie under every rock."

"Pretty farfetched, even for that asshole," said Nelquist.

"Maybe not, Garrick." Ari's hands shook as he gingerly unfolded several thin sheafs of paper from the top drawer of his desk.

Nelquist relit the meerschaum and read the letter written in a graceful script.

August 1, 1959
Dearest Ari,
I tried writing you many times since the end of the War, but each time I failed. I saw the pictures of you and your family in <u>Life</u> *magazine (your wife is handsome and both your children are beautiful--they look just like you!). The article gave me the courage to send this letter.*

So much has happened to me and Italy since the War.

First, I am happy and well. Our family lost everything under Mussolini, but we survived. I now live in Rome and am happily married to Pablo Zarzana. Perhaps you have heard of him? He is the leader of the Italian Communist Party. Pablo is a passionate man who firmly believes in the cause of the Party. I have spoken of you often, and unlike many Italian men, he is not jealous of the love we shared so long ago. Has it been almost a quarter of a century since our toure di amore?

The reason I am finally writing you is to tell you that we have a daughter. When I say we, dearest Ari, I mean you and I have a daughter. Her name is Anna.

After Mussolini arrested my family as capitalistic traitors, we were jailed in Palermo. If we had not been imprisoned, the birth of Anna, outside the sacrament of marriage, would have disgraced the Cappuccino family. Because of this, I am not bitter about my years in Palermo. Anna's welfare gave me the will to survive.

You would be so proud of Anna. People say she looks just like me, but she has your eyes. (How did the newspapers describe them? Luminous and grey, eh?) Anna recently graduated from Milan University in Political Science, with a minor in Medieval Philosophy. (You see that she inherited other traits from you, eh?)

Now the best news!

Anna has been accepted for graduate studies at your beloved Cal and will be arriving in Berkeley for the Fall semester. Perhaps she can even take a Medieval Philosophy class from her father?

I am hoping that this news will not distress you. Anna and I both will understand if you do not wish to meet her, but we are praying that you will forgive me for keeping her a secret from you all these years.

Anna desperately wants to know her American father, and Pablo and I agree that this would be a marvelous gift to her. Anna will call on you after she has settled at the International House. Please meet her, Ari.

You will love her as much as we do.

Amore,

Sofia

"Jeez," said Nelquist, whistling softly. "Didn't know cerebral philosophy types had such balls. A love child? A Commie love child? Christ, If Muck gets hold of this, who knows what kind BS he'll try," he said, tapping the smoldering tobacco into an ashtray.

Nelquist's tone turned somber. "What can wimpy spined academics living in their blissful little ivory tower worlds do about this? We turn up our superior noses at political controversy and let two-bit politicians beat the crap out of us until they get tired and move onto some new punching bag."

Nelquist gripped the meerschaum with a fist. "I thought I gave up my farm boy's aggression when my college boxing days were over, but I'm really getting pissed about this nonsense, Ari. Something has to be done."

"We can organize a united stand against HUAC," said Ari. "If we close ranks, HUAC won't be able to pick us off one at a time."

"Don't expect an easy vote on this one, Ari," warned Nelquist. "Since the Russians launched Sputnik, Cal's hired a raft of those military, technocrat types, and they're beginning to flex their muscles, especially that slimy Werner Von Seller."

Nelquist was referring to the famous professor and atomic scientist whom his detractors called the "Prussian Penguin."

"It'll be a classic battle, Ari. Fuzzy Eggheads versus blood sucking Frankensteins. HUAC has been gaining steam for its witch hunts."

"Since Muck's announcement, there have been a dozen resignations around the country. Ducky Schindler at Yale, Mac Wilson at Harvard, even Toady Warren at Princeton. Christ, you'd think Toady's Nobel Prize would protect him from any old skeletons rattling in his closet," said Nelquist, wedging fresh tobacco into the meerschaum.

The specter of a tumultuous battle within the staid Academic Senate troubled Ari, but HUAC and Muck had to be stopped. Other universities would roll over and play dead, hoping that the hysteria over creeping Communism would subside.

But there was danger in taking such a passive stance. Clayborn Muck's adroit manipulation of television coverage of HUAC hearings and his mission to require loyalty oaths was gathering momentum in an America fearful of Russia's advancements in space.

The loyalty oath seemed to be a harmless document. It merely required professors to swear that they had never been associated with persons, groups, and activities that were "Communist" or "anti-American." The catch was Muck and HUAC were the sole judges of what was Communist or anti-American.

"We've got our work cut out for us, Garrick," said Ari, turning toward Strawberry Creek, watching it leisurely serpentining through the bucolic edges of Faculty Glade. "And whether Cal will survive as an institution of higher education will depend on whether we can stand up to Muck and HUAC's onslaught."

"Ari, the scariest part of all this Commie bull shit is the rumor that Muck is using the HUAC hearings as a launching pad for the vice-presidential nomination at the convention next year!"

Ari shuddered at the thought of "Vice President" Clayborn Muck in 1960, or worse, "President" Clayborn Muck in 1968, a disastrous destiny for the decade of the Sixties!

THREE FOR THE ROAD

"J-o-n-a-T-H-A-N, set the table!" The command, shrill and stern, crackled above the solemn tick-tock, tick-tock of the grandfather's clock. Gertrude Aldon charged about the cavernous kitchen, peering into ovens, sniffing boiling pots, rattling lids and pans. A monument to American 1950's technology, the kitchen was her pride and joy, filled with double ovens and a six-burner stove, a seven-foot refrigerator-freezer, a commercial-size dishwasher, and wall-to-wall built-ins.

Gertrude Aldon was a small-boned woman, slightly more than five-foot-tall, with pale, porcelain-like skin. Her dark brown hair, knotted in a bun, gave emphasis to her clear blue eyes. Under normal circumstances, Gertrude projected an air of indifferent coolness, but when she was angry, the nostrils of her small, pointed nose twitched and flared, belying her aura of composure. Today, her nostrils twitched and flared in uncontrolled fury.

"J-o-n-a-T-H-A-N!" she shouted again, knowing full well that her son had heard her the first time.

I should never have given Cokie the weekend off, she scolded herself.

Gertrude had not cooked in 10 years, but it was not the domestic inconvenience that weighed heavily on her mind. It was the imminent arrival of her brother-in-law, Mike Aldon, and "that woman," Pearl. For perhaps the thousandth time, Gertrude asked herself, *what have I done to deserve this terrible fate?*

When she married Murle Aldon, the people of Clear Lake had warned that the Aldon brothers were as different as night and day. Gertrude preferred the comparison of water and oil.

"Mike is just a little different," Murle had explained."Give yourself some time to know him."

But the more she learned about him, the more Gertrude was convinced her brother-in-law was a disgrace to the Aldon clan. Unlike Murle, Mike had not attended an Ivy League school, but that wasn't the reason she detested him. No, it was his utter disdain for the Aldons' role as the leading family of Clear Lake. Her brother-in-law just didn't care what other people thought!

One of the few things Mike did care about was recounting his Navy days in San Francisco, especially that disgusting story of how he acquired the jagged scar. A souvenir, he had bragged, defending the honor of a young woman.

And then there was the disgrace of that woman, Pearl.

It was three years ago, in 1956, that Mike committed his most disrespectful act of announcing his engagement. Gertrude's initial shock gave way to indignation, then to outrage, when Mike asked her brother, Reverend Leonard Granger, for permission to marry in the Clear Lake Methodist Church.

The impending marriage reminded Gertrude of her stalwart efforts in concealing the history of Aldon Farms from Jonathan. *No need to soil the family name with ancient scandal*, she had reasoned.

On her father-in-law's death in 1953, Gertrude was confident that Miles Aldon had taken the dark secret with him to the grave. Yet, there was that annual $5,000 bequest from Miles Aldon's will that Jonathan often inquired about. By his marriage to that woman, Mike Aldon had stirred up the unwelcome ghost of the Aldon past.

Gertrude had done her best to shield Jonathan from Mike's radical influence, but there had always been a close rapport between nephew and uncle that had been disturbing.

She thought the problem had resolved when Mike moved to Minneapolis four years ago to manage the Aldon Farms sales office, but every month Jonathan would take the bus north up the interstate to visit his Uncle Mike. More recently, over her objections, Ziggy and Jonathan would drive the wheezing Atherton Packard to Minneapolis to buy those dreadful rock and roll records banned on Clear Lake radio station K-HOG.

Gertrude cringed at the thought of ungodly notions Mike may have exposed the boys to. Surely, Jonathan's choice in college was swayed by Mike's crude stories of his Navy days *but what other ways had Mike corrupted her son?*

She prayed that Mike's influence would not infect her son's taste in girls. It was one thing for her brother-in-law to experience unnatural desires, but it was another to expose Jonathan to such perversions!

Yet, Gertrude harbored a gnawing suspicion that Jonathan had known about Pearl all along. That unsettling thought, that her son had been actively supportive of Mike's romance, gave way to a recurring nightmare of Jonathan bringing home someone like that woman, Pearl. Murle had scoffed at her fear, suggesting that she was overreacting. Yet, her nightmares persisted.

In the spring of 1957, Mike Aldon and Pearl Robinson were married by a judge in Minneapolis. Secretly, Gertrude had lobbied her minister brother, Leland, against the consecration of the marriage in the Methodist Church, convincing him of the furor that such a ceremony would create.

"That woman will never set feet in my house." Gertrude had declared to anyone inquiring about her new sister-in-law. Whenever Mike attended business meetings at Aldon Farms, Gertrude retreated to the safety of the family room, watching "The Lawrence Welk Show," "Ozzie and Harriet," and "Leave It to Beaver," television shows depicting what American family life was truly about.

When Jonathan announced his decision to attend college in California, Gertrude had resisted, insisting that her son follow in his father's footsteps to the Ivy League. It had been Murle's idea to let Jonathan try a year in California, confident that their son would soon realize that the Ivy League would best serve his educational needs in preparing him for his future as the owner of Aldon Farms. Gertrude relented only when Jonathan committed to the Three Promises which she believed would ensure the proper guidance for Jonathan living on his own in that God forsaken land, California.

The first promise was that Jonathan would attend the campus Methodist Church. Her brother had already written the minister of the campus church advising of Jonathan's enrollment at Cal. The

15

second was that her son would join Pi Upsilon, her husband's college fraternity. The third was that Jonathan would maintain good grades. Together, The Three Promises would prevent Jonathan from spending too much time in San Francisco where those weird Beat-nuts, or whatever they were called, loitered.

Gertrude had adopted an attitude of calm resignation about her son's move to California, until he announced the shocking details of his travel plans. According to Jonathan, his uncle Mike had agreed to come down, pick him up, and drive him back to the Minneapolis Airport, as she and Murle would be busy with the Clear Lake Labor Day Celebration.

Had Jonathan scheduled his flight on Labor Day, to provide a convenient excuse for Mike to bring that woman, Pearl, to the Aldon home?

Her fears were confirmed by Mike's recent letter with the postscript,

Pearl and I will arrive Sunday around 7:00 p.m. Hope Cokie's cooking is as delicious as usual.

Dinner. Gertrude had fumed. *How dare Mike bring her without an invitation? And where would they stay? Certainly not in the Aldon home.*

Upstairs, in the master bathroom, Murle Aldon listened to his wife's shrill shouts. *Better get moving myself,* he thought.

Murle Aldon was a large bulldog of a man with a thick chest, prematurely silver hair, and a broad, square jaw that reminded Gertrude of Ernest Hemingway. One of his wife's endearing habits was associating people's looks with movie and TV celebrities, although Gertrude became angry when someone suggested she looked just like Margaret Hamilton, the nasty witch of "The Wizard of Oz."

Gertrude was the first to notice the resemblance between Ziggy and Howdy Doody. She bragged that Jonathan looked like the handsome actor, Tab Hunter. She insisted Mike was a dead ringer for movie bad guy, Richard Widmark. Accordingly, Gertrude assumed Pearl looked like the torch singer, Eartha Kitt.

Murle did not relish the role of peacemaker between his wife and brother, but familial duty called. The welfare of Aldon Farms was affected by the growing animosity between the two.

Maybe, he had thought, *once the ice was broken between the two sisters-in-law, the Aldons could expend their collective*

16

energies on improving profits, not in perpetuating ill will.

He had already resolved the sticky conflict by proposing the Three Promises and thankfully Jonathan had dutifully agreed.

Securing acceptance for Mike and Pearl's visit had required a more direct approach.

"Dearest, this is not the end of the world," Murle had begun slowly, anticipating a firestorm of resistance to the proposal he was about to suggest. "If Mike is willing to help us out by driving Jonathan to the airport, the least we can do is have him, he paused, . . . and his wife for dinner."

"But the neighbors? What will they. . .?" she objected.

"Let me finish," he said, placing both hands gently on her shoulders. "I know how you feel about Pearl. But Mike is my brother, and we owe him some consideration."

He continued, "During our marriage, I've provided you everything you've ever wanted, taking you antique shopping in Europe, hiring Cokie as cook for the most modern kitchen in town, building the largest dock on Clear Lake." Murle paused, allowing the truth of his comments to sink in.

"Since Father died, much of the success of Aldon Farms has been due to Mike's efforts in selling our hogs in the Orient."

Sobbing quietly, Gertrude pressed herself to his chest, pained by the awful truth of her husband's words.

"I've been thinking about the neighbors, too," said Murle. "Leonard can help. Ask him to explain to the congregation . . . "

Dabbing her tears with a silk handkerchief, she said, "Oh, no Murle, I couldn't. I . . . I wouldn't." Her voice rose in panic, envisioning her public humiliation.

Murle continued, ". . . about our problem and ask them to pray for us. I'm sure the church will support us 100%," he said softly, kissing her cheek. "There, there, dearest. Leonard and the Lord will see us through our predicament."

He sensed the gears of her brain engaging, as her crying slowed to a sniffle, her shallow panting turning into deep, steady breathing.

Murle's suggestion has a simple boldness that is appealing, Gertrude thought. She could minimize her private anguish by making Pearl's visit a community issue. In her public suffering, Gertrude would be assured an acceptable martyrdom.

During the last week of August, Clear Lake was abuzz with

17

Pearl's imminent arrival, overshadowing the annual excitement for the Labor Day Celebration. Patrons of the Blue Horizon Inn speculated on the outcome. Neighbors and friends greeted Gertrude with choruses of, "Poor dear," and "It will be over soon."

The Sunday before "Gertrude's Ordeal," Reverend Leonard Granger offered a special prayer. He noted the congregation's pride in his sister's noble sacrifice, as Clear Lake's first truly "Modern Methodist Mother."

But for Gertrude, the recurring nightmares persisted.

* * *

The green Edsel zoomed quietly along the highway. The black storm cloud to the south was now out of sight. At the border, the lush verdant fields of Minnesota gave way to the tanned flatlands of Iowa. A fading sign painted on an ancient barn greeted the two occupants with a cheerful,

Welcome to Hog Heaven!

Across the road, a billboard proclaimed,

Start Your Day With Pork!

"Won't be long," sighed the male driver, surveying the familiar terrain of his youth.

Before them, stretching far into the horizon were the thousands of small, white wooden houses in neat, orderly rows, each exactly four feet by ten feet, large enough for a hog to lead a healthy, pampered life until its appointment at the slaughterhouse. Each roof bore the Aldon Farms logo Gertrude had designed in Halloween colors, an orange A and a black F.

A.F. Aldon Farms. Home.

Mike Aldon, age 37, had sandy-colored hair, dark brown eyes, and a handsome, chiseled face marred only by the long, diagonal scar slashing from his left temple, over the bridge of his nose, into his right cheek.

"This, my love, is what you've been missing," he said, biting his lower lip, trying to control his rising anger, as the image of his sister-in-law, Gertrude Aldon, nostrils twitching and flaring, crept into his consciousness.

Reading her husband's mind, Pearl Robinson Aldon said, "Nothing Gertrude can say or do will bother me, darling," She gently touched his jagged scar, that small imperfection that was Mike Aldon's badge of honor.

Turning down the visor, she scanned her face in the vanity mirror. "How do I look? Nice enough for Clear Lake?" she teased.

"Too good for Clear Lake. You look lovely, Mrs. Aldon," he said, marveling at her perfectly coiffed, jet-black hair, the smooth ebony skin and high cheekbones highlighting the exotic eyes that sparkled as she spoke.

A battered Ford rumbled alongside, its occupants dressed in bib overalls and T-shirts, pointing and gawking.

"Is all this attention for me or the Edsel?" said Pearl, giving her sweetest smile and waving.

"Hog country idiots, " said Mike, gunning the Edsel's V-8, leaving the Ford a distant speck in the mirror.

* * *

Jonathan paced back and forth along the front lawn of the Aldon Tudor, as remnants of the rainbow faded into the darkening eastern sky. Dusk, and soon porch lights would pop on along Four Winds Drive. The street, a broad loop graced by ancient maple and oak trees, was paved by grandfather Miles Aldon, the first to build along the lake's shoreline.

Over time, Four Winds had become the address of Clear Lake's most prominent citizens. Uncle Mike had observed that the street had been aptly named, as the four biggest windbags of Clear Lake: Mr. Vickery, owner of the Corner Drug Store; Claudius Frump, the town lawyer; his daughter, Claudia, who had married Uncle Leonard; and, Gertrude Aldon all lived on Four Winds Drive.

The first hint of Mike and Pearl's arrival was a chorus of slamming front doors, as neighbors streamed out of their homes to greet the green Edsel gliding slowly into at the bend of Four Winds Drive.

Driving past familiar faces, Mike Aldon honked the horn at lifelong neighbors. Today they were only curious strangers craning their necks for a glimpse of the woman at his side.

"Friendly people," Pearl observed coolly.

"An old Clear Lake tradition," said Mike, winking and holding her hand firmly. "As a kid, when the circus came to town, we'd

19

line Main Street staring at all the strange, exotic animals."

"Don't be so snotty, darling," said Pearl, smiling, waving.

Jonathan raced to the driveway to greet the occupants of the controversial new car with the inverted pyramid-shaped grill.

Mike leaped from the car, engulfing Jonathan in a warm bear-hug."How's it going, nephew? Ready for the big adventure?"

Walking to the passenger side, one arm draped over Jonathan's shoulder, Mike opened the door with a flourish and a sweeping bow.

"Welcome to Hog Heaven, my love. Clear Lake, home of the infamous Aldon clan," Mike muttered. "And the reason we live in Minneapolis," he added.

Mimicking his uncle, Jonathan bowed, as Pearl slowly and majestically exited the car, greeting Jonathan with a gentle kiss on the cheek.

The historic moment silenced the milling crowd. The first Negro to ever set feet in Clear Lake!

"It's great to see you, Aunt Pearl," Jonathan spoke loudly, so the neighbors would hear."Gorgeous, as ever," he added.

She has a perfect name, thought Jonathan. *Pearl is so elegant and so beautiful.*

He admired her high cheekbones, dark brown eyes, and mane of jet-black hair, her exotic features complemented by a maroon Dior dress.

"It's not half as bad as Michael described," she said, glancing at the throng moving onto the Aldon lawn. "They don't look like they'll bite," said Pearl, giving a small wave to the crowd.

"Don't be hasty, my love. You haven't met Gertrude yet," replied Mike.

From the kitchen, Gertrude had nearly died, watching the crowd of approaching neighbors, the flashing and honking of the Edsel underscoring her impending ordeal.

"Murle!" she called in panic. "They're here!"

"Yes, I know. I heard Mike honking two blocks away," yelled Murle, bouncing down the circular staircase.

She was in the middle of her third deep breath when the front door opened.

Stay calm, Gertrude reminded herself. *You are a Modern Methodist Mother. Straighten your dress. One last look in the full-length mirror.*

"So good to see you, Mike," Gertrude lied, gritting her teeth, avoiding the smiling gaze of the dark-skinned woman.

Mike began the introductions. "You met Murle at the wedding." He paused, "Gertrude, this is my wife, Pearl."

Pearl nodded. "I've heard so much about you," a mocking tone in her voice.

From Jonathan's vantage, he could see his mother's tiny body trembling.

Quite the Modern Methodist Mother, he said to himself.

"And I've told Gertrude quite a lot about you, haven't I, dearest?" said Murle. "Welcome to Aldon Farms, Pearl. Dinner's ready, so why don't we enjoy some of Gertrude's great home cooking," he added, ignoring the lost memory of the last time Gertrude had cooked.

At the dinner table, Murle offered grace adding, ". . .and may Jonathan be blessed with success at college and return home with a better appreciation of the love of his family and the beauty of Clear Lake. Amen."

The meal was an Aldon favorite: well-done roast beef, steamed Brussels sprouts, boiled potatoes, and pumpkin pie. While Murle and Mike chatted about business, and Pearl inquired about Jonathan's freshman courses, Gertrude sat, head down, eating quietly.

"Jonathan, I have a favor to ask," said Pearl, "I have a cousin in Oakland, near the Cal campus. It would be nice if you dropped in for a visit. He's a man of the cloth, a minister, like your Uncle Leonard," said Pearl, peering at Gertrude over a forkful of potatoes. "He's very well known and has his own radio ministry. His name is Reverend Isaac Jones, but he's better known as Reverend Ike."

"I'd be happy to, Aunt Pearl," replied Jonathan.

"Jonathan will be too busy with studies," snapped Gertrude. The specter of her recurrent nightmares loomed in her mind. The last thing Jonathan needed was socializing with Pearl's Negro relatives.

Changing the topic, Gertrude asked, "Where will you two be staying tonight? The Blue Horizon should still have a room or two." It was one thing for this woman to dine in her home, but it was another for her to stay the night, Modern Methodist Mother or not.

Jonathan noted the flush of anger spreading across Mike's face. Before his uncle could speak, Jonathan volunteered, "I thought they would stay with me in the studio."

"I'm not sure they wouldn't rather stay at the Blue Horizon," said Gertrude, her nose twitching and flaring. "Your room is so cluttered with those awful rock and roll records, and . . ."

"We'll be happy to stay with you, nephew," said Mike, cutting Gertrude's protest short.

* * *

The lights of Jonathan's bedroom above the Aldon barn burned well past midnight as the trio sang and danced to Jonathan's favorite records in the musical sanctuary that had been the practice studio for the Amazing Double A's. Sometime after midnight, the three collapsed from exhaustion, Jonathan cured up in a sleeping bag on the floor, and Mike and Pearl entwined like serpents on the narrow twin bed.

From the darkness of the Aldon Tudor, Gertrude exhaled a sigh of relief seeing Jonathan's bedroom lights fading to black. In the twin bed, on the other side of the night stand, Murle slept, snoring blissfully.

Her ordeal was over. Tomorrow, Mike and Pearl would be gone. In time, the brouhaha over the visit would be forgotten. Jonathan would be gone, too, but would soon discover the folly of his decision and transfer to an Ivy League school where he belonged.

Murle is right, she sighed. *The Three Promises will surely protect Jonathan from any corrupting, alien influences.*

Gertrude pulled the stop cord of the ceiling fan, drifting off to sleep, free from the fitful nightmares of the recent past, of the searing image of Jonathan bringing home a smiling dark-skinned girl, someone from the cover of <u>National Geographic Magazine.</u>

4

OF HOGS AND BONES

"Wow, a hundred bucks! Thanks," said Jonathan, examining the face of Ben Franklin on the largest bill he had ever held. Father and son stood on the back porch of the Aldon Tudor, drinking coffee, basking in the warmth of the Clear Lake sunrise.

"A going-away gift," said Murle Aldon. "Treat yourself to something special, son. Mother wants you to buy a new suit for fraternity rush, but I'll leave the choice to you."

Draining the last of the coffee, he said, "Heading off to a breakfast meeting of the Labor Day Celebration Committee. Mother's sleeping off a splitting headache, but she sends her love and reminds you of The Three Promises." He shook Jonathan's hand, then hugged him.

Curling the hundred-dollar bill around his index finger, Jonathan watched his father walk away in his familiar, resolute gait.

Labor Day, a date as important as February 3, 1959, the day he found Buddy Holly's glasses.

* * *

The large white billboard, with green lettering, at the northern boundary of Aldon Farms read,

Leaving Cerro Gordo County- Come Back Again!

9:00 a.m. and the Edsel was a solitary blur along the interstate.

Mike and Pearl hummed along to the Sunday morning church music of Clear Lake radio station, K-HOG. From the backseat, Jonathan peered over the tracts of hog houses, the comforting terrain of home.

Half an hour later, the dry flatlands of northern Iowa yielded to the rolling, green countryside of Minnesota. Turning off a Sunday radio sermon, Mike asked the question burning in his mind since they left Aldon Farms.

"Nephew, how much do you really know about the history of Aldon Farms?"

Nodding at Mike's scarred reflection in the rearview mirror, Jonathan said, "Mother said Grandfather Miles was an orphan who saved his money working in the Des Moines stockyards and moved to Clear Lake to start his own hog farm."

"Did your father add much to that version?" asked Mike arching an eyebrow in the mirror.

"Father's never said much about our family history."

Mike swore softly under his breath and said, "Did you ever wonder why it's your mother, and not your father, who's given you the details of the Aldon family history?"

Jonathan shook his head "no."

"Gratitude to Gertrude," said Mike, "has a nice ring to it." He repeated the alliteration.

"Let me explain. Your father is a prince of a fellow and a helluva farmer, but he's so grateful to Gertrude for marrying him he allows her to embellish the truth. The price of marrying into Boston respectability, I suppose."

"Mother lies?" asked Jonathan.

"Let's just say she stretches some facts and ignores others," said Mike.

"Your uncle is struggling to be diplomatic," said Pearl "Why don't you tell Jonathan the real history of Aldon Farms? He'll inherit it all someday. He has a right to know."

Mike began.

As a child, your grandfather, Miles Aldon, was raised in a home for wayward children in the Bowery of New York City. One sweltering, summer night in 1900, Miles, age 15, crawled out a fire escape and made his way to the railyards, where he found a boxcar filled with drifters, hobos, and other young men, with whom he shared the dream of a better life somewhere in the West.

24

Your grandfather once told me the stench of urine and sweat was so unbearable that, in comparison, the scent of a hog-pen was heavenly.

Whenever the train stopped, Miles and others scoured garbage cans for scraps of food and quenched their thirst from water from leaking hoses.

Des Moines was already the hog butchering capital of America when Miles arrived. He listened to a foreman for Amorall Co. offering jobs to hard-working men, willing to work twelve-hours a day, six-days a week, at ten cents an hour. Hungry and desperate, your grandfather scrawled his name on a two-year contract.

Quickly calculating his grandfather's wages in his head, Jonathan said, "That's less than $30 a month!" he gasped.

Nodding, Mike continued.

Amorall set up thousands of tents in neat little rows in an area next to the stockyards known as Tent City, each row bearing a street name. Miles shared a tent located at Number 4-Pork Bellies Lane, with an Italian kid from Pittsburgh, named Salvatore Lucci.

In those days, hog butchering was crude and bloody. Then, slaughterhouse workers straddled long, wooden chutes running from the railroad cars down to the stockyards. Stampeding hogs were driven into the chutes until they were trapped shoulder-to-shoulder. Knockers numbed the hogs by bashing them over the head with axe handles, making them easy targets for Stickers who slit the throats of the dazed animals. Those gruesome experiences inspired your grandfather to adopt the humane measures that are now an important part of hog farming at Aldon Farms.

Neither Miles nor Salvatore had ever killed an animal before. The foreman, a cruel jokester, gave them butcher knives so long, it took two hands to use.

"I think I may be ill," said Pearl, winding down her window.

"Consider these details a necessary evil in Jonathan's education, my love," said Mike, continuing with his story.

There were confusion, noise, and dust, as squealing hogs were driven down the chutes into the mayhem of the slaughterhouse.

Panicking in the sounds and smells of death, Salvatore froze, unable to kill the helpless hog in front of him.

Angered by the boy's hesitation, the foreman threw Salvatore into the chute, on top of the hog.

'Slit that porker's throat, kid, or I'll fire your ass,' the foreman shouted. Salvatore promptly vomited, retching all over the dazed animal.

"Darling, please," said Pearl, placing fingers to her ears.

"It gets worse," said Mike. "The hog reared up, flipping Salvatore onto the ground, collapsing on top of him."

"Was he killed?" Jonathan shuddered at the thought of being trapped under hundreds of pounds of hog flesh.

Miles jumped into the chute and somehow pulled Salvatore out from under the hog. Salvatore's left leg was crushed and maimed but spared from amputation. The injury caused Salvatore to use a cane the rest of his life. In a rare moment of compassion, Amorall Co. let Salvatore work as a sales clerk in the stockyard store.

"But how could Grandfather have earned enough money from his two years with Amorall to start Aldon Farms?" said Jonathan.

"Patience, nephew. This is where the story gets interesting.

The workers of Tent City were banned in Des Moines. Anyone caught outside Tent City was promptly fired. It was fine for Amorall workers to do the dirty work that made Des Moines prosper, but slaughterhouse workers weren't good enough to rub elbows with the locals.

"What did the workers do with their wages?" asked Jonathan.

Some bought whiskey and cigars from Salvatore at the stockyard store. Many squandered their paychecks in all-night card games. It was clear to Miles that, after two years of hard work, only a few lucky gamblers would leave Tent City with any money in their pockets.

One night, after losing his stake in a Tent City poker game, Miles wandered off to console himself about his run of bad luck. Deep in thought, he crossed the tracks over to the poor section of Des Moines called Colored Town. Turning to retrace his path, he heard loud, raucous voices chanting nearby.

'Seben! Leben! Yo! shouted some.

Lizard Eyes! Ass Dust! Midnight! others yelled.

After a pause, there was a mighty chorus of 'Oh, Shit!'

Miles cautiously approached, intrigued by the excited voices. He glimpsed shadowy figures outlined in the glow of kerosene lamps. Climbing a nearby tree, Miles saw a tight circle of Negro

26

men sitting on their haunches, playing a dice game on a large, muslin bed sheet spread on the ground. The players wagered pennies on the outcome of a pair of dice thrown by players, shouting strange words of encouragement.

Some shouted, 'Joe! Fever! Nina! Big Dick!

Others urged, Jimmy Hicks! Catur!'

A few held their hands together, in silent prayer.

The name of the game appeared to be Oh, Shit, the phrase that ended each dice shooter's turn, followed by hugs of joy by winners and dejected groans by losers.

A thin, well-dressed Negro man with a derby hat, named Bones was in charge of the game. After each roll of the dice, Bones collected pennies from the losers and paid off the winners. The fast-paced game extended late into the night, until players, tired and hoarse, picked up what money was left and drifted into the darkness.

Miles watched spellbound, as Bones counted hundreds of pennies stacked neatly in rows, rolling them into paper wrappers. The night's profits were more than a Sticker's monthly wages!

Intrigued, Miles returned to his hidden perch the next several nights, watching Bones' dice game, eventually deciphering the meaning of the phrases the players shouted.

Seben was the number seven, Leben was eleven. Midnight referred to twelve, Lizard Eyes, two and Ass Dust was the number three. Four was Joe; Fever, five; Nina, nine; and Big Dick, ten. Jimmy Hicks was the name for six, while Catur referred to eight.

One night, after the last cry of Oh, Shit had echoed through Colored Town, Miles was shinnying down the tree when a limb broke, dropping him in a heap near Bones, counting the evening's profits.

Grabbing a pearl-handled pistol, Bones commanded, 'Over here with yer hands up or I'll plug you dead!'

'Don't shoot,' Miles pleaded, raising his hands high, emerging into the glare of the kerosene lamps.

'I'll be damned. What the hell is a white boy doin' in these parts?' said Bones, cocking the pistol. 'Thinkin' of robbin' old Bones, eh?'

'No, No, Mr. Bones,' said Miles, quickly explaining his fascination with the dice game.

'Been spyin' on old Bones, eh?' the nattily dressed Negro

27

chuckled, 'Where you from, boy?'

Miles told Bones about his two-year stint with Amorall and the tent he shared with Salvatore at Number 4-Pork Bellies Lane. Bones tipped his derby hat, a smile creeping across his ebony face. 'So, you want to be a gamblin' man? Well, I think I got me an idea. Here's what we'll do,' he said, tucking the pistol into his belt and explained.

Miles raced back to Tent City, filled with the simple joy of Bones' plan.

'Sal, we're gonna be rich!' said Miles, waking up his tentmate, excitedly detailing the gambler's proposal.

'We'll be partners, Sal,' said Miles. 'All we need are good cuts of lean pork for Bones, and he'll teach me everything about Oh, Shit. Soon we can have our own dice game in Tent City.'

'It's a deal,' said Sal, gripping Miles firmly. 'How 'bout a name for our new business? Somethin' catchy.'

'Thought of one running back from Colored Town,' Miles said. 'How about Al and Sal's?'

Waving his cane in a circle, Sal said, 'Al and Sal's, it is. Miles, this is our lucky night!'

Every day after closing, Sal smuggled lean cuts of pork from the stockyard store, slipping them to Miles for his nightly trip to Colored Town.

During the apprenticeship, Miles learned Bones was born Ezekiel Washington, son of a runaway slave who settled in Boston, working as a servant to a French-Canadian business man who played a parlor dice game called Merde.

Blessed with a knack for numbers, the former slave quickly grasped the concepts of Merde, designing his own layout from an old muslin bed sheet. Bones learned the game at his father's side, inheriting the ancient bed sheet he now used for his nightly dice game. Eventually, Bones changed the name of the game from the French cuss word, merde, to Oh, Shit.

"But, if Bones made so much money from gambling, why couldn't he just buy his own pork in Des Moines?" asked Jonathan, interrupting Mike's story.

Mike explained.

Although Bones was well off, Negroes were not allowed to shop in white-owned stores. The meats sold in Colored Town were Amorall's leftovers. You see, nephew, in Des Moines, both

Negroes and slaughterhouse workers were second-class citizens.

"Jonathan, your mother will never admit how much your family and mine have in common," said Pearl, smiling.

Mike continued.

Working at Bones' side, Miles learned the subtleties of the dice game, placing, collecting, and paying bets. Initially suspicious of Bones' new assistant, the regulars referred to Miles as White Shit, eventually accepting the eager, hard-working white boy as an equal.

"At Bones' Lamplight University, grandfather Miles was taught the same business concepts your father later learned in his Ivy League education," said Mike, laughing.

One *night, Miles arrived late to Colored Town, just as a force of plant security and Des Moines police raided Bones' dice game. He quickly climbed the tree where he had once spied on Bones.*

'Don't know nothin' 'bout no stolen pork,' said Bones stoically. 'Me and the boys here havin' a friendly dice game.'

'Yea,' nodded the others.

'Never go near them stockyards. White folk nothing but trouble,' said one gambler.

No one mentioned Bones' assistant, White Shit.

'Pretty fancy clothes,' said a policeman, caressing Bones' derby hat. 'Maybe a couple of days in the county jail will improve your memories. Take 'em away.'

As the handcuffed gamblers were loaded into paddy wagons, Miles noticed Bones subtly nodding to the dice layout on the ground.

"Bones knew Miles was watching," said Jonathan.

"Precisely," Mike continued.

After the prisoners were hauled away, Miles dropped down from the tree, crawled through the darkness, and retrieved the muslin layout.

Using Bones layout, the former White Shit and his new partner, the crippled Salvatore Lucci, now Al & Sal, set up their own dice game in Tent City. Soon, evenings in the stockyards were filled with the excited shouts of 'Seben! Leben! Midnight! Lizard Eyes! Ass Dust! Joe Fever! Jimmy Hicks! 'Catur! Nina!, and Big Dick!' and always, punctuated by frequent choruses of Oh, Shit!

The game was a sensation, with Tent City residents lining up every night to place bets on the bed sheet layout. Business was so good the partners bribed a Des Moines seamstress to sew fancy felt layouts. From a modest beginning, the dice game grew to eight locations. By the time the boys finished their two-year hitch with Amorall, each had saved several thousands of dollars.

"The rest of the family history is true," said Mike, concluding, "Miles Aldon moved from Des Moines to Clear Lake in the early 1900's, investing his profits from the dice games into land and hogs that are now Aldon Farms."

Jonathan was numbed by the revelation.

Mother and Father had been such hypocrites, he thought. The Aldons owe their success to gambling secrets passed from the Negro gambler Bones to Grandfather Miles. Yet, in the name of respectability, Mother, with Father's acquiescence, disapproved of uncle Mike's marriage to Pearl!

"What happened to Bones and Sal?" said Jonathan.

"A few years after moving to Clear Lake, your grandfather saw a photograph in the Minneapolis <u>Star Tribune</u> of Negroes founding an organization called the National Association for the Advancement of Colored People, the NAACP. In the back row was a tall, thin, well-dressed man with a derby hat, identified as Ezekiel B.Washington, Treasurer."

Suddenly, Jonathan understood the reason for Grandfather's annual gift of $5,000 to the NAACP college fund.

"As to Sal," said Mike continuing, "when Miles left Des Moines, he gave his partner all the dice layouts. Sal moved onto Chicago, where he set up dice games in Speakeasies and during Prohibition made a fortune in gambling, acquiring the nickname Lucky Lucci."

"Lucky Lucci, the gangster?" said Jonathan, his eyes widening.

"A convicted felon, yes. Gangster, no," said Mike. "For years, the FBI tried to convict Lucky on numerous charges, but the only thing the government ever nailed him on was failing to pay income taxes. After serving a few years in Sing-Sing, Lucky Lucci and his son, Lucky Two, moved to the Nevada desert where they built Las Vegas's first casino."

"What do you suppose is the most popular dice game in Lucky Lucci's casino?" asked Mike.

"Oh, Shit?"

"The rules are almost the same, but the name's been changed

30

from Oh, Shit to the more civilized name of casino craps."

As the Edsel reached the outskirts of Minneapolis, Jonathan meditated on the role of fate on human destinies. Grandfather Miles' chance meeting with Bones led to the founding of Aldon Farms and Lucky Lucci's Las Vegas casino. Uncle Mike's Navy days inspired his lifelong fascination with San Francisco, the city he affectionately called 'Frisco.

What did fate have in store for him in California?

Although Jonathan was mindful of The Three Promises he had made, from the recesses of his mind, he heard the incessant echo of the Amazing A's motto,

Shit flies both ways!

5

PAEAN OF SAN FRANCISCO

The brilliant sun skipping across the delicate, golden span, dancing on the northern headland. Puffy, cotton balls drifting over billowed spinnakers, crisscrossing the white capped, blue expanse of Yerba Buena and Angel Islands. An ocean liner gliding through the fabled Gate, its banner flowing in silent tribute to The City. This is Baghdad by The Bay.

The homage, penned twenty-three years ago, had earned Sam Paean the title, "Mr. San Francisco." In a city renowned for civic narcissism, the title bestowed Paean royal status.

Slouching in the leather chair, hunkering over his trusty portable Royal typewriter, Paean sat, transfixed by The City he loved. Taking a long drag from the Lucky Strike, he carefully puffed four wobbly smoke rings. The heady effects of two martinis suffused his body with a warm tingling from his toes to his thinning scalp, as Paean licked the briny aftertaste from the corner of his lips.

With one hand, Paean deftly guided the center hole of the LP into the spindle, flicking on the stereo switch, dropping the diamond stylus on the first band. Against a lush orchestral string background, George Shearing's jazz piano launched into a sprightly version of "What Is there To Say?"

Paean hummed the lyrics,

What is there to do? And what is there to say?

Shearing's hands marched over the keyboard in his signature style of crushed seventh and ninth chords. How well the blind pianist could see the keyboard!

What was there to say about this fair city he had not already said so sentimentally, so eloquently?

The end of the cool, gray foggy days of summer in The City. Soon too, the end of the Nifty Fifties. What would the Sixties bring? Would The City's fabled charm be buried beneath steel and concrete skyscrapers sprouting like monolithic weeds over The City's lovely hills?

Tapping the sides of his aquiline nose, in time with Shearing, Paean closed his slightly almond eyes, drifting into a half sleep.

The City. City of Saint Francis. City of Hopes. City of Dreams. Part Irish, part Italian, part Chinese, part Jewish. All guts and glory, she had been founded by the will and whim of rogues, rejects and romantics, her spirit forged by three waves of immigrants drawn first by the thirst for gold, then by the promise of the great railroad, and, finally, by the lure of laissez-faire commerce.

In California, when one spoke of The City, there was only one. The City of San Francisco.

In 1936, Sam Paean, then a wide-eyed 20-year-old green horn reporter from the hot Central Valley town of Sacramento, crossed the Bay by ferryboat, accepting the job as gossip columnist for the San Francisco *Sentinel*, the City's oldest newspaper.

Whadda job! Whadda life! A hundred bucks a week and all the free booze and food he could put away, just for the privilege of chronicling the bizarre and the beautiful, the wacky and the wonderful, the silly and the sad of this small, compact city.

The column, called Sam's "Paean to The City" featured a deceptively, simple format borrowed from radio legend Walter Winchell. Terse, newsy sentences, separated by three dots.

Tidbits of gossip . . . Who did what? . . . To whom? . . . When? . . . and Where? . . . .

Sam's *Paean to The City* saw all . . . knew all . . . and most important, told all . . . For the legion of Paean's readers, the day began and The City's mood set by the morning's dot, dot, dots. Paean was the civic torch bearer, weaving the magic of The City's history into the fabric of modern life, casting a journalistic spell over a community starving for a connection to romantic "Ess Eff's" bygone past.

Paean gleaned his scoops du jour from informants, snoops, and rumor mongers eager to see their poop in print. On bustling streets, in speeding taxis, in darkened bars, tipsters slipped cryptic messages scrawled on menus, cocktail napkins, business cards, receipts, calendars, and even lace panties. To his adoring public, the ultimate badge of honor was being a source of Paean.

Sam's *Paean to The City*, had clicked along at one-thousand words a day, six-days a week since '36, which Paean had calculated as two-million words of adulation for The City That Knows How. The column was San Francisco's arbiter of good taste and enlightenment, an oracle of social conscience, occupying a position of unmatched power and influence. With a mention, restaurants and nightclubs became overnight sensations, seedy misadventures turned into *causes celebres*, and struggling politicians instant household names.

Paean's love affair with The City had endured longer than any of his marriages to wives who considered the column a royal pain in the ass. His first wife, a dazzling, long-stemmed chorine, had described it as "daily eyetems and sightems sopped up in dark dives" where Sam wangled his free cocktails. The second, the daughter of the French Counsel General, derided his work as the "grist and ooze of San Francisco Gone," while his third spouse, a young society matron, dismissed it as the "dots and whats of snots," the required reading of the nouveau riche clawing up the moneyed slopes of (S)Nob Hill.

For Paean, age 43 and single again, the column was his constant mistress, a source of optimism and a fount of his existence. His well-publicized predilections for tall, leggy blondes and Caddy convertibles would pass in time; but his passion for The City would nurture him until his calling to the Great Dot, Dot, Dot in the sky.

A cable car clanging contrapuntally to the deep, mournful resonance of a distant foghorn jarred Paean from his reverie. He lit another Lucky Strike, letting it burn, as he reviewed the list of possible eyetems for tomorrow's column.

. . . Rumors about a female birth control pill . . .
. . . Jet service for SFO soon . . .
. . . All-time high of $150,000 for Pacific Heights home . . .
. . . Clement St. upset over a Chinese family moving in . . .

Inspiration requires another cocktail, he concluded.

Padding to the bar, Paean carefully mixed the martini San Francisco style. In an aluminum shaker half filled with crushed ice, Paean poured four jiggers of Bombay gin, whispering "vermouth" over the top of the container.

Early in his bar-hopping "daze," Paean had learned the secret to a perfect martini: the mix is shaken, but never stirred. Heeding this truth of mixology, he shook the silver canister gently and rhythmically, up and down, like a maraca for a silent count of twelve. Pouring the contents into a chilled long-stemmed glass, Paean balanced a brace of three green olives across the rim.

After a long satisfying sip, Paean returned to the den, ready for his daily intercourse with his loyal Royal, the gentle coaxing that gave his life meaning, the fondling of the space bar, the delicate caressing of the round metal keys, punctuated by the banging thrust of the carriage.

With two forefingers, he typed,

> *. . . Red Alert! The HUAC attack brings*
> *its Commie dog and pony show to sniff about*
> *the pervasive influence of left wing scholars*
> *at Berkeley. Cal Bears, Beware . . .*

6

CONNIE AND BUTCH

The trio paused before the solitary departure gate, a faded double door leading to the runway. Around them, the skeletons of the new Minneapolis-St. Paul International Airport emerged amid the corpse of the Wold-Chamberlain Field, the site of a failed auto racing speedway once dubbed the "concrete farm."

"Remember me to 'Frisco," said Mike, giving Jonathan a bear hug, "and don't do anything I wouldn't do."

"Leave him alone, darling," chided Pearl. "You sowed your wild oats. Now it's time for Jonathan to have his own fun." She kissed Jonathan gently on the cheek, leaving a bright red lip print below his right ear. "See you at Christmas."

Jonathan crossed the breezy tarmac to an aluminum staircase leaning against the front door of a Lockheed Constellation or Connie of CAT-California Airline Transport- decorated in pink, orange, and red stripes, its nose bearing a childlike smile, a half circle painted beneath two round, black dot eyes

The Connie's propellers coughed and sputtered, spewing smoke from the rear of the jet assisted engines as Jonathan inched up the stairway, his head light, his feet unconnected to anything earthbound. At the top of the aluminum stairway, he turned toward the terminal, the engine noise now deafening. The suction of the propeller blades whipped his tie and billowed his blue blazer.

Jonathan looked back and waved with both arms in slow broad

sweeps to Mike and Pearl outlined in the window of the terminal, saying to himself, *Goodbye and farewell, Clear Lake.*

Ducking his head through the entryway, Jonathan encountered the cabin crowded with a line of passengers moving in slow motion. To his left, he saw the cockpit crew busily twirling dials, pushing buttons, and pulling levers.

To his right, three stewardesses or stews of CAT nicknamed, Kitty CATS, greeted passengers.

They look like starlets, he thought, trying not to stare.

All three were slender, tanned, and long-legged, wearing pink spiked heels, orange skirts with hems slightly above the knee, red tight-fitting blouses, and pink heart-shaped caps sitting on short, poofy hairdos. Each bore a smile as wide as the one painted on the Connie's nose.

According to a recent Life magazine article, Kitty CATS were renowned for their beauty and perkiness and the overwhelming favorites of businessmen. They were all single, between five-foot-three and five-foot-eight inches tall, and could not weigh more than 130 pounds. Whenever a Kitty CAT married, she was mandatorily retired.

"Welcome to CAT flight 4444, nonstop service to San Francisco," oozed the first Kitty CAT, a dark brunette with brown eyes and full luscious lips. "A little something to read," she said, handing Jonathan a copy of the airline's in-flight magazine, *The CAT's Meow.*

"My, my, my. You must have a way with the girls!" teased a pale peroxide blonde with green eyes, admiring the imprint of Pearl's lipstick on Jonathan's cheek.

His face turning scarlet, Jonathan handed his ticket to the third stewardess, a honey-haired, blue-eyed girl with the deepest tan he had ever seen. Her name tag read, *Candy.*

"Jon-a-than Aldon, seat 22D," said Candy, reading slowly from the ticket. "Has anyone told you you're a dead ringer for Tab Hunter?" The dazzle of her perfectly aligned teeth blinded him.

"My mother," stammered Jonathan, "Tab Hunter is one of her favorite actors."

"We don't see many younger people on these flights," said Candy. "Where're you going?"

"College. I'll be a freshman at the University of California," Jonathan said proudly. "In Berkeley," he added.

"Cal?" said Candy returning the ticket. "My little sis will be a freshman too. Maybe the two of you will meet." Her flowery, sweet scent intoxicated him.

"There's another Cal student on this flight, sitting across the aisle from you. You college boys will have the back of the plane all to yourselves," Candy winked.

Jonathan glanced at *The CATS Meow* airline magazine, noting the headline,

Air Travel Boom: 10% of US Have Now Flown

Inching down the narrow, single aisle, Jonathan marveled at the size of the Connie's cabin, cavernous and cigar-shaped, with porthole windows along its fuselage. Men in dark business suits and women in luxurious fur coats sat three abreast on each side of the spacious aisle, fidgeting with overhead air nozzles. He quietly thanked Mother for insisting that he wear his blazer, white shirt, repp tie, and slacks. She had told him how the privileged who could afford to fly always dressed up, especially those traveling to big cities like San Francisco.

Arriving at row 22, Jonathan saw a swarthy, black-haired boy, sitting on the aisle seat to his left, reading a paperback entitled "Lady Chatterly's Lover."

Must be the other Cal student, he thought.

"Is this 22 D?" asked Jonathan.

The dark-haired boy looked up from the paperback, a scowl spreading across his face. "Sit your butt down," he said curtly, pointing to the seat across the aisle, the voice reminding Jonathan of Marlon Brando's movie character in "On the Waterfront."

Jonathan's query had interrupted Butch Tanenbloom's rare moment of doubt. Butch had boarded the Connie at La Guardia, in a euphoric state, but as the flight droned on, he suddenly questioned the wisdom of his decision.

Butch had been an all state high school basketball player as a Junior and a <u>Parade</u> magazine All American, as a Senior. At 6 foot-5-inches tall, he was an imposing figure on the court, taller and stronger than most guards, quicker and more agile than most forwards. Yet, round ball was not the only important thing in his life. From his mother, he inherited a passion for Broadway musicals and movies; from his father, a deep interest in reading; from his grandfather, a commitment to formal education.

Butch viewed a college athletic scholarship as the ticket out of

Brooklyn, a way to satisfy his desire to reach for the stars. He had not been impressed with college campuses until he made a visit to the University of California. From the moment he first set feet on the Cal campus, he knew where he belonged.

It had been February, and most of the country was still buried in snow, buffeted by the harsh winds of winter. At Cal, Butch was greeted by green, rolling hills, and a campus built in a forest. And sunshine! Glorious sunshine that cast a magical, golden glow.

Gazing over the blue expanse of the San Francisco Bay from the campus Botanical Gardens, Butch had inhaled deeply of the fresh, salty air and announced, "California, here I come!"

Now, Butch wasn't so sure. All his life, he had taken for granted what was so wonderfully New York: the theater, museums, ethnic foods, and that certain electricity in the air.

What if he missed the hustle and bustle of the streets? What if he failed to be a star at Cal? What if he became bored with the pastoral beauty of California?

Too many questions cluttered his mind.

Maybe talking with this country bumpkin will keep my mind off things, Butch thought.

Across the aisle, Jonathan removed his blazer and loosened his tie. He studied the clothes of the tall, muscular boy across the aisle, noting the black pinstriped suit and a red kerchief peaking from the left-breast pocket. Above his polished black wing-tip shoes, the boy wore white spats.

Spats? Jonathan had never seen real ones before, recalling Fred Astaire wearing a pair in Mother's favorite movie musical, "Flying Down to Rio."

"So, you're a Cal student, too?" said Jonathan, extending his hand across the aisle. "Jonathan Aldon."

"Butch Tanenbloom," said the dark-haired boy, enveloping Jonathan's hand in a powerful grip. "Jeez, your hands are sweaty," he said, wiping his right hand on his pant legs. "Fly much?"

"No, not really. I've never flown before."

"Piece of cake," said Butch. "First, you put your seat belt on by sticking the male end into the female end like so." He clicked the two ends together with a flourish.

Looking around, Jonathan located the ends of the belt, studied each part, and poked the ends at each other until he heard the sound of the click.

"Too loose," said Butch. "Pull the end of the strap. Here, let me help." Reaching across the aisle, Butch yanked tight the seat belt. "There. If we crash, you'll die in one piece, instead of teeny bits splattered across the windows."

Jonathan swallowed, feeling a lump in his throat.

"C'mon, Junior. Lighten up," said Butch, jabbing with his index finger. "Here are Butch's easy tips on surviving your first airplane ride. First, sweet-talk a beer out of the stew, take a little snooze, read a bit, watch the movie, yak with me. Hey, in no time, we're in 'Frisco. A worse thing that could happen is upchucking in the old barf bag," said Butch, pulling a thin white bag from the seat pocket in front of him. Dangling it by the tips of his thumb and forefinger, he said, "absolutely leak proof."

Soon, their initial tension yielded to an easy rapport as they shared their excitement about attending college in the San Francisco Bay Area. To their surprise, both had been assigned to the same Cal dorm, Dooch Hall.

Following Butch's lead, Jonathan twisted the plastic nozzle above him, straining for cool air, feeling a tingling mix of thrill and dread, as the Connie lurched, picking up speed, and rolled relentlessly forward.

"Here we go!" shouted Butch, as the plane tilted off the runway.

Before them, the Kitty CATS positioned themselves equidistant through the cabin presenting safety instructions. Standing by Row 20, Candy nodded at Jonathan as she pointed to seat belts, exits, and oxygen masks.

"Hey, that stew just winked at you, Junior. Definitely a three-star general," whispered Butch, leaning into the aisle, shamelessly ogling Candy. "Check out that bod! What a set of knockers! Look at those gams!"

"Shhh," hissed Jonathan.

Butch is right, he thought. *She is gorgeous! Can't wait to write Ziggy about the Kitty CATS.*

Groaning, the Connie lumbered toward its cruising altitude, eventually leveling off at 25,000 feet. Moving over to the window seat, Jonathan sat transfixed, taking in the expanse of America's heartland.

"Junior," said Butch Tanenbloom, motioning Jonathan back

to his seat. "I, as connoisseur of female pulchritude, will share with you my famous rating system of the fairer sex," he said, in a serious tone.

"Girls can be ranked like soldiers. Every rank has a specific meaning. For example, every girl is at least a Private just by being female. Fat, ugly, doesn't matter. Now, if a Private screws a lot, she's a Fuck Private. Get it?" Butch beamed at the pun on the Army term, Buck Private.

Jonathan's mind was spinning, as Butch droned on clinically about the aesthetic differences in female breasts, fannies, hips, eyes, lips, hair styles, shapes and sizes that distinguished Corporals, Sergeants, Lieutenants, Captains, Majors, and Colonels in Butch's rating system.

"Now, the cream of the crop, the Generals," said Butch salivating. In rapid-fire succession, Butch delineated the subtle differences among One, Two, Three, and Four-star Generals. "And finally, the Five-Star General, the girl of your dreams," said Butch triumphantly. His mood had improved.

Jonathan watched with fascination as the Kitty CATS wiggled about the Connie, preparing for lunch service. Candy, the prettiest girl he had ever met had actually spoken to him, and his new friend, Butch, had taught him more about girls in one hour than he had ever learned growing up in Clear Lake!

What other surprises are waiting on this airborne flight of fancy? he wondered.

7

FOOD FOR THOUGHT

As the flight droned on, the two new friends swapped views on pop music, Jonathan waxing eloquently about his rock-a-billy favorites, Butch insisting that Eastern Doo-Wop was superior. They found common ground, agreeing that "Rocking Robin" was an all-time great. Singing an impromptu duet of the Bobby Day hit, the two, snapping fingers in unison, were joined by Candy for the last chorus.

"You two are so much FUN," purred Candy.

"Jon-a-than, you're so much FUN," said Butch, mimicking Candy in a high-pitched falsetto. "I'm telling you, Junior. That sweet little stew, Candy, has got the h-o-t-s for you. Listen to the lyrical way she says your name, Jon-a-than. Look at the way she smiles at you. And the way she bends that tight, little ass . . . " His voice trailed off in feigned ecstasy. "Definitely a two-star General."

Returning with lunch, Candy handed each boy a plain, brown bag. "Shhh. Don't tell a soul about this," she whispered.

"Fan-tastic!" said Butch, removing the blue and gold can. "Kerrs! Junior, you know what my Brooklyn buddies would give for a six-pack of this stuff?"

Jonathan shook his head. He had tasted only one beer, a can of bitter tasting, Minnesota brew he had split with Ziggy on high school graduation night.

"Kerrs has a cult following," explained Butch. "It's impossible to find outside of Northern California. College kids drive across the country to pick up a few cases. The secret to its great taste is the water from natural artesian springs of the Sierra Nevada Mountains near Lake Tahoe."

Jonathan read the slogan on the blue and gold can, *Great water makes great beer.*

Producing a Swiss Army knife, Butch unfolded an awl, punching two holes in the top of both cans of Kerrs.

"Anybody who invents a way to open these cans without a church key will make a fortune!" said Butch, offering a toast, "As Bogie once said, 'here's looking at you, kid,' " Taking a long swig, he handed Jonathan the other can. "Great stuff! Have a sip, Junior."

Jonathan hesitated, remembering the bubbly, brackish drink he had shared with Ziggy, tasting like an antacid tablet fizzing in sugar water. Instinctively, he held his nose, bracing for a pungent smell. Surprisingly, the beer was smooth, slightly sweet tasting, its bubbles lightly tingling his tongue and throat. Taking another sip, he released his nose, embracing the aromatic scent of the beer.

"What do you think?" asked Butch.

"Tasty," said Jonathan, this time emulating Butch by holding the can vertically, taking several gulps in a row.

"Okay, Junior. Let's see what Iowa farm boys are made of. Down the hatch! Loser owes a six-pack."

Tilting up their beers, they began their duel. From the corner of his eye, Jonathan saw Butch draining his beer effortlessly in one long, sustained slurp.

Gulping rapidly, breathing between swallows, Jonathan felt his Adams apple bobbing wildly, an air pocket lodging in his throat, blocking the flow of beer, gagging him. Paralyzed, his esophagus expelled beer, spewing an arc of spittle, drenching Butch who recoiled with pretended horror.

Laughing, the two sopped up the disgorged beer with silk handkerchiefs Butch produced from his suit pocket.

"That was some Ka-bloo-ey, Junior," said Butch. "Don't feel bad. Same thing happened the first time I tried to chug. I was at my cousin's wedding reception in Manhattan and upchucked down the backless dress of the maid of honor."

"What's the secret?" asked Jonathan, wiping beads of Kerrs

from the seat in front of him.

"It's a trick called the Brooklyn Hustle," said Butch. "The trick is relaxing your throat muscles while keeping the flow constant. You saw what happens when you gulp. Practice with glasses of water. Cheaper and not as messy. Move up to rot gut beer, then onto Kerrs. If you're good, you'll never have to buy another beer again."

"My, my, you boys have been naughty." It was Candy, armed with paper towels. "What a waste. Looks like you'll need a refill," she said, handing another paper bag to Jonathan containing two more cans of Kerrs.

"We'll make an incredible team," said Butch, producing the Swiss army knife. "With my looks and your charm, other guys won't have a prayer with the babes."

"Butch, what is this stuff?" Jonathan asked, removing two wax paper packages from the lunch bag. In one, the contents looked like green slime and stinky cheese between cardboard pieces of bread. In the other was a pear shaped cactus plant.

"Mmm," said Butch, biting into the exotic sandwich. "Avocado-Limburger cheese on 'Frisco sourdough."

"And this thing?" said Jonathan peeling off a spiny, olive green leaf from a small, dense plant.

"Don't eat the needle end," warned Butch, reading Jonathan's mind. "That's a California veggie called an artichoke. Dip the soft end in the butter or the mayo."

To Jonathan's surprise, the pulpy end of the exotic plant was smooth, tender, and tasty. After devouring the leafy tips, he examined the heavy, fleshy remnant.

"Watch me, Junior," said Butch trimming the sides and bottom, coring the round center, splitting the heart with Jonathan.

Three exotic, new California foods: avocado, artichoke, and Kerrs. thought Jonathan.

Feeling the effects of the Kerrs, Jonathan's lids grew heavy as the in-flight movie flickered on. It was "Pillow Talk," starring Rock Hudson and Doris Day. As the film credits rolled, Jonathan drifted off in sleep, as Butch offered a stream of commentary.

"Wonder if Doris Day is really such a Miss Goody Two Shoes?"

The last thing Jonathan heard was Butch muttering, "Rock Hudson's sex life must be incredible! Generals really go for that he-man type."

* * *

Jonathan awoke to sounds of window shades snapping open, blinding sunlight spilling into the Connie, the movie ending. Rubbing away the sleepy cobwebs, yawning and stretching, he asked Butch, "How was Pillow Talk?"

"Snoozed off myself, Junior, right after that bathtub scene with the telephones. Not as sexy as the reviews claimed," yawned Butch. "Speaking of sex, here comes your little Kitty CAT, Candy," he whispered. "Look at the way she moves, like Jello on springs."

As the warning light to fasten seat belts flashed on, Candy made her way to the rear of the Connie, cheerfully collecting headsets. Blushing again, Jonathan watched her wiggle toward them.

Butch is right again, he thought. *Like Jello on springs.*

"We meet some strange people on these flights," said Candy glancing at Butch, "but you have been s-o-o-o nice, Jonathan. I'm going to give you my little sister's name. She's going through sorority rush. Probably pledge Gamma Delta, the Gee Dees, the sorority with the cutest girls."

"Ah, a source of Generals," quipped Butch.

"I'm sure you would enjoy meeting her," said Candy, jotting on a cocktail napkin. "Here, let me show you a picture."

Candy produced a strip of three black and white photos taken in a photo booth."The one to my left is my older sister Sandy Cane, the one to my right is my younger, Dandy Cane, the one entering Cal."

They could be triplets, marveled Jonathan, examining the photos of the Cane sisters, Sandy, Candy, and Dandy.

Butch whistled softly. "My, my, my. Very impressive. All of you Canes inherited very sweet genes. Three Major Generals!" he said, issuing a thunderous burp.

The Connie circled in a wide arc, in its final approach, affording breathtaking views of San Francisco. Armadas of white sails dotted the Bay, zigging between ocean vessels. For miles in every direction, roads, buildings, and homes carpeted gentle hills, the afternoon sun shimmering like daytime beacons off the

45

buildings of the San Francisco skyline.

Clear Lake is a small puddle in comparison, thought Jonathan.

Candy pointed out the majestic orange span of the Golden Gate and the sinewy arms of the San Francisco-Oakland Bay Bridges jammed with holiday traffic. Jonathan could see the tiny rectangles of cable cars creeping up the hills.

"There it is," said Butch, pointing to a slender white tower standing at the foot of the eastern foothills of San Francisco Bay. "That's Cal's landmark, the Campanile."

Pressing his face against the window, Jonathan saw a large block letter C imbedded on the crest of a foothill above the Campanile.

C for college! C for California! And I'm really here!

8

THE GOLDEN GODDESS

Kate Howell stood before the full-length mirror and studied the image of the typically well-dressed sorority girl. She saw a striking blue-eyed blonde wearing a plaid, pleated skirt, a white blouse with a gold circle pin on the Peter Pan collar, an unbuttoned, dark blue, long-sleeve cashmere sweater, and Bass Weegun loafers. Conspicuously absent were tennis socks, rolled down to the ankles, that would have made the uniform complete.

Kate had adopted this naked-ankle look last spring, and MAD (Mothers Advisory Detail) had not been amused. Before a packed sorority house meeting, MAD issued Kate a Deficiency Notice for violating the sorority dress code.   The sternly worded citation warned,

Remember Who You Are and What You Represent.

The sanction was little more than a slap on the wrist, as Kate could have been grounded for a weekend. Secretly, Kate had reveled in the controversy and its aftermath as, one by one, her Gamma Delta sorority sisters had followed her lead and worn their penny loafers sockless, a style that was now a Gee Dee fashion statement.

The minor reprimand had not surprised Kate's roommate, Joan Dildeaux, who observed, "What did you expect? After all, Kate IS the Golden Goddess."

How Kate hated her nickname-bestowed by a smitten cub reporter of the student newspaper, <u>The Daily Cal</u>- a title that had dogged her during her two years at Cal. But the unchallenged truth was that college boys treated Kate as royalty, a radiant natural beauty who commanded immediate and undivided attention.

She was slender, small-boned, five-foot-five but carried herself taller, an illusion attributable to the perfect carriage and an elegant, graceful stride instilled at the posh Los Angeles Marlborough Girls School where Mom believed Kate would escape the male riffraff of public school: surfers and hot rodders.

Emancipated at Cal, Kate had been immediately thrust into the social spotlight. Kate had been flattered by the public fawning, but she had dismissed the adulation as a function of campus supply and demand, as boys outnumbered girls five to one. How tiresome fancy fraternity parties had become, where she was paraded around like a trophy for a deserving fraternity boy!

Joining the Gamma Delta sorority had not provided respite from the college social whirl. The Gee Dee house was referred to as the House of Beauty, where many a starry-eyed fraternity boy loitered, hoping for a "nod," a date. And among the denizens of the House of Beauty, Kate was the acknowledged queen of the queens, or as the Inter-Fraternity Newsletter described, a true "five percenter," one of the most beautiful coeds on campus.

In the mirror, Kate watched her image drape a large blue silk scarf over her head and tie a dainty knot under the chin. She slipped on a pair of oversized dark glasses.

"There," she said confidently. "A perfect disguise."

"You won't fool a soul," said Joan Dildeaux who had been following Kate's charade with amusement.

Kate slowly pirouetted, her arms gracefully outstretched like a gliding bird. "Why not, roommie?" There was a tone of disappointment in her voice as she gave herself another once over in the mirror.

Joan peered over the top of her thick glasses and rolled her eyes. *Jeez*, she sighed. *Kate really doesn't get it.*

Joan's gorgeous roommate had returned from summer vacation, glowing in a deep orange tan and sporting a glamorous new hairdo. Gone was the short "page boy" so popular among Cal sorority girls. In its place was a new style Glamour magazine called the "flip." The result was dramatic. Kate's flowing flaxen hair highlighted her sparkling blue eyes, complimented the sharp angles of her perfect high cheekbones and underscored her well-defined jaw line.

The rich do get richer, thought Joan.

Joan draped an arm over her best friend's shoulder and grimaced at the bespectacled Plain Jane standing next to the Golden Goddess, noting that the only similarity between the two was their standard sorority uniforms.

God wasn't fair to other women when He created Kate, Joan said to herself. *What I wouldn't give for just one of her classic features. Just one.*

"Kate, you could wear men's clothing and still be recognized."

"Humor me, Joanie. Tell me the scarf and dark glasses make a difference."

"You may as well be Kim Novak walking into the P U house in broad daylight." Joan laughed. She was referring to the Pi Upsilon fraternity across the street. "If you're going to risk getting kicked out of school, you'd be better off learning to walk a little faster."

Joan was awed by Kate's spunk, by her willingness to take risks. But some risks, like this one, seemed much too dangerous, even for someone with Royal privileges. It was one thing to sneak over to Casey Lee's under the cover of darkness, but in broad daylight? If discovered, even Kate Howell, the Golden Goddess would not escape the wrath of MAD.

"Promise you'll be careful," said Joan, giving Kate a hug.

"Promise, Joanie. I'll be back before dinner."

Kate slipped quietly down the fire escape, past the large sleeping porch which would soon be filled with the excited squeals of new Gee Dee pledges.

Touching down on the back patio, she tiptoed past the private apartment of Miss Willa Haversham, the Gee Dee housemother. Through the open window Kate caught a whiff of that southern sourmash whisky Dad and his drinking buddies at the Jonathan Club were drinking these days. "Jack" something or other.

Kate squeezed into a parade of students marching downhill on Channing Way toward College Avenue. The intersection was a battleground of chaotic frenzy, as motorists ignored the blinking signal lights. Parked station wagons and pickup trucks disgorged an army of students and their fall survival gear. Swirling masses spilled onto the far sidewalk fighting for precious toeholds, as the surging crowds lurched one way, then another, engulfing islands of trunks and boxes. A block away stood their destination, Dooch Hall.

To her right, P U's, leaning out their windows taunted the new arrivals with "DORMIES SUCK! DORMIES SUCK!"

Kate looked straight ahead, pulling the scarf tightly to her head, waiting to cross College Avenue.

Good, no one will recognize me in this mess, she thought.

In the middle of the gridlock, a traffic control officer, in dark glasses, undulated elongated arms rhythmically, with practiced precision, like the comic strip hero, *Plastic Man*.

Above the cacophony of incessant car honking, he barked, "Move it or lose it, Dumbo! Hey, can't ya' read? No unloadin' in the middle of the street. Who d'ya think ya' are, moron, a Teamster?" He tooted shrilly at the offender with his whistle.

Kate recognized the Jersey accent of the Waz, one of Casey's friends.

"Hey, Buster, ya' wanna knuckle sandwich?" the Waz shouted at a moving motorist who had flipped him the Bird.

As Kate waited for traffic to clear, she thought back on summer and concluded the best thing had been the visits with grand auntie Martha.

Although Dad and Mom called her Crazy Martha and said she was as "nutty as a loon," Kate found her grand auntie endearing. Despite their sixty-year age difference, the two were kindred spirits who enjoyed a special relationship Mom and Dad would never understand.

What her parents did appreciate was the fact Kate was the sole beneficiary of Crazy Martha's multimillion dollar estate. Therefore, every other Sunday, the Howells had dutifully driven from their home in San Marino, up the coast to Camarillo, to allow Kate to pay her respects to Crazy Martha.

At the Peaceful Valley Old Folks Home, Martha would dismiss Mom and Dad with a wave of the hand, preferring a private audience with her "dear little Katie."

While Dad and Mom strolled the neatly groomed hillside beyond the barbed wire fence, Martha would pluck her full dentures from a silver box, plop them onto her naked gums and plead, "Where are my goodies, Katie?"

It had been a conspiracy of unlikely accomplices. Before each visit, Kate would slip a few dollars to the Howells' faithful Japanese gardener, and Yaz would return with a plain brown bag, no questions asked. Once alone, Kate would present her grand aunt the secret booty, a fistful of rum-soaked cigars.

"Honey, you're the only sane one left in the family," Crazy Martha would cackle, as she ripped off the wrapper of a stogie. "Light me up nice and easy."

Crazy Martha claimed there was Shawnee Indian blood somewhere in the distant family history, a fact no other Howell acknowledged. This, grand auntie explained, was the reason that, unlike the other Howells, she had been born with jet-black hair and dark-olive skin.

"Katie, we've got our own Tonto in the family woodpile," she said with a twinkle in her eye. "Ever wonder why your summer tan doesn't peel off like other blondes?"

Answering her own question, she said, "Recessive Indian genes, Katie." As she puffed a string of perfectly formed smoke rings, Martha said, "A college girl like you should study Mendel's Law of Genetics."

Mendel's Law of Genetics. How ironic!

She had met Casey in Biology 10 where the two had been randomly paired as lab partners. Kate had been immediately intrigued by how differently Casey treated her. He was the first boy since grammar school who actually looked her in the eye when she spoke. And how refreshing that a boy with such a quiet reassuring confidence had never hinted for a date with the Golden Goddess.

And his voice. Deep. Smooth. Mellifluous. She could listen to him for hours. Kate had confided to Joan there were times when Casey spoke, she had imagined closing her eyes and feeling his deep warm voice massaging her very soul.

And when she dared stare into his exotic, dark-brown eyes, she would blush, as the fine hair on the nape of her neck stood perfectly erect.

"Oral sex appeal?" Joan had teased.

It had been Kate's idea to study together at the Gee Dee house, but a nosy member of the House Morals Committee had discovered them alone in one of the date rooms, and a member of MAD had marched Casey unceremoniously out the back door of the House of Beauty.

"Gee Dees should never be alone with nonfraternity boys," a new Deficiency Notice had warned. But Kate knew MAD's concern was that other reason.

Angered by the rebuff, Kate suggested sneaking into Casey's dorm room to cram for exams. He had balked, as a report to the Dean's Office about a girl visiting the all-male dorm would bring social probation for the Dooch Dormies. But Kate had persisted, and Casey relented, accepting the logic of the plan.

There was no chance that a raid by the Campus Police would find her. At night the dorm was dark, and there were too many ways Kate could avoid detection. Two outside stairwells, the dorm elevator, the laundry chute to the basement, and as a last resort, Ollie Punch and Hunch Hitowski's experiments in aerial dynamics were all viable escape routes.

Casey had polled his eighth-floor neighbors, and there had been no opposition. As Royal French explained, "since sorority girls don't date Dormies, Kate's study sessions with Casey will give us cheap thrills."

Neither Casey Lee nor Kate Howell ever learned just how vicarious Kate's visits were, as their every word was overheard by an enraptured Dormie audience. Royal French devised the eavesdrop RF that secretly broadcast all of Kate and Casey's conversations. Marty Silverstein, the Super Sleuth, had bugged the air-conditioning duct of Casey's room with a microphone connected to a transmitter in the All-Pro's KALX transmitter which, in turn, relayed sound to large speakers in the downstairs study lounge. There, Ruby Lips collected a 25-cent admission from any Dormie desiring to hear the sultry voice of the Golden Goddess broadcasting LIVE from the top floor of the dorm.

Their study sessions would give way to intimate discussions Kate had only shared with her roommate Joan Dildeaux.

Conversations with Casey were so different, so exhilarating.

Although he was a gracious listener, Casey never hesitated to challenge and tease Kate about her views, something those goo-goo eyed fraternity boys would never consider. How she loved their private talks!

The second best thing about summer was Casey's cheery postcards. The rectangular tan missives, with two-cent postage, would arrive every Tuesday at the Howell's San Marino estate, bearing the initials "KC," each postcard, a comforting reminder of

52

the spiritual bond awaiting her return to Berkeley.

If Mom and Dad only knew who "KC" was, shock would have been too mild a word, she thought. *Dad had such goofy views about anyone who was different.*

Of the loyal Howell gardener, Yas Yamashita, Dad had observed, "Orientals were born to provide beauty to others. They're hard workers who keep to themselves and never cause trouble." He added, "Those worthless Mexicans can learn a thing or two from Orientals."

Kate wondered what the Howell family maid, Lupe Martinez, thought about Dad's attitude about Mexicans.

"The only difference between Pollacks and Mexicans is the spelling of their surnames," Dad had said with authority. "They're all lazier than sin."

How did Dad's opinion about Polish people square with his high regard for her summer boss, Mr. Z, Anton Zwyzwyzwyski, the manager of Dad's Jonathan Club?

The end of summer and Labor Day had arrived none too soon, Kate thought.

"Step lively, lady!" The Waz's sharply accented voice jolted Kate from her reverie. He pointed to a tiny clearance between two stalled autos.

"Thanks," Kate muttered as she scooted sideways through the opening.

In the middle of the intersection, Kate felt a gentle tap on the shoulder. "Goddess," said the Waz, "none of my business, but 'dem shades don't do ya' justice."

Who else can see through my masquerade? she wondered.

Reaching the stairwell of the Dooch Hall fire escape, Kate paused, quickly scanning up and down Channing Way.

Good, no one watching.

As she began the familiar hike to the eighth-floor, the magnificent vistas of San Francisco Bay and Berkeley's golden foothills enfolded in the brilliant, late afternoon sun.

Yes, Fall is in the air, Kate concluded, feeling a slight nip in the Bay breeze.

Will Casey like my new flip?

How she had missed listening to Casey's deep, sweet voice. And gazing into his exotic eyes.

9

KRUM

Dirk Krum III, President of the Pi Upsilon fraternity, burst onto the sprawling veranda of his second-story bedroom. Krum wore the standard fraternity uniform: a short-sleeve white shirt with a starched, button-down collar, khaki pants, white socks, and loafers. In his hand, he clutched a pair of Army field glasses.

He had inherited the classic features of the Krum clan: the striking looks of a model, prominent cheek bones, sandy, crewcut hair, and brown eyes. But unlike his grandfather and father, Dirk Krum I and Dirk Krum II, Dirk Krum III, had a chameleon change in looks that appeared only when he was angry. Then, his handsome smile degenerated into a sneer, his eyes darkening into smoldering pieces of coal.

Across College Avenue, a long line of humanity snaked out the double doors of the men's dorm, Dooch Hall, down to adjacent Channing Way, jammed with station wagons and taxis disgorging students and their families.

Cursing, Krum frantically focused on the female figure scurrying up the fire escape of the eight-story dorm, appearing, disappearing, then reappearing in the late afternoon sun streaming through the open stairwell that blurred his line of sight.

Perched on the hilly intersection of College Avenue and Channing Way, Pi Upsilon fraternity, or the P U house, as it was known, had been designed in 1904 by the renowned Bay Area architect Bernard Maybuck. Noted for its massive redwood beams, angular shingled roof, and layers of ivy overgrowth, the P U house had commanded a sweeping vista of San Francisco Bay for more than fifty-years, making the P U's the envy of the other fraternities of the Cal Greek system.

But that was before the University had completed the high-rise dorm last year, blocking the P U's once magnificent view of the Golden Gate. Krum had watched the systematic destruction of this peaceful, rustic neighborhood, once graced with Coast live oaks and redwoods. In their place now stood the cold, stark monolith of Dooch Hall, affordable housing for financially disadvantaged students.

For Krum, Dooch Hall represented an unsettling trend in campus living. With its massive concrete columns and large glass windows, Dooch was a sterile box catering to an undesirable element creeping into the University. The Cal experience, once reserved for members of wealthy Greck fraternities, now lay vulnerable to an invasion of students of a lower class.

In Krum's view, the recent influx of undesirables posed a threat to the dominance, if not the existence, of the Greek system. Who would be the standard bearers of taste, excellence, and decorum, if not the Greeks? Krum had warned the IFC, Inter-Fraternity Council, that if allowed to flourish, rabble, like the Dormies of Dooch Hall, would overrun the campus, destroying traditions established and nurtured by generations of Greek fraternity men.

But it was not the survival of the Greek fraternity system that weighed heavily on Krum's mind, as he tracked his quarry in his field glasses.

She was fair and slender, dressed in a plaid, pleated, wool skirt, a white blouse with a Peter Pan collar and a gold circle pin, and penny loafers. The only item missing from the standard sorority uniform was white socks turned down to the ankles.

Only the Gee Dees wore their loafers without white socks. An unsettling deviation from acceptable sorority fashion, Krum thought. More disturbing was the rumor that Kate Howell had initiated this stupid craze.

Impossible. Who would spread such a lie about Kate?

Krum twirled the settings of the binoculars and squinted intently at the moving figure. Despite dark glasses and the silk scarf hiding her face, Krum easily recognized the thin curve of the calves, the smooth slink of the walk, the determined swing of the arms, as she moved quickly up the Dooch stairwell.

Kate Howell!

Why is the Golden Goddess sneaking up the dorm fire escape?

All living groups were segregated by sex, and the university banned students from visiting the rooms of members of the opposite sex. Even in the P U house, females were permitted only in the living room and then, only during formal chaperoned events.

Punishment for violating this rule was immediate expulsion.

Despite Kate's popularity, Krum had noticed she did not date often. True, she was escorted by the most socially correct, the most athletically prominent, and the most politically influential boys on campus to every major social event. Yet, Krum had observed her studying alone at the library, or in the company of her Gee Dee sorority sisters, away from the constant scrutiny of her doting public. It was this quiet confidence, this restrained sense of selectivity, that made her even more desirable.

From the moment Krum first saw Kate Howell, he knew she was the prize he had to have.

Most fraternity boys would give their right nut for a date with her, Krum thought, *for the glory of being seen with her.*

When Kate's shadow reached the top floor of the dorm, Krum saw her knocking urgently on the door next to the landing. The door open slowly, a slender, black-haired male, with an angular face set off by brown almond eyes, quickly admitting her.

Krum adjusted the binoculars to the blinding light of the setting sun and recoiled, shocked by the Oriental face of Casey Lee!

"Oh, God, NO!" Krum gasped, the binoculars trembling in his fists. "It's the fucking Chinaman!"

Resting the field glasses on the wooden railing of the veranda, his face flushed with anger, Krum said to himself, *You'll pay for this, Casey Lee. You and all your goddamned Dormies.*

"Chip! Chip!" said Krum, barking at his roommate, chatting on the bedroom phone, angling for a date. "Dammit, Chip, get your ass out here!"

Sliding open the glass door, Chip Fist lumbered onto the veranda, now darkened by the long afternoon shadow of Dooch Hall. A varsity football player, Chip Fist stood six-feet-four and weighed 250 pounds, a belly nurtured by cans of Hamms beer bulging against a white T-shirt pulled over tight blue jeans, his enormous feet resembling miniature whales encased in rubber

56

beach thongs called go-a-heads.

"Whadda ya need, Dirk?"

Glancing at the sneer on Dirk's face and the darkening of his eyes, Chip knew his roommate was in one foul mood.

"Call an emergency house meeting of the P U Brothers," said Krum. "We're going to teach those Dormies a lesson."

"Bitchin, bitchin," said Chip, his enthusiasm rising at the prospect of violence. "Gotcha, Dirk! See ya downstairs."

From the hi-fi stereo of a neighboring fraternity, Mickey and Sylvia crooned the haunting ballad, "Love Is Strange."

Yes, Krum said to himself, *I'll get you, Casey Lee, the way the Krums should have taken care of the Lees a long time ago.*

10

CITY LIFE

"Looks like the United Nations," said Butch. "Betcha you don't see this in Iowa."

Grinning, Jonathan nodded in agreement. The Connie had transported him from Clear Lake to an exotic, enchanted land that even Uncle Mike's colorful stories had failed to capture. Shouldering their way through the crowded San Francisco airport, the pair was engulfed in a throng of swirling color and the contrapuntal cadence of computing foreign tongues. The furs and topcoats of the Minneapolis passengers were now blandly out of place in the exotic sea of fashion: monks in saffron robes, Middle Eastern men in jellabas, women in a rainbow of sarongs, robes, abayahs, saris, and mu-mus. Turbans, fezes, bowlers, thaubs, berets and sombreros bobbed in a sea of hats.

Collecting their luggage, the two exited the lower level amid a chorus of honking horns.

"Feel that fresh air, Butch," Jonathan shouted, inhaling his first deep breath of California, a curious mixture of Pacific salt air laced with gasoline and diesel fumes.

"Junior, you've been sniffing pig shit too long," Butch clucked.

"How do we get to Berkeley?" asked Jonathan, scanning a long queue of taxis and buses.

"Let's live dangerously," said Butch, nodding toward a solitary, forlorn heap across the street.

It was "woodie," a late 1940's station wagon, with broad

wooden panels, trimmed in yellow and chrome which, according to <u>Look</u> magazine, California teenagers used to haul surfboards to the beach. The windshield displayed a crudely scrawled sign, *Starving Student Needs Work--Cheap Fares & Tours!*

Leaning against the woodie was a ramrod-thin cabby dressed in worn chinos, tattered T-shirt, and long skinny, black shoes resembling rotted bananas, his attention riveted to a copy of <u>Playboy</u> magazine.

"Hey, cabby," shouted Butch. "Got room for a couple of Berkeley students?"

Slapping shut the girlie magazine, the driver rolled it up with practiced precision, slipping it in the driver side visor. At close range, the cabby was even thinner with skin stretched more than six-feet of jagged bone.

Thick chestnut brown hair lay like an emaciated coonskin cap on an angular head. On a large bulbous nose sat hornrimmed glasses. The partially torn pocket of the T-shirt was jammed with a stack of index cards and guarded by a phalanx of ballpoint pens, giving the driver's chest a bulging square breast plate.

"Sure, hop in," said the driver in a squeaky voice."I'll go anywhere for the right fare."

"Four bucks each," said Butch, winking at Jonathan.

"Four gets you a ride, but no tours," said the cabby, picking at a scab on his nose.

"What kinda cheap thrills do we get for a fin?" asked Butch.

"For a fiver, I'll throw in a quick tour of Chinatown and North Beach."

"Can we go by City Lights?" asked Jonathan, referring to the famous Beatnik bookstore.

"Sure, just around the corner from Chinatown," smiled the cabby.

"A deal," said Butch. "A tip, too, if your tour is memorable. Take the shotgun seat, Junior," said Butch, stretching himself across the back seat. "Don't want you to miss a thing in your first visit to 'Frisco."

A tattered permit hanging precariously from the glove compartment displayed mug shots of the driver, emphasizing his enormous nose. Bold black letters read,

ROD ORGAN - Independent Cab Driver

"Hang on, guys," shouted the cabby grinding past first,

thrusting noisily into second, and mercifully into third.

Flipping on the radio, the cabby said, "Hope you guys dig rock and roll." Duane Eddy's guitar boomed "Rebel Rouser" from a speaker in the dashboard and one hidden somewhere behind Butch's seat.

"Look out for that truck!" Jonathan shouted, as the woodie lurched within inches of a slow-moving diesel.

Jamming his foot on the accelerator, Rod made a hard left turn without signaling, zoomed ahead, and cut back in front of the truck, eliciting a deafening blast of the airhorn from the truck driver. Jutting his left hand out the window, Rod flipped a stiff middle finger, as the radio played "Let the Good Times Roll."

"Jeez, Rod. Scared the shit out of me," said Butch. "How fast are we going?" There was a trace of concern in his voice

Pointing to the inert speedometer needle resting on zero, Rod said, "Your guess is as good as mine, Butch. Speedometer hasn't worked in years. Hot Rod Organ delivers on his promise of cheap thrills."

Squeezing the cab onto the shoulder of the road and churning up a dust cloud, Rod Organ raced past a line of Labor Day sightseers dawdling in the slow lane. "Gotta know the territory, guys. Hold on, The City's around the next hill."

"There she is, guys, The City of Saint Francis, 'Queen of the Western Sea,'" said Rod, swinging his right fist side-to-side in a shallow arc.

San Francisco is more breathtaking than any photograph I've seen, thought Jonathan, transfixed by the panoramic view of elegant old buildings, taller than any in Minneapolis, standing tightly among the city's small hills, of seagulls circling lazily over an armada of sailboats filling the bay.

Rod swung the woodie down a ramp, under a black iron archway emblazoned with *International Settlement*, passing two large signs above the waterfront. One, in neon, depicted a *Sherwin-Williams* can pouring color over a flashing globe. The other, painted on the side of a brick building read *Hills Bros. Coffee*, above a five-stories tall, bearded man, in a yellow robe and white turban, drinking a cup of coffee.

Within minutes, the cab was stalled on Grant Avenue, the heart of Chinatown. The two-way traffic was held hostage by a teeming mass of strolling Oriental humanity, oblivious to traffic signals and honking car horns, shouting in a wonderfully strange dissonance, punctuated by the hacking of unseen spitters. Jonathan was overwhelmed by the odors, the foreignness of exotic pungent aromas, a mix of salty, sour, sweet, balmy, bitter, and burnt fragrances.

Dark pagoda-styled buildings, two and three-stories tall, displayed graceful Chinese characters in gold leaf and sing song English translations:

Wong Chong Dry Goods and Fung Ming Restaurant

Stacks of cages filled with braying, cackling animals lining storefronts, next to open, wooden crates of strangely shaped fruits and vegetables. Restaurant windows were filled with tanks of live fish and freshly cooked poultry hanging from hooks. Shops teemed with displays of jewelry, brightly colored curios and massive furniture.

"Jeez," said Butch, pointing to a sign in the window of a herbalist shop. "Powdered deer antlers! That stuff's supposed to jump start the old sex drive when your motor's running low."

"Butch, you've got sex on the brain," said Jonathan.

"Other parts of my body better get some sex soon, or I'll be buying some powdered deer antlers," quipped Butch.

"Oughta feel right at home here, Butch," said Rod, making a sharp turn, pointing to a sign that read "Brooklyn Place."

"C'mon! Chinese invented paper, gunpowder, the compass, and spaghetti, but Brooklyn, too?" chuckled Butch.

Angling the cab onto Broadway, the cabby said, "Edge of Chinatown on your right, Italian North Beach on your left. City Lights coming up." Rod made a slight turn onto Columbus.

"What are those creatures?" said Butch, pointing to a group of young people gathered in front, boys sporting beards and berets; one playing a flute, another pounding rhythmically on a pair of bongo drums, girls in toreador pants and tops, wearing no makeup, cigarettes dangling from their mouths.

"Those are pseudo-Beats hoping to mingle with real Beatniks who won't have anything to do with the phonies," said Rod. "Most of these kids are escapees from states in the Midwest, like Iowa," Rod winked at Jonathan. "The pseudo-Beats put on a little show for tourists to pick up some spare change."

"This is hilarious, really ironic," said Butch. "I've seen Kerouac and Cassady at readings in Greenwich Village, and they don't have beards. Do these yokels really think they're cool by wearing those crazy uniforms?"

"It's Lawrence Ferlinghetti," shouted Jonathan. From the shadows of the doorway emerged the poet and owner of City Lights, a balding, thin man in his thirties, a bemused smile on his clean-shaven face.

"I've got to get his autograph," said Jonathan.

First Ferlinghetti, then Kerouac and Cassady, he thought.

Exiting the cab, Jonathan noted that the attention of Ferlinghetti and the pseudo-Beats riveted on a loud scuffle across the street.

In front of the Tosca Café, two men, one large and muscular, the other short and thin, were dragging a beautiful, busty blonde, dressed in a strapless, sequined evening gown and high heels, into the back seat of a Chevy.

"Those creeps are hassling a General," said Butch, bolting out back of the cab, joining Jonathan in a sprint across Columbus Avenue.

"Take the little guy," said Butch, "I'll handle the heavyweight." "Hey, guys! It's Ok! Don't get involved," yelled Rod Organ. Too late. The boys tackled the two muggers at full speed, wresting them away from the blonde, half in and half out of the Chevy.

Applying a full Nelson he had learned watching TV wrestling, Jonathan swung the smaller man, smelling of Vitalis hair oil, onto the back of the Chevy, pinning him to the trunk.

"Let go of me! Let go of me!" squealed the tiny man in a high-pitched voice.

Butch struggled with the larger assailant who, up close, was as big as a pro football player, the hulk grappling Butch in a bear hug, Butch parrying with a flurry of rights and lefts that bloodied the giant's nose.

"Hurry, Honey, get out of the car!" Butch yelled at the blonde, keeping his body between his opponent and the open back door of the Chevy.

"Take your hands off him, you brute!" shouted the blonde in a deep, husky voice.

"It's ok, doll. Just get out of there!" urged Butch, wrapping the assailant in a headlock between the crook of his right elbow and his right hip. "I can't hold him off forever!"

To Jonathan's amazement, the blonde pulled off her high heels and pummeled Butch from behind, flailing him on the head and shoulders.

Throwing the smaller man to the ground, Jonathan grabbed at the blonde's hands, his right hand gripping her right wrist from behind, twisting away the weapon. As she squirmed away, Jonathan's left hand missed her left wrist, grabbing her hair instead, popping it off in a clump.

Spinning the female around, Jonathan gaped at the blond wig in his left hand and the black, crew-cut hair of the person who had just been wearing it. Despite heavy facial makeup, Jonathan instantly recognized the woman as a man in female dress!

Stunned, Jonathan did not see the high heel in her left hand until it struck him squarely on the forehead, staggering him in a daze of flashing stars.

"Oh, shit!" gasped Butch, now fully enveloped by the behemoth outflanking him.

As the woman raised the high heel to strike Butch, an ear splitting crash jolted the Chevy, crunching steel, shattering glass, sprawling the woman into the gutter, propelling the giant, along with the two boys in a tangled heap to the sidewalk. Rod Organ had wheeled the woodie in a tight U-turn, ramming the side of the Chevy.

"Get in," Rod yelled. "Let's get the hell outta here!"

Scrambling to their feet, Jonathan and Butch scurried around the front of the damaged Chevy and dove into the cab, as Rod peeled out, rubber burning, in a tight turn onto Broadway, vaulting onto the onramp to the Bay Bridge a few blocks away. In the distance the faint wail of police sirens sounded.

"Whee-ooooh," Rod let out a joyful holler. "Chivalry lives!"

"What the hell was that all about?" asked Butch, dabbing away rivulets of blood with his red hankie.

Jonathan, dazed, a large welt growing on his forehead, consoled himself with the knowledge that his attempt at chivalry had not been as costly as Uncle Mike's scar.

"I tried to stop you, guys," said Rod chuckling. "That was the infamous Paulette Du Bois and her two boyfriends. They squabble all over the streets of North Beach."

Ignoring their bruised egos, the two combatants joined Rod Organ in embarrassed laughter as Elvis wailed "Hard Headed

63

Woman" from the woodie's radio.

* * *

From the balcony of the Vesuvios Café, Sam Paean had followed the altercation with amusement. When the two heavies tried to stuff the blonde into the back seat of the Chevy, he had immediately recognized Paulette Du Bois, the noted female impersonator, star of the Broadway nightclub, Pinocchio's, famous for its musical revue performed by beautiful transvestites.

Last week Joe Pinocchio had complained that the frequent brawls of Paulette and her two boyfriends were getting out of hand.

"I can't afford to have Paulette performing with bruises and scratches," Pinocchio had lamented. "When those tourists from Kansas and Iowa come to see the star of my show, they should see the perfect female beauty."

Setting aside his martini, Paean jotted, on a cocktail napkin, the beginning of an eyetem for tomorrow's Paean to The City.

>*. . . Sightem in North Beach: Pseudo-Beats,*
>*acting Cool at City Lights Books, looking*
>*on as two college Joes tried to stop a daily*
>*spat 'twixt gal-guy Paulette DuBois and*
>*her two boy-pals. The Joes saved by a*
>*big nose cabby driving a vintage woodie.*
>*(Ex-Lost Angeles Surfer in The City?)*
>*North Beach Bongos, Beats, and Brawls.*
>*Only in The City that Knows How . . .*

64

11

DOOCHLAND

"Why in the hell are you changing the station?" asked Butch, as the nasal voice of Eddie Fisher suddenly whined over the woodie's stereo system. " 'Oh, My Papa.' What kind of trash is that? C'mon, Rod, turn it back to rock and roll."

"KALX," explained the cabby, "is the Cal radio station. Carries all the local info: traffic, housing, waiting lines, helpful tips, it's all here. The only problem is putting up with the DJ, the All Pro. He plays some pretty weird music."

"That was the HEART GRABBING voice of the one and only Mr. Eddie Fisher," intoned a deep, smooth, and resonant radio voice.

"Campus traffic at a crawl on University and Ashby. Best bet is Gilman to Hopkins up to Oxford."

"Now, as musical BONUS for my loyal listeners, the All Pro spins still ANOTHER Eddie Fisher hit, 'If I Ever Needed You.'"

"The All Pro's got a helluva voice," said Butch. "He probably gets laid a lot."

"Probably not," chuckled Rod. "The All Pro's supposed to be uglier than sin. His nickname is Rooster Face because of his big beak, beady eyes, and drooping chin," said Rod, twirling the radio dial back to rock and roll. "You'll find out for yourselves. The All Pro lives and broadcasts from your dorm, Dooch Hall."

Using the All Pro's tip, Rod Organ had made a smooth end run around traffic jams created by the returning crush of students.

Skirting the southern edge of the Cal campus, the woodie passed rows of stately mansions bearing the Greek letters of fraternity and sorority houses.

Jonathan felt electricity in the air, as each block became an increasingly dense melange of people, trunks, boxes, and furniture. At College and Channing, Rod Organ negotiated the maze of parked cars effortlessly.

"Your new home, guys," said Rod, screeching to a stop next to a high-rise dorm towering over the classic architecture of nearby fraternities and sororities.

"A bonus for the tour and wrassling match," said Butch, handing Rod Organ a five-dollar bill.

"Call me sometime for more cheap thrills in the City," said the bulbous nosed cabby, plucking an index card from the breast pocket of his T-shirt, scrawling a phone number. "Have fun at Cal!"

Jonathan and Butch lugged their bags to the rear of a long line of students and parents. The two craned their necks at the sheer face of Dooch Hall, a monolithic monument to contemporary design, a concrete box with grey columns and large windows forming a rectangular, eight-story fishbowl. Ray Charles boomed "What I'd Say" from a pair of giant speakers on the balcony over the dorm entrance.

"Wow," said Jonathan. "Dooch is taller than all the buildings in Clear Lake," said Jonathan, counting one-hundred rooms. On odd numbered floors, balconies protruded like pouting grey lips, each filled with students cheering a loud commotion on the third-floor balcony.

"We gotta change some bad attitudes around here," said Butch, nodding to a message taped across the windows of the fifth floor proclaiming

DOOCH HALL-HOME OF THE HORNY DORMIE

In the lobby, they saw an imposing mosaic fashioned from thousands of pieces of colored glass in the shape of a double headed, Germanic eagle, wings spread defiantly, its talons clutching a Cal blue and gold banner, emblazoned with *Dooch Hall*. A brass plate beneath the work bore the inscription:

Donated by Robert B. Jean - 9/1/58

Facing the dorm was a glass enclosed dining hall with a sweeping, pagoda roof. Several handmade signs taped to the doors offered gastronomical warnings:

Mrs. B's Cooking, The Shits!
Dorm Food Contains Saltpeter!
Mystery Meat Destroys Brain Cells
Beef Barf-aroni is NOT Italian Food

Butch arched his eyebrows in the direction of a nearby student and his mother in animated conversation. The boy was stocky, with brown crewcut hair, his hazel eyes matching those of his silver-haired mother whose puffy face was layered with pancake makeup.

"Park Avenue shee-shee," whispered Butch, referring to the pair's expensive clothing.

"I don't understand you, Gerald Farthing." The woman's harsh tone reminded Jonathan of his own mother's voice. "Why would you stay in this sterile place, when you can live in that lovely Pi Upsilon fraternity house?" she asked, pointing to the mansion across the street.

Pi Upsilon, the P U's, the name of Father's fraternity, thought Jonathan. One of The Three Promises.

Butch, with both hands akimbo on his hips, mocked the woman by hissing, "I just don't understand you, Gerald Farthing."

"Mom, we've been over this before." answered Gerald. "Both Dad and Grandad were P U's. I'd be an automatic, a third generation legacy, but that's not the point." His voice was tinged with exasperation. "For once in my life, I want to do something on my own."

Do something on my own, in his mind, Jonathan echoed the boy's words, feeling an immediate kinship with young Farthing.

"Gerald, if your father were alive, he would . . ."Mrs. Farthing was interrupted by the loud THUD of a tumbling ball of humanity crashing into a thicket of ferns.

Emerging from a cloud of dust, flicking debris from his disheveled clothes was a roly-poly boy more than 200 pounds supported by two thin matchstick legs, who reminded Jonathan of the twins Tweedle Dee and Tweedle Dum. His close-cropped hair stood upright. Thick, coke bottle glasses magnified the immense brown eyes of his fleshy round face.

In his right hand, the new arrival gripped the remnants of a broken umbrella, its black panels shredded from its metal ribs. A chorus of boo's cascaded down from the upper balconies.

"This Spartan ain't worth shit," said the boy, shouting at a small form leaning over the third-floor balcony.

"Damned thing collapsed before I cleared the second floor, Hunch," he bellowed.

"Junior, tell me this fatso didn't really jump off the balcony?" said Butch staring disbelievingly.

"Who're you calling fatso?" The new arrival peered icily at Butch, his left eye wandering lazily counter clockwise behind the thick lens.

Looking down at Butch's feet, he chortled, "Those really aren't spats? HA! HA! HA! Buddy, what planet are you from?"

Cupping his hands, the balcony jumper yelled to someone on the third-floor. "Hey, Hunch, there's some bozo freshman down here wearing goddamned spats."

Butch tensed; and, for a moment, Jonathan thought there would be a second fight of the day.

"Touche," said Butch, relaxing, extending a hand, introducing himself and Jonathan. "What's this crazy stuff you're doing?"

"Ollie Punch," said the barrel-chested boy shaking hands.

"A simple physics experiment testing the relative tensile strengths of various brands of umbrellas," he explained.

"My partner in aerial dynamics," said Ollie Punch, gazing up at the third floor balcony. "And my partner in aerial dynamics," he repeated in a louder tone.

"AND MY PARTNER IN AERIAL DYNAMICS," he yelled. "Hunch, get your butt down here and meet a couple of new freshmen," he gestured to someone on the third balcony.

"Coming, Ollie." Crawling over the railing of the third-floor balcony, the student opened an umbrella, stepped off, and drifted slowly earthward, both hands clutching the umbrella's curved handle. Landing gently, the new arrival bowed to applause and whistles.

"Standard Roos-Atkins," he said, spinning the umbrella by its handle. Hunch stood less than five feet tall with a cherub face and saucer shaped eyes. A large, round hump arched between his stooped shoulders.

"The most disgusting thing I've ever seen," whispered Mrs Farthing to her son. "Jumping off with an . . ." her voice trailed off.

"My partner in aerial dynamics," said Ollie Punch, "Hunch Hitowski."

"Hitowski, is that Polish?" asked Butch.

"On my father's side," said Hunch in a low muffled voice, "but my mother is Mexican."

"Hunch's real name is Julio. Our BMOC," added Ollie proudly, clamping his fleshy arms around Hunch's hump back.

"BMOC?" said Jonathan, shaking Hunch's tiny, clawlike hand.

"Big Man On Campus," explained Ollie. "Hunch is a real celebrity, assistant chime master of the Campanile, number one carillonneur, Mr. Musical Bang Master of the biggest phallic symbol on campus."

He added conspiratorially, "The only way horny Dormies ever meet any cute girls is tagging along Hunch's guided tours of the Campanile."

"C'mon, Ollie, cut the BS," said Hunch, a sheepish grin spreading across his face.

Mrs. Farthing whispered, "My God, Gerald, a Polish-Mexican midget! A hunchback bell ringer!" She cringed at the thought of what other undesirables lived in Dooch Hall.

* * *

From the rooftop of his penthouse flat on Russian Hill, Sam Paean savored the waning hours of Labor Day with martinis. In the background, Frank Sinatra, backed by Nelson Riddle's orchestra, crooned his signature song for swinging lovers, "I've Got You Under My Skin."

Paean turned his gaze from the reassuring view of the Golden Gate. In the East Bay, he saw the Campanile glistening in the glow of the setting sun. Tapping the side of his aquiline nose in time with the beat, he listened to Sinatra swing,

> . . . so deep in my heart,
> that you're really a part of me . . .

Yes, deep in his heart, as a young man, Paean would have given anything for a Cal education. In the Thirties, college was the private preserve of the children of the rich and swell-egants whose only decision was choosing between Cal or that other Bay Area university, Stanford.

Paean's parents had set aside their savings toward Sam's college education, believing a Cal degree would be the only way Sam would ever get to rub elbows with San Francisco's elite.

But a funny thing happened on the way to college. Paean had been sidetracked by the seductive call of journalism. Thinking back over his newspaper career, he had concluded the choice had served him well. As *Mr. San Francisco*, he had hobnobbed with the captains of industry and rubbed up against the delicious bodies of high-toned society matrons.

And yet?

He wondered, as Sinatra concluded,

. . . I've got you under my skin.

What might life have been with a Cal education?

Paean raised the last of the martini toasting the Campanile, symbol of his almost alma mater.

Cal, I've still got you under my skin.

12

P U STINK

Launched from the roof of the Pi Upsilon fraternity, three rounds of white Number Seven, extra-strength balloons arced silently between the pair of venerable Coast live oaks fronting the fraternity. Water was the standard munition, but for special occasions, the P U's used a variety of fluids: sour milk, perfume, and beer. Today, Dirk Krum had instructed the P U's to fill the balloons with red dye.

The bombs were fired by slings fashioned from long, thick strands of rubber, each eight by two feet, manned by teams of five boys each: two holding the ends of the rubber in a taut, angled direction; two stretching the rubbers to their the maximum elasticity of sixteen feet; and, one gingerly loading bloated bombs into the crook of the human slingshot. Used with precision, The Rubber had an effective range of two city blocks. When carelessly fired, bombs disintegrated, on launch, showering its crew with its contents.

The first missile splattered on the glass pane bearing the letter H of the word Horny displayed on the fifth floor of Dooch Hall, leaving a sienna sunburst of dripping ink. The second struck the railing of the first floor balcony. The third landed squarely on the ferrule of Hunch Hitowski's opened Roos-Atkins umbrella, spraying an arc of red mist.

"What the hell . . . ?" said Butch, gazing skyward for the source of the reddish rain.

The fourth, fifth, and sixth volleys landed in rapid succession, inducing an impromptu tap dance by their human targets, dispersing the registration line, the throng surging forward, scurrying for the safety of the Dooch lobby.

Screams of panic. Jonathan's eyes stinging, Ollie Punch's glasses glistening with a thin layer of red, Hunch Hitowski's grey sweat pants were a shocking pink. Mrs. Farthing, her white suit flecked in crimson, stared in shock at her son Gerald, a bloody red streak oozing down his face.

"Gerald!" she screamed. "He's bleeding! Help him! He's bleeding!" Hugging him to her breast, she sobbed. "I told you not to live in this God-awful place!"

"This way," said Hunch and Punch, motioning Jonathan and Butch to follow, dashing among the concrete columns toward the south end of Dooch Hall.

At the foot of the Dooch fire escape, they were joined by a trio of Dormies who had raced down the staircase. Introductions were quickly made, as salvos of bombs continued to rain down on the entrance of the dorm. One of the newcomers, a lumbering, baldheaded behemoth named Mo McCart, who had a baby face, close-set eyes, and huge arms, towered even over Butch. The second, Ruby Lips, a frail, skinny boy with a smooth, hairless face and deep blue eyes, spoke in a high-pitched voice, underscored by exaggerated feminine gestures. The third, Casey Lee, a tall, sinewy Oriental with a well-chiseled face and slightly almond eyes, carried a burlap sack.

"Damned P U's never let up," said Casey Lee. "If they want to trash property, let's show them how it's done."

Jonathan marveled at Casey Lee's perfectly spoken English, free of any accent. Other than Rod Organ's brief tour of Grant Avenue, Jonathan's only exposure to Orientals had been old Charlie Chan movies and eating chop suey with Mike and Pearl at the Ding How Restaurant in Minneapolis

"Hey," said Butch, "if we're in for a rumble, maybe the little guys shouldn't go." He nodded at Hunch and Ruby Lips.

"Hunch and Ruby are our secret weapons," explained Ollie with a smile. "None of the P U's would ever want to tussle with Ruby. Got any boyfriends at the frat house?" Ollie teased.

"Go hose yourself, Ollie," responded Ruby, gracefully waving two rigid middle fingers. "I wouldn't give those spoiled pretty boys the time of day," he said, puckering his lips.

"The plan will be a Royal French RF special," Casey explained. "Ruby, Mo, and I will create the frontal diversion."

"Grab the P U 's by the balls," hissed Ruby, clenching a fist. "Brute force is the only thing those assholes understand."

Handing the burlap sack to Hunch, Casey said, "Hunch, you, Ollie, Butch, and Jonathan will attack from the rear. Make it quick. We won't be able to hold them for more than a minute or two. Go Bears!"

Dashing from palm tree to palm tree, the commandos darted up Channing Way, as a chant swelled from the P U fraternity house, echoing off the face of Dooch Hall.

"Fuck the Dormies! Fuck the Dormies!"

A faint reply gathered strength, as one by one, Dooch Hall windows slid open, voices from unseen Dormies taking up the cry, led by someone using a public address system on the third floor balcony.

"Frat rats suck! Frat rats suck!"

Crossing College Avenue undetected, the seven split into two groups. Casey, Mo, and Ruby staying low, tiptoed toward the front of the P U house, while the other four raced uphill to the rear of the fraternity house. Hunkered down near the entrance, the trio could see the silhouettes of the boisterous P U's standing at the edge of the roof, shaking their fists triumphantly.

The cacophony of hostility raged back and forth across College Avenue.

It was Chip Fist, swilling a can of Hamms, who spotted the three intruders below. "Dirk, we've got some fucking Dormies down here!"

A cruel sneer spread across Dirk Krum's face, as he recognized the three.

"Well, well, well. It's the Chinaman, the Faggot, and the Neanderthal," said Dirk, as the P U's hooted and whistled.

"If you really had any balls, Dirk, the Third Turd, you'd come down here and say that to our faces," screamed Ruby Lips, pointing at Chip Fist.

"And while you're at it, bring along that big Chip of shit, so Mo can break his arms, and I can lick his lily white ass," Ruby cackled, swaying back and forth, scratching his crotch.

Dirk looked over the faces of the P U's. "Who wants to beat

the shit out of that little homo?"

Every P U hand shot up.

"Ok, let's just jump 'em all, but save the Chinaman for me," said Dirk.

"What's the matter, Dirk?" Casey shouted."Fifty P U prick heads aren't men enough for the three of us? Maybe you need some encouragement."

Casey nodded to Mo, who strode to the ornate, hand-carved redwood sign fastened to two posts sunk into the manicured front lawn. The carefully chiseled writing bore the Greek letters of the house, Pi and Upsilon, and an inscription on the lower, right hand corner.

Donated by Dirk Krum I - September 7, 1900

Mo McCart lashed his massive forearm in a backhanded swipe, exploding against the wood, dislodging the sign from one of the posts. With his other hand, Mo twisted and freed the sign from its mooring. Raising the ancient sign high above his head with both hands, he curled up his right knee, like a flamingo standing on one leg.

Oh, shit, thought Dirk. *That dumb animal's not going to . . .*

Mo broke the sign in half against his thigh, spraying shards of wood across the lawn. He then sailed one-half of the sign like a discus through the leaded stained glass of the front door, demolishing the Tiffany window. With his other hand, Mo flipped the remaining half through the large bay window of the living room in a thunderous explosion of glass.

A cold fury gripped Dirk Krum as he watched the destruction of the P U symbol of tradition and continuity.

It was that Chink's fault, he thought, *Casey Lee, representing everything that was wrong about Cal, the non-Greek alien casting some mysterious spell over Kate Howell!*

"Get the assholes," Dirk shouted. They moved like a human wave, a cascading torrent of human hate, storming down the main staircase, screaming obscenities.

At the rear of the P U house Ollie, Hunch, Butch, and Jonathan vaulted the wall along Channing Way. Pointing to a rear fire escape, Ollie led the way quietly up a wrought iron ladder to the second floor, each squeezing through an open window into a large sleeping porch. In the distance, the Dormies continued to chant "P U's suck."

74

Hunch quickly emptied the contents of the burlap sack onto the floor, a dozen, plastic canisters filled with a waxy substance.

"Light these critters in fireplaces, sinks, and bathtubs, places where there will be plenty of smoke, but no fire," instructed Hunch, dispensing boxes of safety matches. "Be ready for blinding flashes and a horrible smell. If you have a hankie, use it. Stay close to the floor."

"Wait!" They heard the stampeding P U's rushing down the staircase outside, careening off bannisters and walls, screaming "Fuck the Dormies!"

Reaching the ground floor, the P U mob stopped, stunned by the scene of destruction. The late afternoon breeze wafted the floor length drapes over layers of broken glass covering the stately furniture and oriental rugs of the living room.

Suppressing tears, Dirk assessed the damage from Mo's rampage. The front door was ajar. Beyond were the asshole barbarians who had committed this crime against the P U house.

"Get those fucking Dormies," Dirk shouted, charging headlong out the open door. In his rage, Dirk failed to notice the thin trip-wire stretched across the bottom of the doorstep. Ruby and Casey, crouching on each side of the doorway, snapped the wire up to ankle level, tripping Dirk, sprawling him spread-eagled across the porch, followed by a crush of P U's piling on like a line of dominos.

In the confusion, Casey and Ruby leaped from the front porch, the first billows of pungent grey smoke cascading down the main staircase, enveloping the house in a choking, stinging, sulfuric stench.

Stink bombs! The assholes had snuck in behind us, Dirk realized.

Untangling, the P U's scrambled back up the stairs, holding their noses against the crooks of their elbows, warding off the acrid smell, staggering blindly room to room, groping for the invaders.

From the P U sleeping porch, the Dormie commandos heard the stampede of P U's charging up the stairwell.

"Follow me," said Hunch, handing out umbrellas. Snapping open one, the little hunchback sailed out a large, open window.

"Aerial dynamics," said Ollie, steadying himself. "Ok, 'Mr. Spats,'" he said, winking his spinning eye. "Let's see if you can keep up with 'fatso.' HA! HA! HA!" Punch jumped.

The P U's were now a few doors away.

"Junior, let's go!" said Butch leaping. "Watch out below!"

Jonathan closed his eyes. *Shit flies both ways*, he thought, stepping off.

Across College Avenue, the Dormie seven paused to admire their handiwork, nauseous smoke billowing from second and third floor windows, the wail of fire engines approaching.

"Nice touch," said Casey. "Who rang the fire alarm?" he asked, looking for the culprit.

"P U's aren't toilet trained to clean their own stink," said Hunch Hitowski, his saucer shaped eyes wide with satisfaction. "Just trying to be a Good Samaritan."

The first of three fire trucks squealed to a stop, a brigade quickly assembling fire hoses, concentrating streams of water toward an open second story window. Dirk Krum and Chip Fist staggered through the haze of their veranda waving, shouting "No! Don't! No fire!"

Too late. Blasts of water drove the two P U's back into the smokey recesses of their bedroom suite.

Amid screaming sirens, rivers of water, and clouds of smoke, the Dormie seven marched victoriously down the middle of Channing Way. Ruby Lips, lead the march, skipping from side-to-side, arms raised in victory. Casey Lee pumped a fist in the air. Mo McCart flashed two thumbs up. Ollie Punch and Hunch Hitowski locked arm in arm. The two frosh, Jonathan Aldon and Butch Tanenbloom, baptized under fire, basked in sudden glory.

"Junior, I think I'm going to like these maniacs," shouted Butch, grasping Jonathan's shoulder in a powerful grip. "These Dormies are fucking nuts!"

Across Channing Way, Kate Howell quickened her pace. She had tarried much too long on the Dooch fire escape, riveted by the Dormie raid on the P U house. Pulling the silk scarf tightly around her face, she crossed College Avenue, avoiding the chaos and confusion.

No one noticed the Golden Goddess slipping quietly past the fire lines except a disheveled Dirk Krum, leaning on the rail of the second floor veranda, sopping in water and reeking of the rotten egg stench of stink bombs.

13

· R F

From his room on the eighth floor of Dooch, Royal French had closely monitored the raid on the P U's through the powerful telescope mounted on the corner of his desk. As the Dormies marched triumphantly down Channing, Royal smiled at the success of his plan.

It was ironic that Royal French's initials were the same as the term RF, the letters referring to an attitude all Dormies embraced. In polite company, Dormies referred only to the initials as code. Among themselves, they spoke the actual words.

RF stood for the first letters of the esoteric term, Rat Fuck.

The expression originated in a story told at a high school summer camp in the Santa Cruz mountains cosponsored by Jews and Unitarians. The story was told by Ralph "the Lips" Levy of Sacramento who recited it around a camp fire in the summer of 1956.

"Once upon a time, there was a young maiden who dreamed of marrying a handsome Prince. She came upon an ugly rat, who told her that if she would spend the night with him, she would wake up and find a handsome Prince in her bed. The rat was a horrid, dirty, little creature, but remembering the story of how a kiss had turned a frog into a prince, the young maiden agreed to spend a night with the rat.

The next morning, on waking from a most traumatic experience, the young maiden was horrified to find the smiling rat still at her side. 'But Mr. Rat, what happened? You promised if I spent the night with you, I would wake up and find a Prince, not a rat, at my side.'

The rat looked at the young maiden lasciviously. Licking his lips, he announced, 'Sorry, lady, I hate to tell you, but you've just been rat fucked.'"

The term RF had become synonymous with a cunning prank or a deceptive charade, frequently associated with an act of revenge.

How appropriate that I, master of RF, would have the same initials for my name, Royal French thought.

At twenty-three, Royal French was the oldest member of the Dooch Junior class, his enrollment at Cal delayed by the three years he spent with Army Special Forces in the jungles of an obscure country in Southeast Asia called Vietnam.

Royal still kept his black hair closely cropped military style, his deep-set dark eyes underscored by the new contact lenses issued to him by Special Forces. Although his body was still taut and coiled, he had lost that trained edge to react instinctively to stimuli. Royal was now retired from that kind of activity, the reason he could devise paramilitary operations for the Dormies without actually participating in them.

It would be dangerous to resurrect those killing skills, he thought, *deadly dangerous for others.*

Casey Lee had followed his RF to perfection. Now, Casey would have to reward him by fixing him up with a blind date. Maybe a willowy brunette Pi Phi or that busty redheaded Tri Delt, Babs Buxton, or even the Golden Goddess herself! He settled his six-foot-nine frame into the Eames leather and rosewood chair, stretching his legs across the length of the small desk, his palms and fingers clasped in prayer position on his nose.

Yes, that would do nicely, Royal thought. *A date with a five percenter! What a great way to start the semester! When the P U's retaliated (which was a virtual certainty), the Dormies would need other RF's. Those assignments, along with odd jobs for others (secret jobs for smaller fraternities) would yield Royal a tidy little sum and contribute to a pleasant social life.*

Mounted on the wall next to the desk was a four by six foot black and white enlargement of the panoramic view from his room. On the photo, forty-four numbers had been circled in white ink, each representing a window visible through Royal's telescope.

Adjacent to the photo was a typed chart with three columns, the left listing numbers one through forty-four, the middle column, only partially complete, bearing names of girls whose windows corresponded to the circled numbers, the right column listing the names of Dormies credited with identifying the girls in the middle column.

The name appearing the most frequently in the right column was Marty Silverstein, Dooch's Super Sleuth.

Scanning the hillside with his telescope, Royal stopped at an unfamiliar window glowing in the light of a low wattage bulb. Focusing the ends of the telescope did not help, as the setting sun illuminated very few details of the girl hidden in the shadows. He could make out her profile, though. Slender build, perky breasts, a curvy ass. Royal counted from the nearest reference, three buildings north of the Sigma Kappa house which would make that Bay View Terrace, a girl's boarding house. He carefully added and circled number forty-five on the enlargement on the wall.

Ah, a new assignment for Super Sleuth!

14

BUON GIORNO

Muted rays of early morning sun filtered through the forest of Faculty Glade, streaming into the office of Professor Aristotle Scott. Outside the picture window framing the gurgling waters of Strawberry Creek, Brutus, the squirrel, chattered excitedly, claiming the daily offering of his patron.

Ari had reviewed the Saturday mail, saving the outsized envelope bearing the seal of the United States Congress for last.

Suspecting its contents, he still shook with anger, reading, then rereading the legalese of the subpoena.

"YOU ARE COMMANDED TO APPEAR before the House Un-American Activities Committee of the United States Congress, convening in special session on 9:00 a.m., November 3, 1959, in Wheeler Auditorium on the University of California, Berkeley campus, to testify, under oath, as to your knowledge of and association with: (a) any and all persons or groups sworn to the violent overthrow of the government of the United States of America; (b) any and all persons or groups who sympathize with the violent overthrow of the government of the United States of America; (c) any and all persons or groups whose allegiances, associations, and activities may lead to the violent overthrow of the government of the United States of America.

YOU ARE FURTHER COMMANDED TO BRING WITH YOU any and all documents that bear upon your testimony to any and all of the matters set forth above.

FAILURE TO APPEAR OR TESTIFY SHALL BE PUNISHABLE by Congressional contempt for which there shall be levied monetary fines and/or imprisonment, as well as all other penalties imposed by law."

The document was signed by the chairman of HUAC, the House Un-American Activities Committee, the*"HONORABLE CONGRESSMAN CLAYBORN MUCK."*

Picking up the telephone, Ari dialed the campus number of Professor Garrick Nelquist, each spin of the dial whirling like a drill boring into his consciousness.

Does Muck know about Anna? If so, what is he planning?

Answering the phone, Garrick Nelquist detected a tone of panic in Ari's voice. "Ari, did you receive a mucky love note from your buddy, Stillborn? Just got my subpoena today."

Tamping his meerschaum pipe, Garrick asked, "How do you think we should handle HUAC's kangaroo court?"

"I called Chancellor Haynes requesting a special session of the Academic Senate," said Ari, feigning calmness. "Maybe we can drum up a faculty vote denouncing HUAC."

"Hell's bells, Ari. Accept the fact the HUAC hearings will be a three-ring circus. We'll protest to high heavens, denying Commie sympathies, but Muck knows how to play to Middle America's fears about the Russians. The best we can hope for is to maintain our dignity and hang onto our jobs," said Garrick. "Jeez, I'd like to corner Muck in some dark alley and kick that litttle bastard's ass," he added.

Ari suppressed a grin. Education may have smoothed the rough edges from the professor from the small farming town of Modesto, but nothing would mute the spirit of the country boy raised to wrestle cattle and issues with the same dogged determination.

"You may get your chance, Garrick. The HUAC hearings will be televised live. Muck's campaign manager has a buddy over at CBS. Put on your best face and your boxing gloves."

"I'll leave good impressions to glamour boys like the Great Scott. My turn will be bare knuckles and spit. It's about time Muck gets his due."

"That's my sentiment too," responded Ari bravely, but in his heart, he feared for both their fates. "I'll call you as soon as I hear from Chancellor Haynes."

Nestling the receiver back onto the cradle, Ari was startled by the jangle of the phone still pressed to his hand. He let it ring several times, experiencing a gnawing sense of dread completely alien to the Great Scott. The ringing persisted. Picking up the receiver, Ari slowly placed it to his ear.

"Hello?" He said it more as a question than a greeting. Then for some unexplainable reason, Ari held his breath.

A long pause, then the timbre of a female voice, low, silky, and sensual, familiar, yet distant, answered, in a Neapolitan accent, "Professor Aristotle Scott?"

"Yes," Ari responded, his voice tightening, the rush of an old sensation washing over him, a feeling he had buried deep inside more than twenty-years ago.

"This is Anna," the voice said. "Anna Zarzana."

Ari closed his eyes, remembering.

Yes, she had Sofia's voice, so warm it could thaw the polar cap of the North Pole.

There was a longer pause, as Ari felt his heart soaring.

Then the lovely voice, an echo from his youth, said, "Papa, this is your daughter."

15

TELLY VISION

Once you've come to Cal, you'll never be the same.
Casey Lee's remark at the Freshman Orientations Meeting echoed in Jonathan's mind as he strolled Channing Way with Butch Tanenbloom, Gerald Farthing, and Tommy Tubbins, a tall, cherub-faced Engineering major.

The freshman quartet towered over their guide, Hunch Hitowski, the tiny campus bell ringer, who jogged to keep up with his charges. Their destination: Telegraph Avenue better known as Telly to students and locals.

Frosh guided tours had been the brainchild of Ollie Punch. "Telly ain't Main Street, USA," he had bellowed, his wandering eye spinning counter clockwise in emphasis. "The shock of experiencing Telly could send frosh greenhorns packing in an hour!"

At the intersection of Telegraph Avenue, Hunch stopped, allowing the four freshmen time to acclimate to the Telly scene. Auto traffic stretched north and south for blocks, every intersection jammed with immobilized cars, their horns blaring a symphony of deafening dissonance. Waves of shoppers, ignoring flashing traffic signals, engulfed the trapped autos like hordes of ants in search of food, the teeming masses jostling in and out of the warren of stores shoe horned into the long, narrow street.

Outdoor vendors hawking souvenirs competed with restaurant barkers touting foods with exotic sounding names: falafel, dolma, piroshki, tacos, dim sum, lox and bagels, and fondue.

"What's pizza?" asked Jonathan, pointing to a large sign in the front window of

Maehara's-Home Of the 25 Cent Slice of Pizza.

"Never heard of it before," said Jonathan.

Butch chuckled, "Just another tasty dish Marco Polo brought back from China, Junior."

Avocado, artichoke, Kerrs, pizza. What other exotic, California food will I be trying? Jonathan asked himself.

Hunch's tour group pushed through an endless gauntlet of students thrusting leaflets at pedestrians. The multicolored handouts touted obscure causes, lectures, concerts, speeches, and student discounts. Signs and posters were plastered everywhere: on trees, doors, windows, and telephone poles. Bearded pseudo-Beats playing bongos and flutes, jugglers, singers performing in foreign languages, magicians, poetry readers, and street musicians playing all manners of instruments-saxophones, violins, oboes, guitars, harmonicas, bass fiddles, rubber bands, zithers, and mandolins competed for donations.

The freshman four followed Hunch's lead, plunging into the surging crowd, losing sight of the tiny hunchback whose close proximity to the pavement allowed him to spot momentary openings in the sea of humanity. Two blocks later, they spotted him, waving them to the front of a small, dark shop with large gold lettering,

Gifted Florence--Sees All, Knows All

Pressing their faces to the window, the freshmen squinted, adjusting their eyes to the darkness inside, a single shaft of light illuminating a clear crystal ball sitting on a small round table. Two females were facing each other, one heavily made up, dressed in a peasant gown and red turban, tracing lines on the palm of a wide-eyed college girl.

Looking up, the hag winked, puckering thickly coated lips, blowing a kiss at the looky-lou's. Recoiling from the fortune teller's gesture, the boys almost stepped on Hunch.

"That gypsy, a friend of yours?" said Butch, arching his eyebrows.

"Friend of yours, too," said Hunch. "Look closely. Beneath all that makeup is Ruby Lips."

The four pressed forward for a closer look at Ruby.

"Ruby's gets the lowdown on some of the best looking girls on campus," said Hunch with a mischievous grin."They tell Ruby everything including their deepest, darkest secrets. Ruby says, 'girls will be girls!'"

Waving a goodbye to Ruby, Hunch led his charges back into Telly's swirling masses.

"Gosh, I know how salmon feel going up a stream," said Tubbins, bringing up the rear.

At the intersection of Durant, they saw a traffic cop issuing a citation to the owner of a Triumph TR-3.

"Don't gimme any lip, frat rat," said the officer, his voice loud and nasal. "I marked yer tires twice the last hour."

"That's the Waz," said Hunch, "one of our most infamous Dormies. He works as a campus parking control officer or Meter Mel. What power! Loved by none, hated by all," he explained. "Hey, Waz," shouted Hunch. "How's your face?"

"How's yer own face, Hunch," said the Waz. "Just crackin' down on the criminal element of the Greek fraternity system," he said, handing a yellow ticket to the sports car driver.

Hopping aboard a nearby Vespa motor scooter, the Waz shouted, "Don't teach our Dormie frosh any bad habits on your tour." Stomping sharply on the starter, the Waz inched the Vespa along the line of landlocked cars, searching for more parking violations.

Near Bancroft Way, the boys heard a deep, muted voice chirping, "Crunchy Munchy! Crunchy Munchy!"

Behind them was an ancient street vendor, dressed in a white jump suit, black army boots, and a white admiral's cap pushing a white, square pushcart perched on a pair of worn bicycle wheels Cardboard signs taped to the pushcart proclaimed,
Crunchy Munchy Ice Cream.
Jonathan noticed Crunchy Munchy's black hornrims.

Just like Buddy Holly's, thought Jonathan, as he patted his prized possession bundled in the pocket of his windbreaker.

"How's life, Crunchy?" asked Hunch.

"Crunchy Munchy!" chirped the street vendor.

The group watched Crunchy Munchy saluting customers with his right hand and dropping dimes with his left hand into the front pocket of his jumpsuit. Opening the weathered, square aluminum lid, the ancient peddler disappeared into swirling clouds of dry ice, emerging with sticks of Eskimo Pie ice cream bars.

"Five Eskimo Pies, Crunch," said Hunch, flipping him a fifty-cent piece.

Hunch turned to the freshmen and in a low voice said, "He's never said anything but his name in the 13 years he's worked the campus. No one knows much about him, not his name, his age, or where he lives. Crunchy Munchy is Telly's favorite mystery."

"Auschwitz," Butch whispered to Jonathan. "Look at Crunchy Munchy's wrist."

Jonathan leaned forward and saw the dark, crude numbers carved into the ice cream man's wrist. There had been only passing mention of the Nazi death camps in high school history, and his knowledge of Jews was limited to his mother's comment that "those strange people don't eat pork."

A feeling of guilt washed over Jonathan, a need to share the secret he had plucked from the fire of death. He pulled the glasses from his jacket, stripped off its protective covering, closed his eyes and slipped on Buddy Holly's glasses. Since that fateful evening, Jonathan had resisted the urge to try them on, to see the world as his hero had. And now the chilling reality of that vision suffused his body.

When he opened his eyes, Jonathan saw Crunchy Munchy's weathered, smiling face in the center of the lenses. All other images peripheral to his face were distorted and blurred.

Is Crunchy Munchy smiling at me or Buddy's glasses, Jonathan wondered?

"Buddy Holly," said Jonathan, matter-of-factly, touching the surfaces of the skull temples of the glasses.

"Not fade away," Crunchy Munchy rasped, running his fingers down both sides of the skull temples of his black horn-rimmed glasses.

What did Crunchy say? Jonathan asked himself, his eyes wide in disbelief.

"Buddy Holly?" Jonathan said his musical hero's name as a question.

"Not fade away," Crunchy repeated.

Impossible, thought Jonathan, *this ancient Jewish street vendor knows one of Buddy Holly's greatest rock 'n roll songs?*

Just then Jonathan's attention was turned to chanting voices approaching a half block away.

"What the hell is that?" said Butch in a booming voice.

The approaching chorus sounded like, "Whooo Eeee! Whooo Eeee!" the words muffled by the bustling street noise.

Wheeling toward the chanting, the Dormies watched the crowd parting for a line of boys dressed in full length black tuxedo coats, flat white caps, white T-shirts, tan Bermuda shorts, white socks and black loafers. On their faces, the marchers wore black eye masks, like the Lone Ranger. The line of masked boys slithered like an undulating serpent through the throng, skipping from one foot to the other, in cadence with the chanting.

The skipping revelers steadied themselves with their left hands on the shoulder of the boy in front, while their right hands carried silver flasks. There were fifteen-tuxedoed chanters skipping, staggering, and bumping into one another, the chanting growing louder, now discernible.

"WHO? WHO? WHO ARE WE? WE'RE THE MEN OF SKULL AND KEY!"

The sheer crush of the crowd slowed the skippers to a walk, as the tuxedoed boys continued their chant, taking deep swigs from the flasks.

"Out of the way!" shouted the leader. A few pedestrians yielded reluctantly, grumbling as they stepped aside; but Butch and Hunch held their ground against the surging line.

"Back off, scum," the leader barked, looking down at the tiny hunchback, failing to see the massive frame of Butch standing directly behind. Jonathan could smell hard alcohol on the leader's breath.

"Not polite to drink and shout in public," said Butch, twisting the silver flask from the leader's hand. Taking a quick sip, Butch spit the booze at the masked leader's feet. "Cheap bourbon. No class at all," Butch said evenly, flipping back the flask.

Tottering, the leader looked up at Butch's menacing face.

Another Skull and Key member muttered, "Go around him, Dirk. We can take care of these dorky Dormies some other time," steering the P U leader around the milling Dormies.

"Who in the hell are these Skull and Key jerks?" asked Butch.

"A secret drinking society for frat rats," explained Hunch. "Membership is supposed to be an honor," said Hunch,"but sometimes I wonder."

The Dormies watched the Skull and Key member at the rear of the line stagger into a parking meter, fall, then vomit into the gutter.

Grasping the collar of the inebriate's tuxedo with both his claw-like hands, Hunch helped the boy to his feet.

Wiping away bile with his sleeve, the drunk belched mightily, muttered a slurred "thanks"and wobbled gamely after the skipping line of Skull and Key.

Is this a part of the socially, superior fraternity life Mother had often talked about? Jonathan wondered.

"Let's go, frosh. Only a block to campus," said Hunch, "where you'll be changed forever."

Jonathan's thoughts returned to Casey Lee's haunting words, *once you've come to Cal, you'll never be the same.*

16

TRUE LOVE WAYS

The massive redwood doors of the Gamma Delta sorority house had been wired to chimes that played the romantic tune "True Love" whenever the doorbell was engaged.

Joan Dildeaux, who had nicknamed the doors "Virtue's Gates," had been outspoken in her opposition to the musically enhanced doors.

"Utterly poor taste," she had moaned; but her criticism had fallen on deaf ears. While it was true that a goal of the House of Beauty was to promote love and marriage, the chimes were, in Joan's view, "tacky as hell."

Some of the Gamma Delta sorority sisters had accused her of petty jealousy, as Joan was the only homely member of the House of Beauty, a legacy, selected only because her mother had been a member of the Gee Dee house, Class of '39.

Pale, skinny, and slump shouldered, Joan's plain looks were accentuated by severe acne, braces on her teeth, and French designer glasses that magnified her large, crossed eyes. As Kate Howell's best friend, Joan had suffered humiliating barbs of those who referred to the roommates as Beauty and the Beast. She had resigned herself to the fact that the only fraternity boys who gave her the time of day were those hoping she might put in a kind word to the Golden Goddess.

Joan had completed her daily finger exercises on the livingroom Steinway when Virtue's Gates issued a chorus of True

89

Love. Sarcastically, she sang the lyrics of the Bing Crosby-Grace Kelly duet from the film, "High Society," as the doorbells chimed,
I give to you
and you give to me,
True love, true love.
She sighed, walked to the double doors, and waited for the chimes to finish their sappy chorus.

Struggling to open the doors, Joan made a mental note to remind Miss Haversham, the Gee Dee house mother, to have the hinges lubricated. The impatient visitor discharged another chorus of True Love. Joan creaked open Virtue's Gates and encountered the handsome face of Dirk Krum.

Joan thought, *shit, it's the boy asshole!*

There was something pathetic yet evil about the P U President. While many sorority girls considered Dirk Krum the ultimate catch, Joan sensed a darker side of him, an innate quality that frightened her.

"Well, well, well. It's the gorgeous Joan Dildeaux," said Krum, in an exaggerated, unctuous tone, giving Joan a polished wink. Krum secretly winced, hearing his voice send up his usual gratuitous compliment.

God, she's ugly, he thought, trying not to stare at the pimply face with the disconcerting crossed eyes.

You hypocrite, Joan thought, ignoring Krum's patronizing flattery. *If Kate and I weren't such good buds, you wouldn't give me the time of day, you jerk.*

Disguising her revulsion, Joan responded with a toothy grin, producing a grinding sound in her braces. Doing her best impression of Gee Dee femme-fatale, Muffy Peachwick, Joan batted her eyelashes.

"Why, Dirk Krum, you handsome devil. What brings you over here in the flesh? Thought you'd be busy cleaning up yesterday's mess. I heard there were mysterious explosions at the P U house."

She saw his eyes turn to burning pieces of coal.

"Yeah," said Krum, clearing his throat. "Had a pretty bad accident," he lied, "A chem experiment on the second floor got out of hand. Things should be cleaned up in time for tonight's rush party. Is Kate in?"

"How did such an accident happen, Dirk? I can't think of one P U majoring in chemistry." Kate had confided the true nature of

90

the disaster at the P U house, and Joan was enjoying watching him squirm.

"Well, accidents do happen," Krum added lamely. "May I speak with Kate?"

Joan continued to ignore him. "What was all that yelling from the Dooch Dormies? Did they have something to do with your accident?" Joan asked coyly.

"NO!" Krum shouted. "Those worthless dorks just can't accept P U superiority." He added, almost in a whisper, "I'd really like to speak to Kate."

My, my, Dirk Krum is begging, thought Joan.

"She may be in," Joan teased, "but don't take too long. We're preparing for sorority rush."

Depressing the button of the aluminum intercom panel on the wall across from Virtue's Gates, Joan said, "Kate Howell, Visitor."

The usual protocol would have been for Joan to announce, "Kate Howell. Dirk Krum in the living room, Kate." But all sororities had special codes warning of the arrival of undesirable guests, clues describing the caller. Guest, referred to a handsome stranger, while other code words such as Visitor described social undesirables, allowing the Gee Dee listening to the intercom the option of pretending to be absent or unavailable.

"Kate Howell, Visitor!" "Kate Howell, Visitor!" Joan purred the code word for a dork. Only silence at the other end of the intercom. "Kate Howell, Visitor, Kate Howell, Visitor!" Joan repeated, placing emphasis on the word Visitor.

"I guess Kate is out," said Joan, smiling mischievously. Joan shouted into the intercom a third time. "Kate Howell, VISITOR!" "Kate Howell, VISITOR!"

Knowing the intercom codes for all Cal sororities, Krum fumed, understanding what Joan was doing. His face ashen from Joan's gratuitous insult, he pushed her aside, pressing the intercom button himself.

Krum cooed, "Kate Howell, Joan was just joking," he said, projecting his most sincere voice. He glared at the Gee Dee legacy. "This is not a Visitor. This is Dirk, Dirk Krum III. Kate, we must talk."

After an eternity, Kate's muted, but lilting, voice responded, "Down in a minute, Dirk."

91

Emitting a half-hearted chuckle, patting Joan lightly on the head, struggling to keep his temper in check, Krum said, "Cute, very cute."

No, he could not afford to alienate the hideous Joan Dildeaux, but he made a mental note to get even with her for her sick, tasteless prank.

"Anytime I can be of help, Dirk," said Joan, excusing herself with another flutter of batting eyelashes. She bounded up the grand staircase, three steps at a time.

Sitting beneath an original George Nelson bubble lamp, Krum nodded to a stream of Gee Dees moving past the living room. If he were interested in any other girl of the House of Beauty, a phone call would suffice. But for someone destined to be the Love of His Life, an extraordinary personal gesture, such as this unannounced personal call, was required.

At the second floor landing, Joan encountered her beautiful roommate, a pained expression on Kate's face.

She doesn't look thrilled, thought Joan.

"Well, well, well. It's the gorgeous Kate Howell," said Joan, doing an impression of Krum. "I tried to spare you from His Royal Majesty, Mr.Perfect Prick," she apologized, rolling her eyes.

"Thanks, roommie. I appreciate the thought," said Kate, giving Joan a warm hug. "But I think I can handle this Visitor. Wish me luck!"

Wish Kate Howell luck, thought Joan. *With her beauty, grace, and charm, she's got all the luck in the world.*

When Kate reached the bottom of the stairway, Krum did a double take, not immediately recognizing her. This surely was not the Kate Howell he cherished. No makeup, her new long hair style had been tied back in an unbecoming ponytail. She was dressed casually in a gray sweatshirt emblazoned with the Gee Dee insignia, a golden anchor, blue jeans rolled halfway up her calves, and Bass Weeguns loafers without socks.

She's still the most beautiful thing in the world.

"Sorry, I'm not dressed, Dirk." Her gaze made him blush.

"I should have called ahead of time." It was the closest to an apology he could muster.

What was it about this girl that turned his iron confidence to mush?

Kate saw Krum's head bow slightly and his gaze fall to a spot near the tip of her penny loafers.

Why won't fraternity boys look me in the eye, she asked herself, *the way that Casey does?*

Krum cleared his throat and mumbled, "I wanted to personally invite you out after your Presents party."

Presents was the evening when each sorority introduced or presented its new members to the public during a formal party akin to a debutante ball.

"That's very sweet, Dirk; but I think I'll spend the evening celebrating with our new pledges. We're having our party at the Claremont hotel. Of course, you and the P U's are more than welcome to attend."

"Let Joan and the other actives take care of the pledges, Kate."

"I just couldn't, Dirk. I promised Joan I would help. You know how many proud family members attend the affair."

Anticipating the rebuff, Krum had prepared an impassioned plea.

"Kate, listen. You're not just any Gee Dee who has obligations. I mean that it's ok to be fair and responsible; but why tie yourself down with busy work when you can be with me?" There was a desperate tone to his voice.

Giving Krum a smile that melted his heart, she said, "I'm flattered, really I am, but I just can't ignore my duties." Pointing to the golden anchor on her sweatshirt, she said, "Gee Dee's are as stable and dependable as our symbol. As President of the P U's, you must surely understand."

Krum bit his tongue. He glanced up at Kate's dazzling blue eyes but quickly returned his gaze back to the floor.

This elusive quality makes Kate even more desirable.

His roommate, Chip Fist, had warned that his zealous pursuit of Kate Howell might be misconstrued by the P U Brothers as being pussy-whipped.

"You can have the pick of any honey on campus," Chip had argued. "The best way to get to Kate Howell is by making her jealous. How about hustling other Gee Dees? What about Muffy Peachwick?" said Chip, smacking his lips. "Now that's a number worth drooling over!"

Krum had heard the rumors that Muffy was hot stuff, especially after a couple of drinks. But he wasn't looking for easy

93

sex. If he were, he could always visit the girls at the Yearning Arms. No, his obsession with Kate was not about sex. It was about True Love.

"You will be coming to Presents, won't you, Dirk?" Kate inquired. "I'm sure you'll enjoy meeting our new pledges, another great group of girls."

"Wouldn't miss it for the world," sighed Krum.

Yes, he *thought. I'll be at Presents to make my own social statement.*

He envisioned his grand entrance, leading the P U's en masse, lingering to greet Kate warmly, a gesture that would not go unnoticed by any fraternity man harboring any ill conceived ideas that Kate might be available.

As Kate extended her hand, Krum paused. He found this new custom of girls shaking hands disgustingly unfeminine.

Must be that Dildeaux's ugly influence.

He awkwardly gripped Kate's hand, torn by his desire to cling to its velvety touch and his loathing of the masculine greeting gesture.

Withdrawing her hand from Krum's sweaty palm, Kate said sweetly, "See you at Presents."

Turning to leave, Krum heard the door bells chime. Jerking open the massive doors, he collided with the ample charms of Muffy Peachwick.

"Why, Dirk Krum, you handsome devil. What brings you over here in the flesh? purred Muffy, fluttering her long, dark eyelashes. "Nice to see you at the House of Beauty."

"Oh, hi, Muffy," Krum mumbled, exiting quickly as the chimes concluded a chorus of the Cole Porter love song.

Something's got to be done about that doorbell, he fumed. *True Love is the shits.*

17

THE PRUSSIAN PENGUIN AND PEDER'S GREAT ERECTIONS

"Professor Werner Von Seller?" asked the caller.

"Yes," was the response, deeply resonant, tinged with a Teutonic accent. "This is Werner Von Seller."

"Congressman Clayborn Muck calling. I've admired your theories on increasing the power of America's atomic weapons, Professor."

Muck closed his eyes, seeing the image of the famous scientist <u>Life</u> magazine described as *"the quintessential laboratory research genius."*

Von Seller was portly, short-legged, and walked with a slow side-to-side waddle. The waddle and a long pointed nose had inspired the nickname, the Prussian Penguin. On his right eye, the Prussian Penguin wore a monocle that magnified the large, perfectly round eye.

"And I have followed your enthusiastic support of government funding for atomic research, Congressman." The scientist's voice took on a sudden warmth. In his mind's eye, Von Seller saw the short, powerfully built Congressman with the Cheshire grin whom his opponents described as *"the smiling pit bull."*

Professor Werner Von Seller had been a child prodigy in his native Germany before Hitler rose to power in 1933. His parents, wealthy industrialists, fearing the Third Reich's war plans, fled first to Austria, then to Switzerland, and eventually to California.

The teenage Werner Von Seller enrolled at Stanford at fifteen and soon mastered the concepts of nuclear fission and became the youngest member of the Manhattan Project, developing the atomic bombs dropped on Hiroshima and Nagasaki in 1945.

"As you know, I will be conducting HUAC hearings on your campus," said Muck, lowering his voice to a whisper, "I suspect several of your faculty are part of the global Communist conspiracy dedicated to infiltrating and subverting your university."

"I share those concerns, Congressman. There are those on the Cal campus who would, under the guise of liberal education, impede and thwart the great progress we have made in nuclear fission. I welcome HUAC's enlightened investigation of this travesty. With your help, Cal will continue on the forefront of atomic research for the defense of the Western World."

It was the opening Muck had hoped for. "That's why our patriotic movement needs help from dedicated educators like you. The future of atomic research will turn on HUAC's ability to root out Commies and left wing sympathizers."

"How may I assist?" Von Seller sensed he had found an invaluable patron.

"I cannot hope to expose every Communist or sympathizer at your University, but . . ." said Muck, pausing, "if you would be gracious enough to give me a list of a few who you believe are part of the Communist movement, your contribution would be greatly appreciated. For example, my list includes Professors Aristotle Scott and Garrick Nelquist. Whom would you add?"

Von Seller responded carefully. "Scott and Nelquist are certainly prime suspects. I would also include Professors Turpentine Tonkovich, Yale Koblik and Winston Hom. Each has spoken before the Academic Senate against increased budgets for nuclear research. I find such actions highly suspicious."

Secretly, Von Seller had other reasons for hating the three. Tonkovich, a Professor of European History, had clashed with Von Seller on the purposes of Higher Education. Koblik, a Dutch Jew, had given Von Seller the detestable moniker, the Prussian Penguin. Hom, whose family had fled from China in 1949, was one of the few Oriental faculty members, a dangerous trend in hiring. Now, with HUAC's help, he would remove all of them from the Cal faculty in one inspired move.

"I knew I could count on you, Professor!" In truth, Muck needed more suspects to deflect any suggestion he was targeting only Aristotle Scott and Garrick Nelquist.

"If you think of any more names, please let me know. HUAC's chief investigator, Seymour Graft, will be available to assist you. Your loyalty will not be forgotten when Congress considers additional funding for atomic research. I, for one, will not forget your patriotism."

Muck beamed, enjoying his good fortune. He had originally thought HUAC hearings in Berkeley would be fruitless, given the campus's long history of liberal politics. But now, with the assistance of Professor Von Seller, HUAC, the country, and his personal ambitions would be well served.

And, finally, almost a quarter of a century later, Aristotle Scott would pay for stealing the heart of Sofia Cappucino, he thought.

"I will not hesitate to call," responded Von Seller, placing the phone back onto its cradle. He envisioned his future blessed with unlimited funding from the government. He alone would elevate atomic research to its zenith, applying the power of the atom to every facet of American life!

The Prussian Penguin will have the last laugh, he said to himself.

* * *

Hunch Hitowski stopped his tour group at Sather Gate, the symbolic entrance to the campus. Despite the ambient noise from hundreds of students milling about, the gurgling of Strawberry Creek, swirling beneath the balustrades on each side of the Gate could be heard.

"Mary Sather built Sather Gate in memory of her husband, Peder, a prominent Cal alum," explained Hunch. "Beveled masonry columns support the three arches. Each of the four columns is crowned by large glass globes encased in three bronze bands: two longitudes and a meridian. Each globe is topped with a bronze flame-shaped projection aimed at the heavens."

"At night, the light of those four globes shames the moon," Hunch said.

"Mighty poetic, Hunch," said Butch.

97

Hunch continued. "The three arches are sculpted from bronze panels, dark green from almost fifty years of oxidation. The large central arch is a curved piece of bronze accented with laurel leaves. The oval of the central arch bears the insignia of the University: a star, a book, and the motto, *"Fiat Lux,"* which means, *"Let There Be Light,"* Hunch explained.

"The two smaller arches, on each side, are rectangular bronze filled with filigree swirls."

"See the spaces on the tops of the four columns?" asked Hunch, pointing to blank areas below the glass globes. "Originally, there were eight marble plaques, bas reliefs of four nude men and four nude women on the fronts and backs of the columns."

"Mrs. Sather didn't know they were nudes until the day the Gate was unveiled." A grin crept across Hunch's face. "She was shocked and ordered the sculptor to remove the nude panels. Mrs. Sather was especially offended by the male nude above the memorial inscription to her late husband."

Hunch pointed to the words chiseled into the masonry column second from the right.

Erected in Memory of PEDER SATHER, 1810-1886.

"It took workers a week to gingerly pry the nude panels off. San Francisco newspapers had a field day, noting the male nudes above the inscription as *'Peder Sather's Great Erection.'"*

"Gosh, what happened to the nude panels?" asked Tubbins.

"That's one of the great campus mysteries," replied Hunch. "Mrs. Sather demanded the nudes destroyed; but the sculptor wanted the panels saved for posterity, or at least until society accepted nude sculptures on public monuments. Legend has it, the artist swiped the panels in the dead of night, and hid them in Mary Sather's other campus monument to her dear departed Peder."

"There's another Sather structure?" asked Jonathan.

Hunch nodded. "Yes. When Sather Gate was completed in 1910, Mrs. Sather had already started construction on what would eventually be known as *Peder's GREATEST Erection,* Cal's wonderful, world renowned Campanile," said Hunch, gesturing toward the tip of the magnificent white bell tower several hundred yards away.

"In my spare time, I've roamed the floors of the Campanile

looking for the nude panels, but found nothing," sighed Hunch. "Not a trace."

"Ok, frosh, the moment of reckoning," Hunch said solemnly, clapping his hands, "the ritual turning you into an official Cal student. Pass beneath Sather Gate and repeat Casey Lee's prediction that you'll never be the same.

Hunch stepped gingerly under the middle arch of the Gate and turned, extending his hand back toward the four freshmen."One at a time, cross through Sather Gate and change your life forever."

Butch crossed first, his shoulders squared, head erect. Hunch shook Butch's gigantic hand vigorously. "Welcome to Cal, Butch, you'll never be the same."

"Never be the same," echoed Butch.

Jonathan was next, crossing through the entry of the campus with a giant leap, Hunch slapping him on the back, squeezing his arm. "Welcome to Cal, Jonathan. You'll never be the same."

"I'm already not the same," said Jonathan, thinking of everything he would report in his first letter to Ziggy.

Tommy Tubbins followed, walking slowly backwards through Sather Gate.

"What the hell are you doing, Tubbins?" asked Hunch, turning the baby-faced freshman around and shaking his hand.

"I don't want to change too quickly," he explained.

Gerald Farthing hesitated, looking at the four urging him through Sather Gate.

"C'mon, be a sport," shouted Butch, "step on through."

"Do a cartwheel," urged Jonathan.

"Gosh. Just do anything," urged Tubbins, eyeing the growing crowd of curious onlookers. "I'm getting nervous for you."

"Do it your own way, Gerald," shouted Hunch.

For once, Gerald Farthing surrendered to his instinct.

"Call me Jerry," he said. "At the top of your lungs, call me Jerry."

"What?" his companions shouted simultaneously.

"All my life, I've hated my first name, Gerald. It was given to me by my grandmother. My parents have never let me use a nickname. Gerald, rhymes with sterile," he laughed.

"If I'm never going to be the same, I want to change my name from Gerald to Jerry. Jerry rhymes with contrary."

"You can do better than that, Jerry," said Hunch. "From this time forward, I dub thee, Jerry Fart-ing!"

"Fart-ing! Fart-ing! Fart-ing!" the Dormies on the other side of Sather Gate chanted, cupped their hands to their mouths.

"Fart-ing! Fart-ing! Fart-ing!" a crowd of onlookers took up the chant.

"Never be the same!"Gerald yelled with glee.

Backpedaling ten paces, the former Gerald Farthing flipped onto his hands, and walking upside down, staggered through Mary Sather's Gate as the newly christened, Jerry Fart-ing.

For the four Dormie freshmen, Jonathan Aldon, Butch Tanenbloom, Tommy Tubbins, and Jerry Fart-ing, their Cal education had begun!

18

OSKI, HERE'S TO THEE

The gentle, sloping hillside of Faculty Glade forms a grassy amphitheater protected from the breezes of San Francisco Bay by Stephens Union, the sprawling Tudor squatting on the shady banks of Strawberry Creek and by the grove of Monterey pines shading the entrance to the venerable wood shingled Faculty Club. Beneath a dazzling midmorning sun, a buzzing swarm of eager freshman students occupied the rolling emerald carpet of Faculty Glade, awaiting the start of Freshman Orientations. Bemused upperclassmen, having survived their own freshman year, jammed the upper terraces of Stephens Union, spilling onto the brick cobbled footbridge over Strawberry Creek.

"Butch, this crowd is larger than the whole town of Clear Lake," said Jonathan, struggling with a gnawing sense of insignificance.

"Junior, can't be more than a few thousand, like Park Avenue on a slow shopping day," said Butch, allaying the apprehension he sensed among the Dooch freshmen huddled at the foot of the Glade.

At Casey Lee's urging, the Dooch freshmen had arrived early to secure front row seats. Above them, on the top of the hill, stood a small podium and several microphones.

Scanning the crowd, Jonathan concluded Ollie Punch was right when he said boys outnumbered girls four to one.

A series of loud explosions interrupted their banter, a cloud of white smoke and the acrid scent of cordite wafting over the startled crowd. Beyond the haze, an extended drum roll preceded an ear splitting trumpet fanfare. The Dormies felt them before they saw them saw them, an army whose precision marching shook the earth like a musical temblor.

Jonathan heard echoes of slow, steady applause descending on them from the horde of upper classmen behind them in Stephens Union, now standing, clapping in unison to the beat of unseen musicians. Loud cheers followed by whistles, the music growing closer, the ground shaking more violently.

Spilling over the crest of the hill, blotting out the rays of the sun, appeared an army of blue and gold. Led by a tall drum major wearing a towering fur hat, the all-male California Marching Band, two hundred strong, charged into Faculty Glade. The juggernaut, with a platoon of tuba players bringing up the rear, serpentined its way through the throng, fanning out, forming a script Cal near the cobblestone bridge of Stephens Union, performing a medley of Cal fight songs.

Crewcut yell leaders, dressed in white shirts and khaki Bermuda shorts roamed the crowd, urging freshmen to clap in time with the music.

A furry creature prowled among the throng, a small bear with an oversized head, dressed in a gold letterman's sweater stuffed with pillows, baggy blue pants, shoes as big as beaver tails. The cartoon head had two large black eye holes, brown freckles, and a smile wider than the one painted on the nose of the CAT Connie.

"OSKI! OSKI! OSKI!" the upper classmen chanted, greeting the Cal mascot

On hearing his name, Oski produced a bottle of beer from the front pocket of his letterman's sweater and a length of transparent plastic tubing. Uncoiling the tubing, bear mascot inserted one end into the bottle, the other into one of his eye holes and drained the beer in one, long sustained sip. To the shouts of "OSKI, MORE Beer!" the bear mascot produced two more bottles, quickly draining their contents with the plastic tubing, the golden fluid flowing effortlessly through Oski's eye hole.

"Jeez, unbelievable," chortled Butch. "The Brooklyn Hustle with a straw! Oski bear is great!"

"Gosh, Oski must have an incredible bladder," said Tommy

Tubbins.

Pompom girls, clad in short blue and gold skirts, pranced acrobatic dance routines. While the smiling girls kicked, twirled, and hopped to the music, Oski dropped to his knees beside them, wiping imaginary drippings of sweat, peering up their skirts, as the crowd from the terrace chanted, "HORNY OSKI!"

"Those pompom girls must be picked for their brains; because with their looks, none of them are better than a Lieutenant," shouted Butch.

Springing to his feet, Oski, in animated steps, greeted freshman girls sitting near the band with exaggerated gestures, alternately hugging and fawning them, pretending to guess the size of their busts. Above, the crowd from the terrace roared its approval with shouts of "OSKI FEELS GOOD!"

"Be kind, Butch," said Fart-ing. "Maybe they've got sparkling personalities."

"Yeah, betcha they all cook and sew. And all the girls like 'em," retorted Butch.

Boy, I wish Ziggy were here to see this, thought Jonathan, a tingling sensation racing up his spine. The energy and emotion pulsating through the crowd was as infectious as the night of Buddy Holly's concert.

"Here come the boring speeches," said Fart-ing, nodding toward two men approaching the podium from the direction of the Faculty Club. Both wore dark suits and hornrimmed glasses, one a student with blond crewcut hair and an air of smug nonchalance, the other silver-haired, radiating a sense of dignified authority. The younger man fiddled with the sound system, muttering a series of "testing, testing, testing."

A chant swept down from the Stephens Union terraces, "WE WANT OSKI! WE WANT OSKI! WE WANT OSKI!"

Ignoring the giggles from the crowd, the speaker smiled and said, "Welcome to Cal. I'm Ralph Van de Kamp, a member of the Zate House and your student body president."

"I know you freshmen are anxious for the start of Greek rush activities," Van de Kamp added. "and whatever naughty things you Dormies do behind closed doors."

Butch led a loud chorus of hisses.

"Whatever your living situation, you'll find your Cal days memorable."

103

And you'll never be the same, said Jonathan, repeating Casey Lee's words to himself.

Turning to the distinguished older man, the student body president said, "It's my pleasure to introduce the Chancellor of our great campus, Roger Haynes."

A polite round of applause greeted the spectacled, silver-haired man. Turning off the microphone, he spoke without notes.

"I don't blame you for preferring Oski to us windbags. I'd love to have Oski's carefree life," said Chancellor Haynes, in a booming voice echoing over Faculty Glade.

"You, the members of the Class of '63, represent the best and brightest students from around the country and the world. To qualify for admission, you were in the top twelve percent of your high school class, but the reality is that your class is actually drawn from the top five percent. I hope you'll experience many happy times, leaving with indelible fond memories."

"However, I must warn that you will encounter very difficult and trying times in the pursuit of your education and degree. Take a moment and introduce yourself to the students to your right and left."

The Dormies mockingly went through the charade of introducing themselves to each another.

Chancellor Haynes continued, "The sad fact is that two of every three of you will not graduate in 1963," he said, allowing the statement to sink in. "Fierce competition, emotional stress, financial concerns, changes in goals, delays in achievement will combine to sidetrack even the most well intentioned plans."

"Over the next four years, you will experience the painful agony and blissful ecstasy of academic endeavors in the most challenging educational environment in the world. Many used to achieving A's in high school, may find that getting C's will require every ounce of work and dedication."

"Some of you will find the going too arduous and transfer to some other college. Sadly, some of you may flunk out. Others will not withstand the intense pressure of competition."

Murmurs of shock and disbelief rippled through the crowd.

"I know that many, including some of your parents, have promised you that college will be the best time of your life, and I hope that this prophecy will come true."

"I must warn you that there is a struggle going on with which

104

you must be concerned. No, I don't mean the struggle between the Soviet Union and America for superiority in space, although that is an issue of pressing importance. I am referring to the battle to define the purpose of a University education."

"There are those who argue that the primary purpose of a great University is to support the wishes and goals of its government. Some professors and educators believe that the role of a modern university requires immediate and far reaching changes. They suggest that scientific research should be the most important activity and dissent should have a secondary importance on a modern campus."

"Others believe that the mission of a great University is to stimulate the mind, to nurture the soul, to challenge the intellect, and to satisfy the conscience. To this end, the University exists to promote the free and unfettered exchange of ideas, to instill the discipline of rationale thought, to critically distinguish between fact and fiction, hypothesis and hyperbole."

"Until recently, an overwhelming majority of the faculty supported the latter. But the winds of change blow strongly within our halls of ivy."

"I urge each and every one of you to dedicate yourself to your academic pursuits, keeping in mind that your Cal education is not an end in itself, but rather a tool by which you can and will be a meaningful member of society."

"Ultimately, you will learn that being a Cal Bear is both a way of life and a state of mind. Your experiences here will change your life forever, hopefully for the benefit of both you and mankind. I wish you well in your pursuits and hope that you will come to understand the motto of our campus, 'Fiat Lux!' or 'Let There Be Light!'

He paused and added, 'Go Bears!'

En masse, the freshman Class of '63 rose, applauding.

Student Body President Ralph Van de Kamp returned to the podium.

"Thank you, Chancellor. It's a Cal tradition to conclude all official events with the singing of the alma mater. Most of you haven't learned the lyrics, so I'll ask Chancellor Haynes and the upper classmen up there in Stephens Union to help me. Soon, I expect all of you to know it as well as the words to 'Happy Birthday', or 'The Mickey Mouse Club' song."

Turning off the sound system, Chancellor Haynes sang, in a booming, sonorous voice, the Cal alma mater. Soon the upper classmen joined, in three part harmony. The lyrics and music sent chills down Jonathan's back.

California,
Here's to thee;
Honor to thy name;

Alma Mater, carry on
To fortune and to fame.

Queen beside the Western Sea
Rule our destiny;

Stand for right,
Let there be light,

California,
Here's to thee!

The Class of '63, three thousand strong, issued a thunderous "GO BEARS!"

19

OH, MY PAPA

For Ari Scott, the sounds of the Campanile bells were comforting as the sight of the majestic, slender white tower itself. Standing at the base of the campus landmark, he felt the music of the carillons course through his very being. As a student, he had often spent the noon hour absorbing the sounds of the carillonneur's artistry 300 feet above. Whether the selection was Mozart, Cal's alma mater, a hymn, or the national anthem of a visiting dignitary, Ari could depend on the bells suffusing him with an aural, kinetic energy, soothing his soul, nourishing his spiritual needs.

He had crossed the pathway from Stephens Union, past venerable South Hall, oblivious to the stream of students hailing him. As a man of philosophy, Ari was unaccustomed to grappling with the twin pangs of excitement and anxiety - the excitement of anticipation, the anxiety of rejection.

In honor of his daughter Anna's Italian heritage, Ari had suggested meeting at the Campanile, the Cal bell tower that was a smaller replica of the original in Saint Mark's Plaza in Venice. Ascending the steps of the esplanade, the Campanile's carillons shook the ground beneath him with the Cal fight song, "Our Sturdy Golden Bear." Ari fidgeted, feeling like a teenage boy waiting for the arrival of his first blind date.

Impossible! More than 20 years had passed since the toure di amore he thought.

Each clang of the Campanile's bells vibrated his body like a tuning fork, quivering and humming endless questions.

Would she like him? Whom did she look like? What would they talk about?

He sought solace through word association. Footrace. He envisioned the footrace between HUAC supporters like Werner Von Seller, the Prussian Penguin and the loyal opposition led by Garrick Nelson, racing for the hearts and minds of the campus over the issue of loyalty oaths. Ari cringed, envisioning the ordeal of such a tumultuous political footrace.

Fondly, he recalled a time when footraces had a loftier bent. As a young man, Ari had been a brilliant student, breezing through his philosophy studies with honors, but it was in track that Ari had secured his notoriety. A world class miler, Ari had represented America in the 1936 Olympics in Berlin. In the finals, overcoming a painful foot injury, captured the gold medal in the metric mile.

The feat took a backseat to Jesse Owens' four gold medals over Hitler's Aryan horde, but Ari captured his share of press. As the New York <u>Herald</u> noted, *There is poetic justice in an American graduate student with the Greek philosopher's name winning the metric mile, a natural Olympic hero!*

He recalled, with a flush of pleasure, the rising tide of cheers, beginning the final lap in third place, well behind his American teammate, Clayborn Muck and the favorite, Latvian champion Gunnard Lange. He could still feel the rush of adrenaline deadening his ankle pain, as the throng chanted, "Ari, Ari, Ari." Sprinting past the fading Clayborn Muck and lunging at the tape, Ari nipped Gunnard Lange by half a stride.

The Western press hailed him *"The Great Scott,"* the *"California Golden Boy,"* captivating Europe with refreshing modesty, self-deprecating humor, and *"luminous grey eyes."*

At the 1936 Olympics, his luminous grey eyes caught the attention of Italian breaststroke swimmer, Sofia Cappuccino. In competition, Sofia's voluptuous figure proved to be a disability, her buoyancy no match for her reed-thin rivals, but the press duly noted it was Sofia who received the crowd's undivided attention and enthusiastic applause whenever she appeared in her form-fitting bathing suit striped in Italy's red, green, and white.

Many male athletes sought Sofia's affection, none more ardently than Clayborn Muck, the scion of Eastern Establishment, a young man accustomed to the spoils of rank. To Muck's displeasure, it was the unaffected, naive Aristotle Scott, who captured Sofia's heart.

Ari recalled, with sweet fondness, how innocent he had been, a virgin, the affliction of a dedicated young athlete. Yet, responding to Sofia's passionate lead and insistent ministrations, Ari learned what he had missed during his teenage years.

After the Games, Sofia guided Ari through Italy, in what she called their *toure di amore*, romantic days and nights amid the splendid ruins of Rome, the beaches of the Italian Rivera, the ancient canals of Venice, the magnificent art of Florence, exchanging the undying pledge of lovers.

They saved her birthplace, Milan, for last. Sofia's father was Giussepe Cappuccino whose inventions included the coffee brewing machine bearing his name. At the Cappuccino estate, the couple announced their desire to marry, Ari formally asking for Sofia's hand. A traditional Italian, Giussepe would not grant his consent to a prospective son-in-law who was not yet gainfully employed. Hiding their disappointment, they plotted their future. Ari would return to Cal and finish his doctorate program, and Sofia would remain in Milan, working for her father.

During the next two years, he and Sofia exchanged lovesick letters and erotic remembrances of their *toure di amore*, but the news from Europe was frightening, as the Nazis began their Blitzkrieg across Eastern Europe. Following the progress of the war intently, Ari lost all interest in his studies. In July, he read the devastating AP wire story that Mussolini had arrested so-called *bourgeois capitalists*. The list of families included the renowned Cappuccino family of Milan.

Late in the fall, Ari received Sofia's last letter, dated July 4, 1938, delivered by an Italian exchange student who had smuggled it out, informing Ari that she and her family were imprisoned in Palermo.

Was Sofia alive? Was she well? Would he ever see her again?

Despondent, Ari volunteered for the Red Cross, hoping to obtain information about Sofia and the Cappuccinos. Yes, there was a civilian prison at Palermo, but it was impossible to verify the names of its inmates.

When America formally entered the War, Ari volunteered for

the OSS, serving as an intelligence officer during the invasion of Italy. As the Allies pushed northward up the Italian "Boot," Ari clung to the flicker of hope that he would find Sofia.

At Palermo, he found only ruins. Locals confirmed there had been a prison, but it had been leveled by Allied bombing and abandoned by the Fascists in the face of the advancing Allied army. A survivor of the Palermo prison recalled a Cappuccino family, but they had died before the Allied invasion.

Ari retraced their *toure di amore* from the Italian Riviera, through Rome, Florence, and Venice, searching refugee camps, asking for any information about the Cappuccino family from Milan. In Milan, Ari walked the grounds of the Cappuccino estate destroyed by artillery fire, tearfully remembering their vows of love. *Sofia was dead.*

After the War, Ari returned to Berkeley, completing his Ph D program, accepting a position as Professor of Philosophy at Cal. In a few years, his classes became favorites, especially among female undergraduates attracted to Ari's handsome blond looks, and luminous grey eyes. One such student was a Gamma Delta sorority girl named Cecelia Cee Cee Chandler, daughter of a pioneer California newspaper family.

Still in mourning, Ari ignored the keen interest expressed by the thin, honey-haired, soft-spoken Cee Cee. But the Chandler family had a long history of getting whatever it wanted. Cee Cee, in her quiet, steady manner, eventually captured Ari's affection.

In 1949, they married in Piedmont, a wealthy hillside enclave east of campus, in a mansion that was the wedding gift of the bride's father, William Randolph Chandler, publisher of the San Francisco Gazette.

In 1951, a son, Marcus Aurelius Scott, was born, and two years later, a daughter, Monique Chandler Scott, both tow-headed like their mother, but both inherited their father's luminous grey eyes.

Now, ten years later, comfortably ensconced in the trappings of uncomplicated, upper class life, Ari basked in the glow of success. His rise in academia had been smooth and orderly. His scholarly papers on his favorite topic, Higher Truth, garnered him international acclaim.

Ari was considered a campus neo-Renaissance Man, finding time to coach the Cal track team, stirring his athletes with rousing pep talks, generously sprinkled with inspirational quotations from

Greek philosophers. Earlier in the year the <u>Saturday Evening Post</u> had featured him in an article entitled, *Aristotle's Coaching Philosophy - Cal's Great Scott.*

It was two years ago, while perusing a 1957 issue of <u>Life</u> magazine, Ari read an article on the emerging power of the Italian Communist Party and its charismatic new leader, Pablo Zarzana. Scanning the item, he had almost missed the small black and white photo tucked in the lower corner, a family portrait of the Communist leader, his wife, and daughter. Staring at the woman's face, Ari had lost his breath. The face was rounder, the eyes more recessed, but the spectacular figure was still full and sensuous, the untamed hair, still jet black.

The caption identified the three as *Italian Communist leader, Pablo Zarzana, his wife Sofia, and daughter, Anna.*

Sofia was alive!

Ari often thought of writing, of sending a telegram, of reaching out to touch the magic of his first great love. But on each occasion, his courage failed him.

Youth and love, he told himself, *had passed him by.* The Olympics, Sofia, and their *toure di amore* were faded memories of a distant time, ancient as Medieval Philosophy.

Ari's reverie was interrupted by the chime master's rendition of True Love, *an echo of that silly doorbell at the Gee Dee house,* he thought.

Christ, Ari whispered to himself. *Could he tell Cee Cee and the children about Anna? What would their reaction be? And what would his father-in-law, William Randolph Chandler, do?*

The Old Man had just declared his candidacy for governor of California, and news of Ari's illegitimate daughter would be more than an embarrassment, it would be a political disaster!

The image of the Old Man scowling at him with his bushy, owl-like eyebrows, arching in utter disdain made him shudder. Although he had easily adapted to the Chandler family's gracious lifestyle, he had always been uneasy in the Old Man's presence. There was something troublesome, a sense of foreboding.

Ari heard delicate footsteps behind him, hesitatingly contrapuntal to the sure hand of the Campanile's chime master.

"Professor Scott," a silky voice tinged with a hint of an accent, caressed him, raising the hairs on the nape of his neck.

Ari turned, his eyes hooded, delaying to the last, this moment of truthful confrontation.

"Yes, Anna?" he asked slowly opening his eyes. For a moment, he was magically transported back to the moment he first spoke to Sofia Cappucino.

Anna stood before him, as her mother had more than two decades before, radiating the same voluptuous beauty, the familiar haughty sense of mischievousness, the identical mesmerizing hint of passion that had captured the heart and soul of the Great Scott.

Old, familiar feelings came flooding back. For a moment he saw the young Sofia of his youth, but an inner voice told him it was only nostalgic imagination.

It was the luminous grey of Anna's eyes that spoke the undisputable truth. They stood silently, the sounds of the cascading carillons engulfing them. With the back of his hand, Ari gently traced the contours of Anna's cheek, touching the rivulet of a solitary tear flowing down her finely sculptured face.

They embraced gently, silently, father and daughter sharing this moment of blissful reunion, oblivious to the inquisitive stares of passers by.

High above, in the bell tower of the Campanile, Hunch Hitowski, swinging gracefully among the ropes of the carillons, clanged the bells with authority the song, "Oh, My Papa," a special request of KALX disc jockey, the All Pro.

The little hump back bell ringer swore to himself,

Oh, My Papa? Played on the bells of the Campanile? Absolute heresy! All Pro, you and your damned Eddie Fisher owe me big time!

112

20

CLASSES AND MASSES

5:30 a.m.

Under a full September moon, they appeared as apparitions, bundled in sweaters and wind breakers, spilling out into the streets, shuffling like zombies down the eastern foothills for the biannual campus siege known as Class Registration.

The day before, during his radio show on KALX, the All Pro had repeated the rumor that the administration would be closing the south side of campus, funneling students through Sather Gate. The news spread like a wildfire throughout the fraternities and sororities. In truth, the All Pro's announcement was an integral part of Royal French's Reg Line RF.

Jonathan, Butch, Tommy Tubbins, and Jerry Fart-ing jogged four abreast along Bowditch. Approaching Bancroft Way, above the din of thousands of marching feet, they heard the piercing whine of a policeman directing traffic. Behind them, clusters of Dooch freshmen labored to keep up with the quartet's swift pace.

The hour before, they had been rousted out of bed by the dorm Scholarship Committee and herded into the cavernous lounge where they gulped cups of bitter, thick hot mud called "Mrs. Beerwagen's brew." Stereo speakers blared Johnny Horton's "The Battle of New Orleans" at an ear splitting level.

Wearing his Army Special Forces camouflage fatigues and a green beret, Royal French conducted the briefing standing before an enlarged campus map leaning on an easel entitled

Secret Entrances to Campus Buildings.
Royal looks like a giant green orchestra leader, Jonathan thought.

"The first truth of student life is that there's a war out there," said Royal, slapping a rubber-tipped pointer against his thigh.

"And Class Registration will be your first test of battle. The key to academic survival is getting the courses you want, not leftovers," he said, turning to the map. "This will be one of your secret weapons. Marty Silverstein, our Super Sleuth, charted a map for your use."

The Dooch Scholarship Committee handed out smaller versions of the map, as Royal explained with military precision, the details of his Reg Line RF.

At Bancroft, the four freshmen saw the outline of a tall, thin police officer shouting directions with a bullhorn from the back of a flatbed truck stacked with traffic barricades. He wore a leather jacket, helmet, and, despite the dimness of the predawn hours, dark glasses.

"Dis entrance is closed. I repeat. Dis entrance is closed," the officer shouted into the bullhorn. "Go to Telly and enter through Sather Gate."

Crossing Bancroft, Jonathan and Butch pretended to stretch and jerk an unseen rope across the width of the street. On the near side, Tubbins and Fart-ing feigned struggle with the other end of the invisible strand.

Shouting "Stop!" "Look Out!" "Stand Clear!" the quartet tugged the imaginary cord, seesawing back and forth across the three-lane, one-way street. Startled by the tug-of-war, the parade of students stopped, allowing the rest of the Dooch freshmen to scamper unimpeded across Bancroft, all according to Royal's Registration RF.

As the freshmen passed, the officer tilted up the dark glasses and winked. It was the Waz.

"Hey Daddy-O's," the Waz hissed, "only fifteen minutes before all hell breaks loose," he shouted. "Hustle your Dormie asses over to the Campanile. Hunch and Mo are waiting."

Clip, clop. Clip clop. The first layer of fall foliage swirled up, as they ran in an even pace along a moonlit path, their elongated shadows matching them step-for-step. Above groves of eucalyptus trees, over a half mile away, they saw the outline of their

114

destination, the Campanile.

"Big bird" said Fart-ing, pointing to a manicured lawn to the left, a huge bronze pelican gleaming in the moonlight, its giant wings raised skyward, mouth agape in silent tribute.

"Are we there yet?" huffed Tubbins. "Gosh, I'm dying."

Winded, they bounded up two flights of stairs to the base of the Campanile where other Dooch freshmen huddled in the glare of flashlights. In the distance, they heard the muted shuffling of armies of unseen students, marching through Sather Gate.

"You're late," shouted Ollie Punch. Even in the dim light, Jonathan could see Ollie's eye spinning dizzily in its socket.

From a side door of the Campanile emerged the beefy outline of Mo McCart carrying stacks of small cardboard boxes in each of his massive arms, balancing one box on his smooth, bald head. In the circle of flashlight beams, Hunch Hitowski rationed out rectangular computer cards.

Casey Lee explained, "Hunch found these Reg Cards stored in the guts of the Campanile. These little cardboard beauties are the only proof you're enrolled in a class. As Royal said, these computer cards control your academic destiny."

"The normal procedure is to wait in line for Reg Cards," said Casey. "That's where everybody is heading for. After picking up Reg Cards, you stand in lines to register for classes using the Reg Cards. The kicker is that there is no guarantee there will be any space left in a class by the time you get to the front of the line."

"Jeez, what a waste of time," muttered Butch. "I could be stacking Z's, sleeping instead."

Casey continued, "Across the top of each card is a coded color stripe indicating the number of units for a course. Some have tried to make their own Reg Cards, but no one knows how to imprint the coded stripes."

"Frat rats try to beat the system by saving places in line in front of popular classes, while others get their Reg Cards. The problem is that they can save all the places they want, but no one can enroll for a class without an official computer card."

"We're also giving each of you a few blanks without the coded stripes. In an emergency, the blanks may be useful," said Casey.

"After registration, we'll meet at the Mining Circle at noon for the Big C Sirkus and another of Mrs. Beerwagen's salt peter specials."

The Dormies scattered, as the Campanile's carillons struck 6:00 a.m. Cheers echoed across campus.

Quickly traversing the brick paths of the Campanile esplanade, Jonathan and Butch marched westward, passing rows of English Plane trees, their tentacle branches pointing heavenward like gnarled fingers. The two had decided to enroll in English 1A and Political Science 1A, taught by two of the most popular professors on campus, Jacob Aural and Garrick Nelquist.

Royal French had warned that it would take a combination of the Super Sleuth's map, quick feet, and luck to land spots in both classes.

The early rays of morning peeking around the Campanile, bathed ancient South Hall, a four-story ivy-covered, brick office in an ethereal, red glow, illuminating the low relief panels of cast iron depicting California native fruits and grains.

Stately, mid-Victorian in feel and Second Empire Style in design, South Hall was one of the first buildings completed on the Cal campus in 1873. It stood as testament to a time when the campus was a cluster of buildings dotting the wilderness of the East Bay foothills.

Students swarming the front porch of South Hall spilled down the ornate front steps for fifty yards in every direction. A few new arrivals, waving computer cards, pleaded "let us through." Some yielded begrudgingly, but most held firm, keeping an anxious eye for friends bringing them their own computer cards.

"Let's see if we can find the secret entrance," said Butch. According to Super Sleuth's map, it was hidden behind a bush along the north wall. Circling the milling crowds, the pair saw a dense, two-story bush abutting the ancient brick facade. Easing sideways into the thicket, the two pushed aside layers of prickly branches.

"Junior, Royal's RF is on us. Where the hell is this secret door?" said Butch, scanning the crumbling brick around his head.

"Here," said Jonathan, scraping away a pile of dead leaves with his foot.

Dropping to their knees, they smoothed away a thin layer of dirt, feeling the outline of a metal plate. Grasping the edges of the plate, they whispered in unison, "One, two, three, lift!"

"Jeez, this weighs a ton," grunted Butch.

Alternatively lifting and twisting, the two separated the metal

116

plate from its mooring, revealing a rectangular opening of a darkened hole.

Butch descended first, lowering his six-foot-five inch frame into the abyss, feet first, disappearing into the darkness with a quiet thud.

"Piece of cake, Junior," said Butch, from the darkness, "a drop of a foot or two."

Jonathan followed, landing in the musty dankness of a subterranean room, invisible tentacles of cobwebs tickling his cheeks.

"Gotta be a light somewhere," said Butch, fumbling in the darkness. "The pyramids must smell sweeter than this hell hole."

Touching a cool surface before him, Jonathan traced the unseen contours of irregular shapes and sizes, some rounded, others angular.

Click. Butch found a string to an overhead bulb. An eerie orange light flooded a half basement. Scraping away dust from the bulb, Butch said. "Gotta be kidding. Ten watt bulbs went out with the Depression! Look at this old shit. Must be a storage room."

Squinting, Jonathan studied the objects before him. "Butch!" A rising excitement gripped him. "These have got to be . . ." his voice almost cracking, ". . . the missing panels from Sather Gate!"

Before them, buried beneath layers of gracefully spun cobwebs, standing end to end, were eight marble panels sculptured with nude human forms, four women and four men.

"Now I know why Mrs. Sather didn't want these nudes on her beautiful gate," said Butch, studying the anatomies of the bas reliefs. "The women are ok, maybe captains or majors," he said, tracing the outline of a bare breast with an index finger. "But, Junior, look at the teeny peckers on these guys! What a disgrace!"

The boys sidestepped to a paint-encrusted exit at the end of the room. Twisting a rounded brass bolt, Butch creaked open the door. "Douse the light, Junior."

They tiptoed along a darkened corridor toward a sliver of light at the far end of the hall. Above, hardwood floors squeaked from the weight of impatient students. They crept up a small stairwell leading to the first floor.

Opening the door gingerly, the two eased into a noisy mob,

jostling for position along a wide hallway. Jonathan tugged Butch's sleeve, pointing to an ornate wood-paneled staircase. Holding high their computer cards, the two freshmen shoved their way past the grumbling throng jammed on the steps of the staircase. Royal French's Reg Line RF was working to perfection!

Rounding a corner of the second floor, they encountered a cluster of five bulky boys, leaning against a set of double wood paneled doors of Room 200. A wooden sign on the door read
Professor Jacob Aural
They were dressed in the standard fraternity uniform of white, short sleeve, button down shirts, khaki pants, and loafers with white socks. Around their necks, each wore a string of dead fish with bulging, black, button eyes and shiny scales glistening in the diffused morning light. Swigging beers hidden in rumpled paper bags, they burped and muttered, "P U's rule."

"Nobody registers until the P U 's are done," snarled the leader, a short, powerfully built freshman with no neck, teetering from side to side, "unless you're willing to share your computer cards." He pointed to the treasures in Butch's hand, the other P U's pressing forward, nodding in approval.

Butch's body tensed, ready for a fight.

"Too many. Let's try a diversion," Jonathan whispered.

"Sure guys, got enough for everyone." Grabbing a handful of the unstriped computer cards from his back pocket, Jonathan casually tossed them in the air.

"Reg cards! Reg Cards!" The P U's charged en masse, pushing past Jonathan and Butch, swiping at the elusive cardboard rectangles fluttering gently above.

"REG CARDS! REG CARDS!" echoed the crush of other students rushing from behind to snatch the airborne prizes.

The two groups crashed at full force along an irregular line of scrimmage marked by the torn remnants of Reg cards. The P U's were outmanned by the sheer numbers of the flying wedge of screaming students, consuming them like hungry sharks in a feeding frenzy.

Side stepping the flailing piles of humanity, Jonathan and Butch pounded on the door to Room 200. Waving blue Reg Cards at an elderly security guard, they entered.

Signing in and having their computer cards punched, the two exited by a back stairway, moving on to register for another coveted, freshman class in nearby Wheeler Hall.

Wheeler Hall, a massive Classical styled, grey, four-story building sat on the incline of a steep hill. On the upper floors were two pairs of Ionic pilasters, surrounding roundheaded recessed windows. Above, on top of six Ionic colonnades, gigantic Grecian urns offered scholarly tribute to the heavens.

Crowds of freshmen registrants serpentined from Wheeler's nine arched entryways downhill toward Sather Gate. From the lobby of the Auditorium or "Aud," came muffled chants of "OPEN THE DOORS! OPEN THE DOORS!"

Using Super Sleuth's map, Jonathan and Butch located a small door along the tree-shaded side of Wheeler marked, *Trash Removal Only*. Their goal: Political Science 1A, a popular freshman choice, taught by Professor Garrick Nelquist whose early, vocal opposition to HUAC had made him a campus celebrity.

Inside, Jonathan and Butch fought their way along a hallway leading to Wheeler Aud packed with jostling students contesting every inch of the corridor. The heat of compressed bodies was stifling, inducing hacking and coughing. A few fainted, their unconscious forms propped against the hallway walls by the sheer crush of hopefuls.

Guarding a main entrance to the Wheeler Aud was a tall, thin policeman wearing dark glasses. waving elongated arms.

Motioning, the Waz yelled, "Let dees two guys through." Jonathan burrowed behind Butch's towering frame, wedging past shoving, grunting students, squeezing into the packed auditorium.

"Just under the wire," said the Waz, slamming shut the massive doors. "The other Dormie frosh have come and split."

Emerging from stifling heat of Wheeler Aud, the two paused, leaning against the granite-sheathed building to staunch the rivulets of sweat streaming down their faces.

"This is brutal, Junior. Worse than fighting through picks in a basketball game," said Butch. "Gonna head over to Cal Hall for a World History class. See ya at the Mining Circle."

Jonathan reviewed his list of freshman classes.

English 1A and Poli Sci 1A gave him six.

He would cross the Plaza to Dwinelle Hall and sign up for a 3 unit Rhetoric 10 class, in honor of Mother and a 3 unit Business Administration 10 class, in honor of Father, bringing his units total

119

to 12.

The next logical stop would be to move onto the T-Buildings, temporary wooden buildings, left over from World War II, tucked away in a secluded eucalyptus grove. There, he would register for the 2 unit Reserve Officer's Training Corps, dubbed "ROT-C," that, by law, was mandatory for all freshmen and sophomore males. In honor of his memorable flight to Cal, Jonathan had decided to enroll in Air Force ROT-C.

Then he would hike up the hill, past the Campanile, to the Freshman Chemistry Lab, and register for his last course, a 5 unit Chem1A class, taught by one of Cal's Nobel Prize winning professors. This would bring his total to 19 units, three more than recommended by the Dooch Scholarship Committee; but Jonathan felt confident about his ability to handle the academic load.

Making good grades will be the easiest of The Three Promises, Jonathan thought. *English 1A, Poli Sci 1A, Rhetoric 10, Bus Ad 10, Chem 1A, Air Force ROT-C, all sound like snap courses.*

He had never studied much in high school but was selected co-Valedictorian with the mayor's daughter, Dawna Carpenter.

College courses can't be more difficult than high school classes, can they? Jonathan wondered.

21

LONGING AND BELONGING

Easing his slender, delicate frame into the bathroom stall, Ruby Lips bolted shut the metal door. In his three years at Cal, he had surveyed public bathrooms on campus with the same systematic zeal Marty Silverstein, Super Sleuth, used in searching for hidden entrances to campus buildings. This seldom used men's room or "head" tucked in the lower recesses of Doe Library, near the Archives, was his favorite. More popular campus restrooms offered Ruby no appeal, for it was not the noise, bustle, and lack of privacy that repulsed him. It was the inferior quality of the bathroom graffiti.

At Stephens Union, the school administration repainted men's restroom stalls every semester, but soon the doors would be defaced with tired, low brow scribblings such as

Dormie shit = two flushes
P U asses suck canal water
and the most common graffiti on campus:
Muffy Peachwick does it with anyone.

Here in the depths of Doe Library, Ruby reveled in the quiet solitude and the superior quality of the graffiti, civilized and intellectual offerings penned by unknown authors neatly etched by pencil, not a pocket knife, providing space for editorial comment.

Before him was a recent musing by a member of this secret, literary society.

She offered her honor.

121

He honored her offer.
And all night long
It was on her and off her!
Ruby wished his social life were as simple as "he" and "she." Although he had understood his sexual orientation as a young boy, his openness had both frightened and alienated classmates raised in an era of Eisenhower normalcy. Dooch Hall had been an unexpected refuge. Although the Dormies did not embrace his lifestyle, they refrained from public taunts of "queer" and "faggot" that had haunted him since childhood. For the first time in his life, there were people who accepted him as a person, not some freak of nature.

Ruby had often thought it strange that the Dormies had become his first real friends, the concept of strangeness probably the key. Where else could such diverse strange individuals as Hunch Hitowski, Ollie Punch, Royal French, the Waz, Super Sleuth, Lizard and the All Pro peacefully coexist? Even the two most conventional Dormies, Casey Lee and Mo McCart, were themselves strange. Casey, the Dormie leader was an Oriental, surprisingly successful in a Caucasian, All-American world, and Ruby's buddy, Mo, the behemoth varsity football player, displaying a sensitivity abnormal for a jock.

And what about those freshmen? Butch Tanenbloom and his outrageous spats? And that Jonathan Aldon, a frat rat looking cherub, enjoying his status as a Dormie!

In the larger picture my sexual preference may not really be that strange, he thought.

On occasions, when his income as assistant to Gifted Florence permitted, Ruby would splurge by taking the AC Transit bus to San Francisco, seeking out his own kind in a charming area of the City called the Castro where attractions and businesses catered to people like him. But the Castro was about promiscuity, and as much as Ruby enjoyed variety in companionship, he wanted something long term, something permanent, something romantic. Yes, love.

It was in the Castro that he learned of the new term for people who were proud and accepting of whom they were. It was both a password and a badge of pride. The word was Gay.

Thus, it was with surprise and curiosity that Ruby noted a new message penciled in the corner of the door of his favorite head.

122

Discreet? Gay? TH8-6969. Only after midnight.
*Was there a special someone on campus for him? Someone
who wasn't afraid to acknowledge the joy and longing of the
human spirit?*

   Intrigued, he jotted the phone number in the small notebook he
kept in the breast pocket of his shirt.

   On the left side of the stall door, a member of the secret,
literary society had printed the philosophical quotation,

To Do Is to Be - Nietzsche

Underneath, a commentator had offered a rejoinder,

To Be Is to Do - Kant

To which Ruby added a third, in neatly printed letters,

Doo Bee Doo Bee Doo - Sinatra

* * *

   Emerging from Wheeler Hall into the bright, morning sun,
Jonathan stood, awed by the scene before him. From the top of
the steps, the slope of the hill opened onto a grand plaza teeming
with thousands of students. *A human ant hill*, he thought.
Jonathan felt alone, adrift in a sea of humanity ebbing and flowing
around him.

   "Dwinelle Plaza," explained the distinctive, familiar voice
behind him. "Intimidating, isn't it?"

   Turning, Jonathan encountered the smiling face of Casey Lee.

   "Don't let the numbers scare you," said Casey. "In all that chaos
is a definite social order. Look at the trees in Dwinelle Plaza and
tell me what you see."

   Scattered about the Plaza, like islands of refuge, stood ancient
trees encased in concrete rings. Around each gathered clusters of
students, their excited banter competing with the gurgling of
nearby Strawberry Creek.

   "The people around the trees know each other," said Jonathan.

   "It's more than that," said Casey. "The trees in Dwinelle Plaza
are where fraternity and sorority members hangout on campus.
Between classes, Monday through Friday, you can always find the
same people at the same trees. Super Sleuth has another map
spotting the gathering places of the eighty fraternities and
sororities."

   "What do the Greeks do at those trees?" asked Jonathan.

123

"You are witnessing the Greek dating ritual," said Casey, pointing to a nearby oak whose massive, shady branches cast a shadow thirty feet in every direction. "Look closely at what is happening around that tree."

Standing around the tree in a half-circle, a dozen boys, identically dressed in tan wind breakers, white, button-down shirts, khaki pants, white socks, and brown loafers, puffed cigarettes. At the base of the tree stood a pyramid of empty cigarette boxes. Half of the group stood, one foot perched on the tree's concrete ring, their backs to the Plaza; the rest, with hands in their jackets, craned their necks in the direction of a nearby tree where groups of sorority girls chattered excitedly.

"Dating ritual?" said Jonathan. "Don't see any of those guys talking to any girls."

"Part of the rules, Jonathan. You'll notice that, although none of the guys are actually talking to any girls, they're still checking them out. That tree is the mighty Wheeler oak, the P U tree."

"The ones with a foot up on the ring are upper classmen," explained Casey. "The socially cool guys who'll be on the phones tonight calling sorority girls they saw here in Dwinelle Plaza, but it's up to the 'birddogs', usually lower classmen, the guys with their hands in their pockets, to scout for prospects."

Casey pointed to a tree beyond the Wheeler oak, the object of the ogling P U birddogs. "That loquat tree is the gathering place of Gamma Delta, otherwise known as the House of Beauty. The Gee Dees are so popular that girls from other sororities stop by for small talk just to be noticed by frat rats."

"But what about Dormies?" said Jonathan. "Don't we have our own tree in the Plaza?"

"As the Bard once said, 'aye, there's the rub,'" said Casey. "At Cal, tradition is everything. The Greeks have claimed the trees in the Plaza for three generations. Dormies are the new kids on the block. If we attempted to take over any of those trees, the Inter-Fraternity Council would declare war. We can handle the P U's one on one, but there's no way in hell we could fight the entire IFC."

"It isn't fair," said Jonathan. "The Greeks don't own those trees."

"Tradition has nothing to do with fairness," said Casey,"but it has everything to do with power. When we get our share of power, we'll be part of the tradition."

"Will we ever have our own tree in the Plaza?" said Jonathan.

A sly grin crept slowly across Casey's face. "In due time, Jonathan. See that tree?" he said, pointing to a small oak at the western edge of Dwinelle Plaza. "That's where the Jewish fraternity guys meet. They didn't get their own tree until the IFC Peace Pact of 1931 when the Jewish houses got full voting rights within the Inter-Fraternity Council.

Somewhere near the Gee Dee loquat tree, two female voices yelled in unison, "Casey, Casey Lee!" Two pairs of arms arced like syncopated metronomes from girls dressed alike in white blouses with Peter Pan collars and gold circle pins, deep-green cardigan sweaters pushed up to the elbows, pleated green and yellow plaid wool skirts, and penny loafers without socks. Casey Lee waved back at the two, one a skinny, homely brunette with acne, wearing thick, black glasses; the other a slender, beautiful blonde with long flowing hair

"See you at the Mining Circle, Jonathan. We're counting on freshmen to help us score at the Big C Sirkus."

Jonathan watched Casey stroll with an easy grace past the Wheeler oak toward the Gee Dee loquat tree. He saw anger and hate welling up in the P U faces following Casey's every step. One P U, a beefy lad the size of a small house, pointed emphatically at Casey while another with a cruel sneer nodded, fists clenched. Whatever was discussed between Casey and the two Gee Dees was brief, the beautiful blonde explaining something, the homely brunette nodding frequently. When the blonde gave Casey a goodbye hug, Jonathan noted the P U with the sneer staring intently after the Dormie leader, as Casey disappeared into the frenetic masses of Dwinelle Plaza.

If looks could kill, thought Jonathan, *Casey would be dead.*

125

22

FOREPLAY

"THIS is the ALL PRO, your voice of campus radio KALX, Channel 69, broadcasting LIVE from the BEAUTIFUL, SYLVAN SETTING of the Mining Circle, site of the 49th annual, BIG C SIRKUS! A special visitor to this year's Big C Sirkus is K. Lumm, the famous photographer from <u>LIFE</u> MAGAZINE!"

The All Pro's smooth, mellifluous voice belied the gross imperfections of his face: small, beady eyes, a prominent hook nose, thick gray lips, frizzy black hair, and a constant five o'clock shadow. Microphone in hand, he tilted his head suavely toward the <u>Life</u> photog snapping candid shots of the event.

"It's a GORGEOUS September Day. Warm. Clear. CAL BLUE SKIES. Golden Gate and Bay Bridges framing glassy waters of San Francisco Bay, the kind of day that makes San Francisco BAGHDAD BY THE BAY, the term coined by the <u>Sentinel</u>'s popular columnist, Sam Paean."

"Speaking of Sam Paean, *Mr. San Francisco*, is one of the judges for the Sirkus today, along with Student Body Prez Ralph Van de Kamp, and Big C Sirkus Queen, a LOVE-LY member of the HOUSE OF BEAUTY, Gee Dee KATE HOWELL! Honorary King for this year's Sirkus is none other than our BELOVED purveyor of street sweets, The CRUNCHY MUNCHY MAN!"

Behind the judge's table stood a large white scoreboard bearing a column of neatly stenciled Greek letters of fraternities competing in the Big C Sirkus. At the bottom, in uneven printing was a hand scrawled notation of a last minute entry, "Dooch."

At the judge's platform, Sam Paean jotted notes for tomorrow's column. He would have preferred tippling martinis and chronicling the antics of North Beach eccentrics. Yet, with the sweeping Bay vista before him, the intoxicating nip of eucalyptus in the crisp fall air and the alluring presence of this beautiful blond coed beside him, he could not envision a more pleasant way to pass this splendid September day.

"While the teams are warming up, a special request. From those PERKY DOLLS of the Pi Phi house to those HANDSOME DEVILS, the Fiji's."

The All Pro flipped the thick black vinyl donut over the stubby spindle and dropped the needle arm gently onto the first groove of the 45-rpm record. With his other hand, he twirled a dial on the console, increasing the volume of the coffin sized speakers mounted on each side of his outdoor radio studio. The Teddy Bears sang "To Know Him Is to Love Him."

* * *

Completing the uphill climb from campus, Jonathan emerged from a grove of blue gum eucalyptus into a broad, flat circle of grass dominated by a living testament to classical Beaux Art design, the three-story Hearst Mining Building.

Wide steps led to a vestibule articulated by three sturdy Tuscan porticos framed in stately glass archways two-stories high, their delicate wooden frames trimmed with fan lights and embellished with carved medallions. Large granite wreaths graced each side of the archways. A copper skylight across the top of the gabled red tile roof shaded intricately patterned moldings, punctuated with six sculpted corbels of the lively arts.

The Mining Building is a gingerbread, jewel box, Jonathan thought.

Temporary bleachers ringed the Mining Circle. Dotting the perimeter, like tribal camps, stood crisp, brightly-striped tents flying fraternity pennants emblazoned with the Greek letters of their house names. Swarms of jabbering, back slapping well wishers and kibitzers flowed in and out of the tents. Festive shouts greeted the "woooosh" of each freshly tapped beer keg.

Scanning the throng, Jonathan located the frame of Royal French, standing like a human Campanile above the Dooch contingent. The fifty Dormies huddled by a battered olive drab tent, in a worn patch of grass at the far end of the Mining Circle.

"Junior, where the hell have you been?" asked Butch Tanenbloom, trotting up, handing him a lunch bag. "Saved you some of Mrs. B's shit on a shingle. Let's go! Royal French is making team assignments, as soon as the Dooch tent is decorated."

Pushing through the crowds, the two freshmen made their way to the tattered Dooch tent. A skinny Dormie, wearing large dark glasses, directed a brigade of freshmen splashing buckets of brightly colored paint over the olive drab tent, transforming it into a canvas of swirling rainbows.

"That's Bobby B. Jean, better known as the Lizard," explained Royal, nodding toward the artist."Hell, I thought this old Army surplus would do. But no, our resident artist insists on making a cultural statement."

Jonathan recalled the mosaic of the double headed Germanic eagle mounted in the Dooch Hall lobby with the brass plate inscription, *Donated by Robert B. Jean.*

"What does the Lizard call this technique," asked Butch? He had viewed many unusual styles at the New York Museum of Modern Art, but *buckets of splashing paint?*

"Psycho-something," said the Waz.

"Psychedelic," corrected Hunch Hitowski. "Lizard believes the mixing of bold primary colors connects the beholder with his basic emotional core, touching the essence of the universe."

"Highfalutin' bull shit, if you ask me," said Butch."Dormies throwing paint on a tent is art? If Lizard's psychedelic art ever makes it big, I'll eat my shorts!"

Ignoring the barb, the Lizard, flicking his tongue in and out like his reptilian namesake, admired the dripping, congealing masterpiece. He had chosen lime, orange, cherry, lemon, and pineapple hues, inspired by the flavors of "Lifesavers" candy. Comparing the Dooch tent with the fraternity tents ringing the Mining Circle, the Lizard grinned with satisfaction.

Now the Dormies can compete in the Big C Sirkus with artistic inspiration, he thought.

"Aldon!" Ollie Punch huffed to Jonathan's side. "Hunch says

you've got a pair of glasses like Crunchy Munchy's. Let me have them for a couple of hours."

"Yes, but . . ."

"Look, we've got an emergency. Crunchy broke his and can't get a replacement until tomorrow," Punch explained. "A little PR with the Honorary King of the Big C Sirkus is not going to hurt us, right, Aldon?" Ollie flashed a Cheshire grin, his left eye spinning wildly in a counterclockwise direction.

Jonathan reached into the pocket of his windbreaker and produced his prized possession, unwrapping it from its protective plastic wrapping.

"Please be care . . ."

Ollie snapped up Buddy Holly's glasses and waddling like a human beach ball on stilts toward the judging stand, shouted over his shoulder, "Won't harm a flea, Aldon."

"Dormies, huddle up," barked Royal French, leading the Dormies into the Lizard's dripping, psychedelic creation. Outside the crowds swelled as fraternities took up their favorite chants. Above the din, the All Pro spun the Everly Brothers' plaintiff ballad, "Let It Be Me."

"The Sirkus is scored like a track meet," explained Casey Lee, scanning a clipboard filled with calculations.

"The top five of each event are awarded points from 5 for first place down to 1 for fifth. Total points at the end of all the events determine the winners. The key to winning a trophy is to place in as many events as possible. 15 total points should be enough to win something."

Royal added, "It would be a real coup for us to bag a trophy. Our strength will be in Frisbee and Free Style. Any points picked up in the other events will be gravy. The P U's and SAE's are heavy favorites, but I'd watch out for the Kappa Nu's. They've recruited talent just for the Sirkus."

From the back pocket of his battle fatigues, Royal pulled an entry form, filling in names of the Dooch team.

"Mo, you and Hunch will take care of the Joust. Casey, of course, will enter the Frisbee toss. Ollie, you and your big mouth will try Goldfish Swallowing. Ruby will be our secret weapon in Free Style."

"The frosh will have to fill in some of the events," said Casey. "How about Beer Chugging?"

"Butch is great," said Jonathan, volunteering his friend's prowess in the Brooklyn Hustle.

"Piece of cake," said Butch yawning.

"Coin Toss?" asked Royal.

"I'll take that one," said Jonathan, raising his hand.

"That leaves Phone Booth Stuffing for the rest of the freshmen," said Royal, completing the entry form.

Casey Lee spoke slowly, a fierce edge in his voice. "The Big C Sirkus gives us a chance to earn a little respect, score some brownie points with the sorority girls, and maybe change the image of Dormies as wimpy dorks."

"I resent that last remark," said Ruby Lips, feigning disgust.

"Actually, I think you resemble that last remark, Ruby," retorted Ollie Punch.

"Concentration is the key," said Royal French, advising the Dooch freshmen. "Don't let the crowd scare you. Now that you've survived Class Registration, you're ready for anything."

Casey continued, "Dooch is the first non-Greek living group that has been allowed to compete. It took a lot of help from some of the good fraternities, like the Sig Ep's and the Jewish houses to get us into the Sirkus. The P U's thought they could keep us out by having the Inter-Fraternity Council charge us a one-hundred dollar entry fee."

"Jeez," said Super Sleuth, amid a chorus of whistles. "A hundred bucks! How in the hell can we afford it? That's the dorm social budget for a month!"

"Don't sweat it, Marty," assured Casey. "As usual, Royal has an RF to raise the C note."

"Hey," said Dick Phuncque a balding, pimply faced Dormie, wearing a slide rule like a sword on his belt. "What are the rest of us gonna do while you studs are whipping frat rat asses?"

"Ah, I'm glad you asked, Phuncque," replied Royal. "You weenie-wimp Eng-gineers are gonna get us back our one- hundred dollar entry fee, and . . . " Royal paused for effect, "as a bonus, you'll get to slobber all over those good-looking Sally sorority girls."

"Phuncque, as a weenie-wimp Eng-ineer, this could be the highlight of your social life for the year!" teased Ollie Punch.

In the whooping and hollering that followed, the Dormies did not hear the clanking and clattering of approaching vehicles, but soon felt the trembling vibrations of grinding machinery.

"I believe our hundred-dollar RF plan is here," said Royal.

From a nearby fraternity tent, a voice tinged with awe, shouted, "Holy cow! A World War Two halftrack!"

"Ok, Dormies, give a hand," shouted Royal leading the group out the tent.

Parked outside, growling noisily, belching green smoke, sat a half truck-half tank war machine with thick front wheels and oval rear caterpillar treads, escorted by the Waz, aboard his silver Vespa.

An Army soldier sat behind the wheel of the open air vehicle. Another squatted at the rear, next to stacks of cardboard crates. Both snapped to attention as Royal approached. Dismissing them formally with a touch of a right index finger to his brow, Royal greeted both with warm handshakes.

"Good to see you Cap'n French," said the driver.

"How's civilian life treatin' you, sir?" asked the other soldier.

"Better than the jungles of Indo-China?"

"Different kind of jungle here," replied Royal with a grin. "What do I owe for the load?"

"Straight from the PX, chilled like you ordered," said the driver. "Tossed in some ice," he said, pointing to the cargo marked *Kerrs Beer-This Side Up.*

"Consider this a payback for saving our asses on that night mission in the Mekong, Capt'n," said the driver.

The two soldiers snapped to attention, holding their salute. For a moment, Jonathan thought he saw the glistening of a tear in Royal French's eyes as he returned the salute ramrod stiff.

"Ok, let's move the brew into our tent," said Royal.

Forming a single line, the Dormies gingerly passed cases of Kerrs from one to another into the recesses of Lizard's artistic creation, the crowd buzzing with the news that the Dormies had unloaded a shipment of the rare, delicious beer!

"Phuncque," ordered Royal. "Have your weenie-wimp Eng-gineers set up those tables along the rear! Get a couple garbage cans from the Mining Building for the ice. Casey, give me a hand with the sign."

Royal held a neatly printed sign in place as Casey Lee stapled its corners to the flap of the Dormie tent. It read,

KERRS - One Dollar a can. (Sorority girls FREE)

"Wow! A buck for beer? Hell, that's highway robbery!" said Super Sleuth. "Kerrs is only a quarter a can . . ."

". . . when you can find it." Royal finished the sentence for him.

"Do you think the Greeks will spend that kind of dough on Kerrs?" said Super Sleuth. "We've got twenty-five cases of Kerrs. Six hundred is a lot to sell at a buck a can!"

"Simple supply and demand," said Royal. "The Greeks have the dough but can't find Kerrs in quantity anywhere. What's a buck to a rich frat rat?"

Royal nodded toward the crowd pressing toward the Dormie tent. "Watch. The Greeks will swallow their pride and spend the money, especially when all those lovely Sallies begin drinking their free Kerrs. Here they come!"

Amid squeals of "free Kerrs," a crush of sorority girls jammed into the Dormie tent, the Dormie Eng-gineers dispensing cans of Kerrs slowly, teasingly, gleefully, ogling the pretty girls.

Stunned groups of fraternity boys converged on the Dormie tent, watching the Sallies savoring swigs of the legendary beer.

"Don't buy from those fucking Dormies," shouted Dirk Krum, stoking the handle of a beer keg pump. "Drink our own Hamm's," he said.

"Shit, who cares who's selling it," said Chip Fist, plucking a bill from his wallet. "Christ, it's Kerrs! I'm getting a six-pack. Want some?"

Within minutes, the Dooch tent was jammed with excited Greeks waving wads of bills. Sorority girls clamored for the attention of the Dormie beer-tenders, shouting for seconds on their freebies.

"The Dooch weenie-wimp Eng-gineers won't be able to sleep for days standing within smelling distance of all those great looking Sallies," said Ollie Punch, his spinning eyeball focusing on the ample charms of Muffy Peachwick who had just finagled two cans of Kerrs from a drooling Dick Phuncque.

23

SIRKUS CIRCUS

"Let the GAMES of the Big C Sirkus BEGIN," announced the All Pro. "The FIRST event, Telephone Booth STUFFING!"

As the All Pro explained the rules, teams lugged phone booths onto the Mining Circle like metal cocoons. "THIRTY seconds to CRAM in as many freshmen as possible. One point per person, and THREE points deducted for any team tipping over its booth," the All Pro announced.

Referee's whistle! Bodies squirming in laughter and pain. Some teams like the P U's used brute strength, wedging in piles of flailing arms and contorting bodies. The Dormies, following Royal's strategy, stacked orderly rows of freshmen, like human sardines in fetal positions. Tommy Tubbins and Jerry Fart-ing were the first row. Other frosh followed.

"Almost a dozen!" shouted Royal. "There's still room at the top!" Royal and Casey boosted two tiny freshmen, Johnny Welt and Christof Pappass, into the top of the booth. Twelve! One more to go.

"TEN, nine . . ." the All Pro began the final countdown.

"Burrow straight in," said Royal, pushing Jimmy Nayfee, the smallest Dooch freshman into the top of the packed phone booth.

"Can't breathe," gasped Tubbins from the bottom of the pile.

"Jeez, who farted?" shouted a voice from within the writhing pile of humanity.

A contagious giggle, then a chuckle rippled through the baker's dozen, blossoming into hysterical laughter.

"THREE, two . . . "

"That's not a fart," said a muffled voice. "It's Dave Prestone's breath!"

The Dormie phone booth, pulsating from uncontrollable laughter, shook, tilted, teetered, then dropped backwards beyond the point of no return, crashing the 13 Dormies in a disheveled heap as time elapsed.

When final body counts were tallied, the Kappa Nu's were first with 12, the P U's second with 11, the Dooch Dormies third with 10 (13 minus 3 penalties for the tipped phone booth), SAE's fourth with 9, Sig Ep's, a distant fifth.

"Not a bad start, Dormies," said Royal. "Third, only 2 points behind."

"Event NUMBER TWO!" announced the All Pro. "The FRISBEE CHUCK! Total distance for three throws."

"Casey's got a damned good chance," said Royal. "With aerial input from Ollie Punch, Casey has elevated Frisbee to art form."

The Dormies watched fraternity chuckers sprinting to the foul line, power tossing Frisbees cross-armed downhill toward the base of the Campanile, most efforts bringing jeers from the crowd as the saucers, catching updrafts, stalled, veered, and plummeted to the ground.

"My God, it's T.A. Brewster," said Fart-ing, pointing to a handsome dark-haired boy with a taut athletic build warming up."He won the Manhattan Beach Frisbee Championship!"

T.A. Brewster whipped his Frisbee in a power throw, a snappy, cross-armed delivery that whistled in a flat, elliptical arc, sailing toward the Campanile before touching down 200 feet away, drawing appreciative "oooh's" from the crowd.

P U's Chip Fist muscled into second place with a 190-foot cross-armed heave defying the cross winds in a high trajectory.

"Go, Casey!" the Dormies yelled.

Casey Lee's first effort was a deceptively slow, smooth, cross-armed throw that, dancing on top of cross currents, bobbed and floated, touching down into third place, 165 feet away.

For their second throws, contestants used an underhanded, flipping motion resembling the rolling of a bowling ball.

With a crisp snap of the wrist, T.A. Brewster's flip sailed 120 feet. Chip Fist, thrusting his muscle-bound arm away from his twisting body, struck his own hip, sending the disc fluttering like a wounded duck 80 feet down hill, still good enough for second place.

Dormie cheers mingled with P U boo's as Casey Lee lined up for his second throw.

"Hey, Chinaman, go back to where you belong," shouted a drunk P U.

Raising an index finger, Casey tested the wind, stopped, and taking two quick steps, snapped the Frisbee sharply from his right hip like a gunfighter drawing a pistol. The saucer skimmed over the grass and stayed low, hugging the road toward the Campanile. At 100 feet, an updraft caught the Frisbee, lifting the disc 10 feet vertically where it sailed leisurely in a straight line, touching down gently 200 feet away.

Score after two throws: Casey Lee first with a combined score of 365 feet, T.A. Brewster in second with 350, and Chip Fist a distant third at 270 feet.

"Now, Casey's *coup de grace*," said Royal confidently.

Chip Fist rested a stiff thumb along the ridge under the rim and snapped the disc in a sidearm motion from behind his right ear, the velocity of the throw dissipating as the Frisbee flip flopped from one tack to another in an "S" shaped arc, crashing 90 feet away, giving the P U a total of 360 feet.

T.A. Brewster sandwiched the rim of the saucer between the web of the thumb and index finger, resting four fingers on the Frisbee's topside. With a running start, the Kappa Nu used a whipping, straight armed, discus delivery, sailing the flying disc out in a tilted attitude, soon straightening out to a distance of 100 feet, reclaiming first place with a combined distance of 450 feet.

As the Dormies shouted encouragement, Casey Lee limbered up for his final throw. Turning toward the judges' platform, he tipped his Frisbee to Kate Howell, a gesture that induced a sneer from Dirk Krum

Standing in a wide stance, Casey bent his knees, and with a swift flick of the wrist, sent the Frisbee through his legs from behind. The saucer flew straight and true, waist high, landing 95 feet away, for a combined total of 460 feet.

CASEY WINS!

Standings, AFTER TWO EVENTS, announced the All Pro, "Kappa Nu's, first place: 9 points. DOOCH DORMIES, a

SURPRISING SECOND with 8, P U's third with 7."

"Next event," intoned the All Pro, "Goldfish SWALLOWING! Contestants have ONE MINUTE. Only fish actually swallowed will count. NO POINTS for fish flopping out of a contestant's mouths!"

"C'mon, Big Mouth!" yelled the Dormies, as Ollie took his place at a long table stocked with clear, water bowls filled with live goldfish swimming in lazy patterns.

"Gosh, how long does a goldfish flop around in your belly," asked Tubbins.

"They don't suffer too long," said Hunch. "Human stomach acids are pretty deadly."

"ON YOUR MARKS, gentlemen," said the All Pro. "Get set, GO!"

Contestants plucked goldfish with small mesh nets, plopping them quivering into their open mouths. Novices, flapping their lips wildly, struggled with their wiggling thrashing prey. Veterans, tilting back their heads, puckered their lips and sucked their prey into their gullets with a single gulp. Watching, Jonathan felt bile percolating into his mouth, remnants of Mrs. Beerwagen's lunch that Butch had described as shit on a shingle.

With effortless efficiency, the SAE, P U's, and Kappa Nu's matched each other slurp for slurp. At the 30 second mark, Ollie trailed by only a few swallows, the rest of the field gasping and gagging far behind.

"TIME'S UP," announced the All Pro.

"Shit," said Ollie Punch, issuing a prodigious belch. "I should have checked out the fish bowls first. The frat rats who beat me knew which bowls had the tiniest fish. The one I got had goldfish as big as minnows!"

"Still a great job," said Royal. "Picked up a point and a half. We're still in the hunt."

"SCORE AFTER THREE EVENTS. Kappa Nu still leading with 13 points. Slipping into second, the P U's with 10 points. Dropping to third, the DOOCH DORMIES with 9 and a half points. Closing the gap is SAE with eight points."

"The NEXT EVENT, the ever popular BEER CHUGGING!"

"Pressure, Butch," said Casey. "Can you handle it?"

"Have no fear, Butch is HERE!" he said, pointing his index finger toward the ground.

"Where'd the Dormies drag up that thing?" shouted a P U.

"Spats went out with black and white movies," yelled another.

Butch glared at the hecklers, tapping the side of his nose defiantly with an erect middle finger.

In the middle of the Mining Circle were stacked pyramids of Hamms, 15 cans high, each bearing triangular holes from a church key opener. As other chuggers gripped cans tightly at the ready, Butch nonchalantly placed his left hand behind his back and yawned.

"Gosh, Butch sure knows how to tick people off," said Tubbins.

Referee's whistle! Other contestants sipped, gulped, burped, and coughed down their beers, slamming down the empties. Butch, deploying the Brooklyn Hustle, methodically inhaled the contents of the cans, flipping empties over his shoulder.

"Jeez," shouted Super Sleuth, "Butch's downed a six-pack!

Thirty seconds, and it was already a rout as Butch outdistanced his rivals with a machine like precision.

"SEVEN, EIGHT, NINE!" astonished sorority girls took up the count.

"TEN, ELEVEN, TWELVE!" The crowd screamed at Butch's boffo performance.

"Ten seconds and three beers left," yelled Jonathan. "C'mon, Butch!"

The crowd was on its feet. At the center of the maelstrom of noise, Butch reminded himself,

Stay calm, big fella. Big finish. Here goes!

Tossing down beers twelve and thirteen, Butch sailed the aluminum carcasses at the P U tent. Waving to the Dormies, he knocked down number fourteen. With a flourish and a lipsmacking "ahhh," Butch emptied the fifteenth can, tossing it into the air as the whistle sounded.

"Ladies and gentlemen," announced the All Pro, "a NEW CAMPUS RECORD! FIFTEEN cans in SIXTY SECONDS! Our new champ, from Dooch Hall, BUTCH TANENBLOOM!"

Hoisting Butch on their shoulders, the Dormies circled the Mining Circle in a victory lap, taunting the P U's with shouts of DORMIES RULE! DORMIES RULE! DORMIES RULE!

"Our NEW standings, at the halfway point. Kappa Nu's still leading with 16 points. VAULTING INTO SECOND, DOOCH

DORMIES with 14 ½ points, edging the third place P U's with 14 points."

Leaning to his left, the All Pro, microphone in hand, horned into a closeup K. Lumm, the <u>Life</u> photographer, was taking of Kate Howell, the Golden Goddess.

"When we come back from our commercial break, KALX will bring you the EXCITING conclusion of the 49th annual Big C Sirkus! STAY TUNED!"

24

MUCK AND GRAFT

"Are you certain, Seymour?" said Congressman Clayborn Muck, unable to conceal his rising excitement.

Seated in a leather chair in Muck's suite at the Claremont Hotel, above the Cal campus, was Seymour Graft, Chief Investigator of HUAC, the House Un-American Activities Committee.

"Straight from J. Edgar Hoover's right-hand man, Tallefson, passed along by the CIA," said Graft, a French Gaulois cigarette dangling carelessly from the corner of his mouth. "A direct link between the international Communist movement and the University of California, Berkeley."

Seymour Graft had an angular face with narrow set eyes, twitching nose. A wispy moustache from a small, round mouth.

"Great work," said Muck, rifling through the packet of black and white photographs and single-spaced typed notes.

"Traded the FBI that stuff we had on Jack Kennedy and Marilyn Monroe," Graft said in a hacking cough.

Wish Seymour would get rid of that stupid hat and tan trench coat, thought Muck. *Humphrey Bogart, he was not!*

But Muck reminded himself that Graft was so effective in doing HUAC's bidding, unearthing tidbits of dirt, sniffing out Commie connections, and compromising bureaucratic sources that he could live with Muck's eccentric affectations.

"Anna Zarzana, daughter of Italian Commie Boss, Pablo

139

Zarzana, snuck right under the nose of Immigration and enrolled at Cal as a grad student," said Graft, puffing a wobbly smoke ring above his head, then hissing a stream through its center.

"FBI says it was those fucking Kennedys who pulled it off," said Graft. "Before the War, when the old man, Joe Kennedy, was Ambassador to England, he was a drinking buddy of Anna's grandfather. According to the CIA, Grandpa Cappuccino was some kind of an I-tralian industrialist in Milan. A favor, for old time's sake, I guess," he said, twirling his wispy moustache, pooching another circle of cigarette smoke into the air.

Muck smirked. How he despised John F. Kennedy, the millionaire's son with the boyish handsome looks and Irish Boston charm. *Too ambitious! Too Catholic! Too liberal*!

Despite the well oiled political machinery and all that money, Muck thought, *John F. Kennedy will surely lose his Presidential bid next year.*

According to Muck's timetable, five years from now, in 1964, after establishing himself as America's preeminent anti-Communist Crusader, the White House would be in his reach. Muck studied the grainy enlargement of the smiling, waving girl boarding a Pan Am Connie in Rome bound for New York. *Such a pretty girl! Pity she's a Commie!*

For a moment, something from the dim recesses of his memory tugged at his consciousness. He reexamined the black and white photo again. Something oddly familiar about the voluptuous outline of her figure, the pout of the smile. Closing his eyes, Muck dismissed the thought. *No need to be concerned about details now. in due time, Seymour Graft will ferret out everything he needed to know about the girl.*

"You will, of course, keep close watch on her," said Muck. "Who she sees, what she does, classes she takes. We'll need evidence showing her connection with campus Commie sympathizers."

"Should be easy, Boss. She's staying at the I-House. No special surveillance problems there."

The International House or I-House was the campus address for hundreds of foreign students, from more than seventy-five countries attending Cal, returning to their homelands as future leaders. Built in 1930 through the generous donations of the John D. Rockefeller, Jr. and David Rockefeller families of New York, the domed Spanish colonial castle, with a Moorish accent was located at the northern edge of Piedmont Avenue immediately adjacent to Memorial Stadium, enjoying the distinction of being the only co-ed living group at Cal, one wing for men, one for women. The international flavor of I-House with residents of every race and color was in stark contrast its neighbors, the all-white members of Cal's Greek fraternities and sororities.

"Gonna take this assignment myself. Should get some real incriminating stuff soon," said Graft, producing a miniature camera, the latest in spy tools he had acquired from his contacts at the FBI. He thought to himself, *Yes, Seymour, you lucky dog. This lovely Commie tail will provide some titillating photos for my private collection.*

How he loved to lurk in the shadows, unseen by his prey, quietly photographing their every movement with the new infrared film. Especially unsuspecting, beautiful girls emerging from the shower!

Graft felt heat in his loins, anticipating the loving shots of this Commie girl, Anna Zarzana, emerging from the shower, imagining what feminine charms she would be revealing to his omnipresent prying eyes.

"Good," said Muck. "There'll be a special bonus for you, Seymour, if you get something special on Professor Ari Scott."

"Piece of cake, Boss. Already bugged the phones of Professor Scott and Professor Nelquist like you asked."

"Seymour, do me a favor," said Muck, flicking a fifty-cent piece across the width of the desk.

"Sure , Boss, name it," replied Graft, scoring another bulls eye with a stream of cigarette smoke.

"Buy yourself some American cigarettes. Looks bad for HUAC when its Chief Investigator smokes that foreign crap."

Muck thought, *What sacrifices to good taste I've had to make in my crusade against the insidious, International Communist conspiracy!*

25

TO THE LOSERS, THE SPOILS

"A NEW event this year, the COIN TOSS," announced the All Pro. "Contestants will have two throws at the target, a stretched length of rope ten yards away. The closest of each contestant's tosses will count."

"Our first contestant, from the first place Kappa Nu's, that well known penny pitching ace, MONTY MAITLAND!"

"Kappa Nu's can take a big lead here," sighed Royal. "Monty Maitland makes a living pitching pennies at the Sproul Hall steps."

Maitland, a stocky boy with thinning hair and cocky stride, planted his right foot slightly behind the mark and, leaning forward, flipped a coin like a miniature Frisbee toward the target. The shiny, spinning penny made a high, lazy arc, landing in a spray of sand near the rope.

"Six inches!" announced the official, measuring the distance of the coin to the rope.

"Jonathan," said Royal, pulling the freshman aside. "I've watched Maitland many times. He can be beaten if you ignore his insults. Breathe deeply and don't let him get to you."

Jonathan watched intently as Monty Maitland assaulted other contestants with a stream of barbs, distracting them just enough to maintain his lead.

"Shoe's untied! Not nervous, are you? Don't foul!"

P U hisses greeted Jonathan as he approached the mark for his first toss. Jonathan had chosen a fifty-cent coin rather than a penny, the weight of the half-dollar closely approximating the weight of the small, flat stones stacked at the end of the Aldon dock.

Gingerly he hefted the coin in the palm of his left hand as he eyed the rope, imagining he was ready to bomb the buoys floating beyond the Aldon dock on Clear Lake.

"Don't choke, southpaw," shouted Monty Maitland.

Yes, Jonathan said to himself, fingering the coin between his forefinger and thumb. *It's about the same distance.*

In his mind's eye, he saw the familiar bobbing buoy, emblazoned with an orange "A." Pretending Ziggy was standing next to him aiming at the other buoy, he counted to himself, *One, Two . . .*

On the count of *Three*, he flipped the coin underhand in a high arc as he and Ziggy had done thousands of times before. The half-dollar kicked up a cloud of dust as it buried itself beneath the sand.

"Four inches!" announced the official.

Jonathan, the Clear Lake freshman, in the lead!

It was a stern-faced Monty Maitland who walked with deliberation to the mark for his second throw. This time he carefully measured the distance of his toss.

"Don't shit your pants!" Butch teased.

Leaning on his right knee, Monty Maitland rhythmically cocked his right wrist once, then twice, Frisbee fashion. With a smooth flick, he sailed the copper coin in a high arc, eliciting shouts of encouragement, the penny ending its flight with a plop near the taut rope.

" One-half inch!" shouted the official, the crowd breaking into applause.

"We've got at least second place, Jonathan," said Casey Lee with a comforting hand on his shoulder. "Relax, no pressure now."

The crowd rose as Jonathan walked slowly to the mark.

"Go, Jonathan!" shouted the Dormies, praying for a miracle.

Monty Maitland stood to the side with arms folded. "I don't have to say a word, Dormie. This competition is OVER," he said with a broad grin on his face.

Jonathan closed his eyes, envisioning the crystal blue waters of Clear Lake, smelling the hog laden scent of an Iowa summer, and tasting the toe-zone heavy in the air. He flipped the coin cleanly, pointing his raised arm at the tail of the trajectory of the shimmering fifty-cent piece.

Shit flies both ways! Jonathan shouted to himself.

The crowd exploded in an "OOOOH," as the missile struck the rope, bouncing high like a jumper on a trampoline.

A perfect shot! Jonathan was buried under a pile of screaming Dormies.

"THREE WAY BATTLE for the lead with only two events remaining!" shouted the All Pro into the microphone. "Clinging to first by a hair is Kappa Nu's with 20 points, followed CLOSELY by the Dormies with 19 1/2. The P U's third, with 17 points."

"Next event, THE JOUST! Single fall elimination until we reach the final six. Two out of three falls for the FINALS!"

"JOCKEYS, mount your beasts of burden!"

Emerging from the P U tent, Chip Fist, a can of Kerrs in each hand, squatted on his haunches, as Dirk Krum straddled Chip's blocky shoulders, one hand cradling a lance fashioned from a mop handle, its striking end, a pillow tightly wrapped in burlap. Both wore black football helmets with the silver inscription, *P U's Rule.*

Facing them was the Delt team of two thin, handsome boys. The beast of burden was a tall lanky lad on whose bony shoulders sat a short muscular jockey. Both wore helmets of the Delt colors, pastel blue and white.

Dirk Krum spat over his beast's right shoulder. "Ok, Chip, let's show 'em why P U's rule."

The P U's toyed with the Delts, Dirk feigning jabs with his lance, Chip standing in place casually sipping from his two cans of Kerrs.

"I'm bored, Dirk. Let's finish these pretty boys off," shouted Chip shifting the P U leader into attack position.

"P U rules!" shouted Dirk as Chip lurched forward in powerful, short steps. Deflecting the Delt lance with his free hand, Dirk struck the beast on the temple sharply with a swift stroke with his lance, followed by a quick jab to the chest of the jockey, the Delts collapsing under Dirk's one-two punch, as the crowd roared its approval.

"Next," announced the All Pro, "the Zates and the Dormies."

The Zates, a fraternity of dashing party goers, were soundly cheered by adoring sorority girls.

144

"Go, Zates!" student body President Ralph Van de Kamp urged his fraternity brothers.

A chorus of jeers and laughs greeted the Dooch twosome. Stripped to the waist, Mo McCart with his massive, rippling muscles resembled a bald headed version of the cartoon character Alley Oop, towering over Hunch Hitowski clad in a tattered T-shirt and cut off blue jeans. The Dormie duo wore brightly painted helmets, two swirling, psychedelic creations of the Lizard.

"Which one's the beast?" shouted a member of the crowd.

"It's a baby humpback whale out of water," yelled another.

"Who barfed on your helmets, Dormies?" said a P U

Placing a bear-sized hand over Hunch's small, rounded back, Mo said, "Pay them no mind, Hunch. We'll let our actions speak for themselves."

At the whistle, Hunch leaped on the broad girth of Mo's mammoth shoulders, scrunching low behind his head, like a turtle retreating into its shell, providing an almost invisible target for the Zates.

The crowd cheered as the Zate jockey jabbed in vain at Hunch's hunkered down form. Maintaining a controlled stance, Mo held his ground as the Zate lance bounced harmlessly off Hunch's rounded back.

"Ok, Mo, let's do it," said Hunch.

In a sudden thrust, Mo McCart rammed his head into the solar plexus of the Zate beast, eliciting an "oooof" as air rushed out of his lungs. The Zate team staggered, then keeled forward. Raising up from his defensive position, Hunch pushed the Zate team to the ground with a swift jab of his lance.

Around the Dooch tent, Dormies cheered wildly, but around the Mining Circle, a hushed silence descended among the Greeks, as the Zates dusted off their embarrassment and exited the field of combat.

Alternating matches from the two brackets, the list of competitors was whittled down to three semifinalists from each, the P U's, SAE's, and Sig Ep's remaining in A bracket, the Dormies, Kappa Nu's, and Theta Delts surviving bracket B.

At the P U tent, Chip Fist spat out a broken tooth. "Another reload of Kerrs, Dirk?" Chip asked, wiping traces of blood, sweat, and grime from his eyebrows.

Dirk shook his head furiously, glaring at the swirling, multi-

145

colored, psychedelic tent.

First, there was the matter of unfinished business, revenge!

Inside the Dormie tent, Royal French addressed his Dooch team. "Mo, you and Fist are about the same size, so don't let him get leverage under you. Hunch, Krum gets careless when he smells a kill, so sucker him in. Then strike when he's overconfident."

Two competing chants arose as the two teams entered the Mining Circle.

P U's RULE! P U's RULE! P U's RULE!

GO DORMIES, GO! GO DORMIES, GO! GO DORMIES, GO!

At the whistle, Chip charged Mo on all fours, driving a head butt to Mo's knees. Deftly sidestepping the tipsy P U, Mo slapped away both cans of Kerrs. Above, Hunch caught Dirk cleanly on the cheek, toppling him, drawing bright red blood. The crowd issued a lusty roar.

Kneeling, Dirk dabbed the laceration, glancing at his oozing essence, his face blushing a scarlet matching the color of his wound. He pursed his lips in a fierce sneer.

"No one fucks with the P U's," he shouted, remounting Chip Fist's shoulders. "Kill the bastards!" he shouted, pounding the top of Chip Fist's head.

As Chip lurched toward the Dormies, Hunch hugged Mo's neck tightly, expecting a blow from Dirk's lance. Instead, both P U's tackled their adversaries, Chip grabbing Mo's shoulder, rocking him back and forth, as Dirk grabbed Hunch in a headlock, prying him off Mo's back.

Both lances clattered to the ground as the foursome, arms and legs akimbo, grappled in hand to hand combat. Dirk's superior leverage took its toll, as Hunch's grip on Mo's neck gradually slipped away. With a defiant thrust, Dirk chucked Hunch to the ground with a thud, like a sack of potatoes.

A tie! One fall each!

"No way in the hell those fucking Dormies are going to take us," said Dirk. The searing memory of Mo McCart ripping apart the ornate hand-carved P U lawn sign flashed through his mind.

"Soak my lance with that stuff," said Dirk, holding out his weapon to a freshman pledge emptying the contents of a bottle marked *Ammonia* over the burlap end of the lance.

"Done, Dirk," sniffed the pledge, tears streaming down his face from the pungent fumes.

Once again, the two beasts of burden charged, colliding with a sharp thud. Fist and Mo grappled, each struggling for balance, necks bulging, countenances contorting. Hunch hunkered down into his defensive posture.

"Shit! Sit up and fight like a real man, you little hump back midget," shouted Dirk, bouncing another jab harmlessly off Hunch's back.

While Mo and Chip teetered back and forth in a slow, grotesque waltz, Dirk saw the opening he needed. Turning his aim from Hunch's backside, Dirk jabbed at Mo's head, rubbing the ammonia-tipped lance into his face.

"Aaarrrhhhh!" screamed Mo, a burning pain engulfing his eyes.

Hearing Mo's scream, Hunch raised up. Dirk was waiting, his thrust landing squarely on Hunch's nose, engulfing his nostrils with the paralyzing odor. Hunch's lance fell away as he cupped his hands to his face. Chip jolted Mo backwards, as Dirk struck Hunch repeated with sharp blows to the chest. The Dormie duo whirling blindly, collapsed slowly to the ground in pain.

Amid the celebration of the cheering P U's, Dirk handed the poisoned lance to his subaltern pledge, shooing him away.

A silent pall descended over the Dormie tent. The P U's had defended their crown, besting the SAE's in the final round, the Sig Ep's placing third, the Kappa Nu's finishing fourth.

The Dormies had been shut out in the Joust!

"Cheating sons of bitches!" Royal swore, his killing instinct emerging.

"Ruby, it's up to you," Casey sighed to the Dormie anchorman.

Ruby Lips pursed his lips in an imaginary kiss. "No sweat, Casey. Watch me strut my stuff."

The All Pro announced the latest standing, "A TIE for FIRST PLACE going into the FINAL EVENT of the Big C Sirkus. Kappa Nu's and P U's with 22 points each. In THIRD, the Dooch Dormies with 19 ½ points. SAE's FOURTH with 16 points and in FIFTH, Sig Ep's with 9 1/2!"

"Our judges will award points for NOVELTY, AGILITY, AND STYLE!"

The Sig Ep two man team skipped sideways across the Mining Circle, gingerly playing catch with an over sized water balloon that did not break. The judges held up scores preprinted on white cards.

Kate Howell: 6. Ralph Van de Kamp: 7. Sam Paean: 7. Average score: 6.67!

Three SAE's, clasping each other's ankles, somersaulted as a human wheel across the Mining Circle.

Score: Kate Howell: 8. Ralph Van de Kamp: 9. Sam Paean: 9. Average score: 8.67!

The P U entry, an inebriated pledge with a string of dead fish dangling from his neck, flipped onto his hands and began a tortuous journey upside down across the Mining Circle. Weaving then tottering, side-to-side, then back and forth, the drunk ended his ill-fated trek, falling flat on his back barely halfway across Circle amid a chorus of hoots.

Score: Kate Howell: 3. Ralph Van de Kamp: 5. Sam Paean: 4. Average score: 4!

The P U's had blown their first place tie with the Kappa Nu's!

The Kappa Nu's positioned themselves for the championship, their entrant effortlessly traversed the Mining Circle juggling four raw eggs.

Score: Kate Howell: 7. Ralph Van de Kamp: 8. Sam Paean: 7. Average score: 7.33!

"Ruby, we can catch the P U's if you pull this off. Nine points will do it," said Casey, studying the scoreboard.

A host of hoots and whistles greeted Ruby Lips as he sashayed from the Dormie psychedelic tent with two armloads of neon colored hoola hoops.

"Pansy faggot!" yelled a P U.

"Don't hurt yourself, sweetie pie," shouted another.

Ignoring the insults, Ruby gyrated one hoola hoop slowly on his hip in a clockwise direction. The hoots turned to giggles as Ruby set another hoola hoop on his hip in motion in the opposite direction. Laughter turned to amazement as Ruby twirled two smaller hoops in opposite circles around his neck, then pairs of hoola hoops spinning on each outstretched arm, one at the wrist, the other at the elbow.

Ruby accelerated the speed of the eight spinning hoops, and with his left leg fully extended off the ground, setting into motion a ninth and tenth hoola hoop as he turned a full circle on one leg! A wildly wheeling, whirling dervish, a one-legged flurry of pastel halos.

As the Dormies cheered, applause swept the crowd. Ruby finished by sailing all ten hoola hoops with backspin toward the center of the Mining Circle. When the hoops reached the limit of their momentum, each reversed, returning to Ruby's waiting arms. Plucking five hoola hoops with each hand, Ruby thrust his arms airborne to thunderous cheers!

Scores: Kate Howell:10, followed by Sam Paean's 10, then Ralph Van de Kamp's reluctant 10!

A PERFECT SCORE!

The Dormies mobbed Ruby, lifting him in a victory march around the Mining Circle. Blowing exaggerated kisses, Ruby Lips cast his hoola hoops, one at a time, into the crowd.

"The FINAL SCORES," announced the All Pro dramatically, "Winners, step forward to receive your trophies from our Big C Sirkus King, CRUNCHY MUNCHY!"

"Fifth place trophy to the Sig Ep's.

Fourth place, the SAE's."

Applause began to mount, as All Pro continued, "AND IN THE CLOSEST COMPETITION IN THE HISTORY OF THE BIG C SIRKUS, in Third Place, the P U's with 24 points.

RUNNERS-UP with 24 ½ points, the DOOCH DORMIES! And Winners of the 49th Annual BIG C SIRKUS, KAPPA NU with 25 points!

Kappa Nu's edge Dooch for first by only ½ point!

DORMIES SECOND!

P U's third!"

The All Pro spun Rick Nelson's version of "Gotta Travel on," as the Waz spun figure eight wheelies on his Vespa. Crunchy Munchy, wearing Buddy Holly's glasses, waved regally from his throne, as Sam Paean autographed copies of his column. Kate Howell held court for a host of her admirers while roomie Joan Dildeaux stood faithfully at her side.

DORMIE CELEBRATION ! ! !

Tubbins and Fart-ing hoisted Ruby Lips on their shoulders for the Life photographer. Royal French toasted Ollie Punch with a Kerrs. Muffy Peachwick congratulated the entire Kappa Nu team for their victory.

Casey demonstrated his behind the legs Frisbee toss to T.A. Brewster, as Monty Maitland exchanged a joke with Jonathan.

Butch showed off his spats to a pair of sorority girls, one a Major, the other a Colonel, as Super Sleuth looked on. While Lizard artfully applied swirling patterns of salve to Mo and Hunch's facial burns, Dick Phuncque and the weenie wimp Engineers paraded around the Mining Circle with the Dormies second place trophy.

No one noticed the intruders with rancid fishes dangling from their necks, crawling under the back of the unattended Dormie tent, scooping up the stacks of neatly bundled dollar bills from the sale of Kerrs, and quietly fleeing in the direction of the P U fraternity house.

26

SCHEMING AND BOWLING

The Campanile carillons gonged the midnight hour across the sleeping Cal campus. Three well-dressed males sat in luxurious leather chairs before the great hearth of the Pi Upsilon fraternity house, remnants of the evening's fire still crackling. The annual P U alumni dinner had concluded, and older generations of P U's, energized by drink, old songs, and brotherhood, had stumbled back to reality.

Gone were the debris and residue of the embarrassing stink bomb attack by the detested Dormies at a repair cost of five thousand dollars! The P U house had been restored to its former, elegant state, the traditional bastion of stable comfort, the campus home to three generations of superior P U fraternity men.

"This humiliation must end," said Dirk Krum III, slamming the beer bottle against his thigh. "The Dormies must be stopped."

All week, Krum had received condolences from other fraternity presidents about the P U's third place finish in the Big C Sirkus. The callers had avoided mentioning the disturbing fact that, as Runner Up, the Dormies had come dangerously close to winning the entire damned thing!

Krum had not divulged the P U's theft of the Dormies' beer sales from the Big C Sirkus. Almost six-hundred dollars! Part of the money had been spent on replacing the hand-carved, P U lawn sign destroyed by Mo McCart during the raid. *Poetic P U justice*, he thought.

151

"Yeah, fuck the Dormies," said Chip Fist flipping an empty beer bottle into the fireplace.

The third member of the group, Chauncey Remington, sipped Courvoisier cognac from a snifter, patiently listening to the inebriated rantings of his fraternity brothers. Remington had a handsome, well-defined face, with a thatch of chestnut hair combed straight back, emphasizing dark brown eyes framed by speckled hornrim glasses. It was rare for any P U to wear glasses in public; but, at the senior age of 23 and a second-year law student, Remington oozed with his responsibilities as the P U Graduate Advisor.

The Pu Graduate Advisor had never condoned Krum's violent responses to the lowly Dormies across the street. Remembering the lessons of popular revolutions in Western civilization, he had warned against provoking and galvanizing the anger of this new, growing element of campus.

"Let these sleeping dogs lie," he had urged, as he watched in fascination, the rise of Casey Lee and Royal French as charismatic leaders of the Dormies.

"But who is really to blame for the Dormie problem?" asked Remington. "Dirk, you've been looking at this problem backwards. The real culprits are faculty supporting admission policies for nontraditional students."

The P U Graduate Advisor was referring to Cal's recent recruitment of lower income students, offering them low interest loans and affordable student housing such as Dooch Hall.

"If the current admissions policies were reversed," said Remington, "time will be on our side. In a couple of years, after Casey Lee and Royal French graduate, the Dormies will lose their leadership. If not, others will take the place of Lee and French, and in a few years, nontraditional students will be in such large numbers, they will organize and win student body offices, take over the Daily Cal newspaper, and usurp all other campus institutions the IFC has always controlled."

Krum and Fist nodded in agreement.

There had never been a non-Greek student body officer in the history of Cal student politics.

Such a calamity during my presidency of the Inter-Fraternity Council next year would be a disastrous legacy, Krum thought.

"Hell, they could even take over a tree in Dwinelle Plaza,"

152

burped Fist.

"The real problem," said Remington, "has been the fuzzy headed liberals who have gained control of the faculty. Who led the fight to appoint Roger Haynes Chancellor over our own P U alum, Bob Bateson? Who championed the new admission's policies?"

"Professor Garrick Nelquist," said Fist, following Remington's logic.

"With a boost from Professor Aristotle Scott," added Krum. "Nelquist couldn't have done it himself."

"Professor Scott sure swings a lot of weight, now that his father-in-law is running for Governor," Fist burped.

"Yes," said Remington, "but since Old Man Chandler supports HUAC, he's not happy with his son-in-law's very liberal views. My dad says Chandler will put the kibosh on Scott to avoid embarrassment to his campaign." Chauncey's father was the chairman of William Randolph Chandler's Election Committee

"The best way to stop the Dormies is to get rid of their faculty sponsors," said Remington, planting the seed of an idea. "Possibly we can help HUAC rid the faculty of radicals like Nelquist and Scott?"

"Easy," Krum said, a sneer sweeping across his countenance. "We know campus liberals will demonstrate against HUAC. It's an old Cal tradition that always gets a lot of press."

"We'll infiltrate the demonstration, spark an anti-HUAC riot, and generate public sympathy for Congressman Muck and his Committee," said Krum. "The liberals on the faculty will then be easy pickings."

"Bitch-in, bitch-in," said Fist, sensing violence.

"If we could only alert Muck to our plan," said Krum.

"Say no more," said the P U Graduate Advisor in a patronizing tone. "My Dad can arrange a meeting with Muck. I'm sure the Congressman will find your plan intriguing."

Glancing at his watch, Remington rose. "Excuse me, men. Got to make a call. It's still early in the Islands, and it's been hell trying to get through on the lines."

Krum and Fist watched Remington bounding up the grand staircase toward his room in the penthouse.

"Fuggin-A," slurred Fist, "When I hit my middle-twenties, I sure hope I get as much nookie as Chauncey. I hear girls go nuts over older guys."

Ignoring Fist, Krum thought only of the brilliance of Remington's proposal.

In one fell swoop, the P U's would discredit the liberal wing of the faculty, shut the door on Dormie admissions, and perpetuate the fraternity way of life at Cal for generations to come! The IFC would be eternally grateful, and once more, the P U's would rule!

Now, if only Kate Howell appreciated my genius . . .

* * *

Handwritten notes had been taped across the doors of their rooms. Each index card read,

Frosh, beware! Your time has come!
- The Dooch Bowling Team

"Junior, what is this crap," said Butch, pulling off the note "Does Dooch have a bowling team?"

"Don't know, Butch," said Jonathan, "But it looks like every door on the third floor, except the All Pro's, got the same note."

1 a.m..

The echo of the Campanile's solitary peel tumbled down from the Big C.

Skeleton keys quietly opened the rooms of the third-floor freshmen. Jonathan awoke with the suffocating sensation of a hood pulled over his head, arms pinned violently behind his back by unseen intruders yanking him off the bed, trundling him out the door. In the darkness, Butch's muffled voice issued a stream of epithets, bodies ricocheted like pinballs against the walls of the hallway, as the two freshmen kicked vainly to break free. The kidnappers burst through another door carrying their struggling victims.

The third-floor bathroom thought Jonathan, feeling the presence of many others shouting,

"BOWL 'EM! BOWL 'EM! BOWL 'EM!"

Jonathan's right hand broke free, groping, then grasping a metal partition between the urinals. Many hands wrenched away his temporary hold, then turning his body upside down.

Somewhere near his head he heard the sound of a toilet seat clanking against the tank. The hood ripped from his head,

154

Jonathan stared down at the swirling waters of the toilet bowl, two huge brown turds floating leisurely like brown serpents amid the swirling eddies.

Voices continued to chant,

"BOWL 'EM! BOWL 'EM! BOWL 'EM!"

Jonathan felt Butch's body thrashing violently in the next stall. He heard Jerry Fart-ing screaming "NO! NO! DON'T! DON'T!" above the sound of flushing toilets. With renewed strength, Jonathan struggled to break free.

No use. Too many hands.

"One, Two, Three" shouted his captors, and Jonathan felt the shocking cold of the toilet water rushing over his hair. Holding his breath against the impending submergence, he fought an urge to gag. He felt the clammy touch of the sticky turds against his forehead.

Suddenly, as swift as his descent into the murky waters of the commode, he was righted, pulled from the stall, carried across the hallway, passing the line of hooded, freshmen victims awaiting their turn at bowling.

In the study lounge, whistles and applause greeted him. Nearby Butch, a towel over his wet, black hair, gasped for air.

"You have been officially bowled and baptized as a Horny Dormie, entitling you to all the privileges of our ilk," said a perspiring Ollie Punch standing beside the smiling faces of Ruby, Casey, Hunch, Royal, Lizard and the Waz.

"If I weren't so pooped, I'd kick all your asses," huffed Butch. "That's not funny. Closest I've come to eating shit!"

More cheers greeted the arrival of a dripping Tommy Tubbins carried by Mo McCart, Super Sleuth, and the All Pro.

"The turds were just for effect," gloated Ruby, holding up a jar of peanut butter. "You don't think we'd push your faces into real shit? Rolled those little babies with my own dainty hands."

The Dormies roared, even Butch and Jonathan laughed at the bowling RF. More cheers as upper classmen carried Jerry Fart-ing into the study lounge. Ashen faced, Fart-ing rushed onto the balcony railing and vomited over the side, retching spasmodically in the spittle and phlegm of his barf.

Across the hall, amid the sounds of flushing toilets, the choruses continued,

"BOWL 'EM! BOWL 'EM! BOWL 'EM!"

155

27

ORAL AURAL

A polite applause rippled across the South Hall lecture room, as a large, brown and black German shepherd ambled leisurely past the lectern, plopping down in her usual seat of honor in the warm morning rays of the eastern window. All thirty seats of the classroom were filled, and another dozen "crashers" stood at the rear, hoping for dropouts among the lucky registrants.

"Quite a dramatic entrance, eh, Junior?"

When the two freshmen had entered Professor Jacob Aural's English 1A class, Jonathan had motioned Butch to a pair of seats at the rear corner of the room, hoping to hide, praying he would not be called to recite on this first day of class.

The applause swelled to an ovation, as a silver-haired professor dressed in a tweed jacket, repp tie, and dark glasses entered. In his left hand, he carried a thick notebook; in his right, a gold handled walking cane. Stopping at the lectern, Professor Jacob Aural acknowledged the affectionate greeting by nodding and smiling.

"Sandy's the real reason this class is so popular," he began in a cultured but friendly tone. "She's listed in the course catalogue as my assistant, but you realize there are two different celebrities named Sandra D," he joked, referring to the dog's namesake, the popular beach blanket, movie star.

Sandy barked twice in response.

"If each of you would take the same seat for each class, it would facilitate class discussion." The professor ran his fingers over a page of the opened notebook. "I'll call the roll alphabetically, and each of you will introduce yourself in a firm, clear voice stating your name and hometown."

"He doesn't seem blind," said Jonathan.

"Shhh," whispered Butch. "His hearing is supposed to be better than radar."

"Let's start at the front of the alphabet. Mr. Aldon."

Instinctively, Jonathan hunkered down into his desk.

Professor Jacob Aural ran his fingers over his braille notes. "That's Mr. Jonathan Aldon, correct?"

"Here," said Jonathan, a catch in his voice.

"Please stand so we can see you, Mr. Aldon. And do speak up. It's difficult hearing someone sitting in the rear corner of the room."

"Jeez," said Butch, "How in the hell . . ."

Rising slowly, red faced, Jonathan said, "Jonathan Aldon, sir, from Clear Lake, Iowa."

"Much better, Mr. Aldon. Clear Lake, Iowa America's heartland and hogland?"

"Yes sir," said Jonathan, wishing he were invisible to the professor's probing mind.

"Perhaps, Mr. Aldon, you will provide a Middle American point of view?"

"No, sir," said Jonathan, feeling quite alien, "I came to Cal to escape Middle America."

A sorority girl in front of Jonathan, with a brief case embossed with a gold "*R. Tess,*" giggled.

"But we're all immigrants, Mr. Aldon, bringing to this great University, this educational melting pot, if you will, values ingrained by your families and home communities. No matter how hard you try to escape your cultural bonds, they do shape your thinking, your ability to reason, and your understanding of your fellow man."

The seeing-eye dog growled throatily.

"See, even Sandy agrees. Next, Mr. Bartholomew," Professor Aural continued calling the roll of students, commenting on each student's hometown.

As he listened, Jonathan was intrigued by the sounds of the exotic, Spanish names of California cities.

How mundane Clear Lake sounded compared to romantic

communities with Spanish names like San Juan Bautista!

"Ah, Brooklyn, Mr. Tanenbloom," said Professor Aural, reaching the bottom of his alphabetical roster "Perhaps, you will be our designated East Coast voice."

"An honor, Professor," said Butch, bowing.

"Our first question today. Why should freshmen have to take English 1A?" Professor Aural surveyed the class, using his ears like antennae seeking a signal. As his head turned in Jonathan's direction, Sandy D. barked twice.

Jonathan hunkered down behind the girl, *R. Tess..*

"Thank you, Sandy. Mr. Aldon!"

Jonathan gulped, looking helplessly at Butch.

Butch quickly scrawled a note, in large letters, on a piece of paper.

Jonathan read Butch's note aloud,

"IMPACT OF LITERATURE ON MODERN LIFE"

"Excellent observation, Mr. Aldon," said Professor Aural. "And why do you think literature is so important in modern life?" He emphasized the word "think."

Again, Jonathan looked to Butch for help.

"Critical thinking," whispered Butch.

"Improve our critical thinking," blurted Jonathan.

"Very well, Mr. Aldon. Tell us how the reading assignment for today helps us in critical thinking?"

Sandy D. yawned, then blinked in the sunny spotlight.

"For example," continued Professor Aural, "what does *Catcher in The Rye* contribute to critical thinking?"

Jonathan looked at Butch in panic, as he had not read the class assignment.

Butch leaned over, whispering another response.

"Thinking aloud, Mr. Aldon? Or is that Mr. Tanenbloom talking to himself?"

"Just critical consulting, Professor," said Butch, inducing laughter from the class, easing Jonathan's anxiety.

"Nice recovery, Mr. Tanenbloom," Professor Aural chuckled."Critical thinking does involve a sense of humor."

He continued, "All right, Mr. Aldon, you're off the hot seat today. But you must be better prepared if you expect to gain anything from this class."

Sandy D barked three times, underscoring Professor Aural's

advice.

Relieved, Jonathan swore he would heed Professor Aural's warning, reminding himself that maintaining good grades was one of The Three Promises.

28

TROUBLE IN PARADISE

Ari Scott stood in his walk-in closet of the master bedroom of the Piedmont mansion, fumbling his third attempt at knotting the black tie of the tuxedo. It was impossible to concentrate on minutiae, as his mind retraced the exhilaration of the day in The City with his daughter, Anna Cappuccino Zarzana.

He had intended to take her sightseeing, but their instant bonding had relegated the usual tourist attractions of Fisherman's Wharf and North Beach to background settings for deep, animated conversations.

He had escorted her to some of his favorite saloons, noting with paternal pride, the envious looks of men appraising, appreciating her stunning beauty. Over the years, he and Garrick Nelquist had spent endless hours in these haunts, drinking and discussing the affairs of the world. Nelquist had dubbed the bar tour the "Pub Crawl," in honor of the time the two, sotted by wine, negotiated North Beach, on their hands and knees, searching for a cab back to the East Bay.

There was so much to know, so much to learn: two decades of events, hopes, and fears. How they had laughed and cried! How he loved the way she called him "Papa."

It was clear Anna had inherited Sofia Cappuccino's strong will, her mother's lust for life, and her teasing sense of humor. In his daughter's presence, he was transformed into the man he had long forgotten, the romantic adventurer of his youth.

On her part, Anna basked in the love of her father, discreetly refraining from mentioning that Sofia had shared with her daughter, in intimate detail, the course of her romance with Ari during their *toure di amore*. She immediately comprehended the depth of her mother's passion for this dashing American who had given her his grey luminous eyes.

"*We* will do our best to suppress some of those nasty liberal ideas of yours at Mummy and Daddy's, won't *we*?" Cee Cee Chandler Scott cooed from the deep recesses of her massive, separate dressing room adjacent to the master bath.

Cee Cee spoke in the clipped, singsong diction peculiar to graduates of the Anna Bransome Boarding School for Refined Young Girls. Cee Cee had maintained her classic beauty, the finely chiseled chin, the sparkling blue eyes, the perfectly coiffed hair cascading effortlessly down the side of her face like the movie actress Veronica Lake.

Although pretty coeds had always been a staple of his classes, it had been Cee Cee's voice, with its cultured tone, its precise phrasing, and dramatic pauses reeking of privileged upbringing that enchanted him. He had teased her about the kind of voice training that permitted a Bransome alumna to speak without moving her jutted, lower jaw, diction that Cee Cee had cheerily described as "unchy."

But after a decade of marriage, her once appealing manner of speech had become the grating reminder of long lost charm. How Ari hoped their daughter, Monique, would not acquire the tell tale affectation of an Anna Bransome student.

The grand mansion nestled high on the promontory of the Piedmont hills with its commanding view of the Bay had been owned by the Chandler clan for decades. To his chagrin, Cee Cee was fond of reminding him that no other Cal faculty member could afford living in Piedmont.

Cee Cee had committed her trust income to creating her interpretation of domestic paradise, replete with an expansive glass conservatory filled with lush tropical plants and cages of exotic birds, squawking macaws, toucans, cockatoos, and cockatiels, where she hosted meetings of the matrons of the Junior League. Cee Cee referred to the room as "Ari's aerie," although Ari had confided to Garrick Nelquist he considered the room Waikiki kitsch, a smaller version of Trader Dick's, the ersatz

Polynesian restaurant in The City popularized by columnist Sam Paean.

"Daddy's hosting some of his biggest donors, and *we* wouldn't want to offend them, would *we*?"

Ari ignored the obvious admonition. Since the Old Man had declared his candidacy, Cee Cee had been relentless in reminding him of the prestige of being the son-in-law of the future Governor of California. "You'll be the most important person on the faculty," she said.

"When did *we* go to the Buena Vista, Scotty?" The query, accusatory in tone, intruded on his reverie, as he began a fourth attempt at the black tie.

The Buena Vista, better known as the BV, was a bustling San Francisco waterfront bar where Irish Coffee had been introduced to the United States. He had collected matchbooks for Anna during their recent pub crawl but had forgotten to give her the souvenirs before dropping her off at I-House.

"Garrick loves the BV," Ari lied. Lord, how he hated her habit of rummaging through his pockets. "The owner is an old friend of his from college."

That statement is true, he said to himself.

"Wish *we* wouldn't frequent sleazy bars, Scotty."

Throughout their marriage, Cee Cee had developed the irritating habit of using *we*, instead of *you,* when chiding him.

"Daddy says your friend Garrick is a Commie sympathizer HUAC will be going after. Hopefully that isn't true!"

"Garrick isn't any more a Communist than I," said Ari.

"I see we've been going to Enrico's Coffee House and Gold Street too," Cee Cee said, pulling more of Anna's souvenirs from his trousers. "And *we*'ve been to Pinocchio's?" a tone of shock in her voice.

Ari suppressed a grin. Enrico's was a famous North Beach gathering spot for Bohemians and free thinkers, Gold Street, the hangout for young Montgomery Street businessmen, and Pinocchio's, a night club renowned for its gorgeous female impersonators, especially the notorious Paulette DuBois.

Cee Cee continued her interrogation. "Isn't Enrico's near that Communist bookstore, City Lights? And Pinocchio's, isn't that the disgusting queer place? *We* should be more careful where *we* may be seen in public."

"Those places can't be that awful," he retorted, "some of your friends have been there." He had overheard Cee Cee's society girlfriends twittering how they had worn Beatnik outfits to visit the two famous North Beach hangouts.

"*We're* not like anyone else, Scotty. Bad publicity would hurt Daddy's campaign!"

"Yes," he sighed. " *We* will be more careful," he promised, noting the deep frown on his reflection in the mirror.

How would he explain Anna to Cee Cee? What would the Old Man do if he learned that Anna's stepfather, Pablo Zarzana, was the leader of the Italian Communist Party?

Ari shuddered at the possible fallout.

29

PYRE & FIRE

The conflagration roared 20 feet into the night sky, greeted by thousands of howling college boys packed into the Greek Theater. Empty booze bottles cascaded into the inferno, tailless meteorites, launched by the pajama clad, beer swigging, cigar puffing mobs. The Greek Theater was an amphitheater sculptured into a hillside eucalyptus grove, a concrete semicircle facing an elevated, three-sided stage of Classical design. Eleven vertical aisles divided the steep bowl into curved seating areas of 19 rows each. On the floor of the arena were ornately carved, stone high back chairs reserved for the house presidents of members of the IFC, the Inter-fraternity Council.

Patterned after the theater at Epidaurus, the Greek Theater was first used for a commencement speech in 1903 by President Teddy Roosevelt. Now, over a half century later, the Greek Theater was reserved for large gatherings such as the Academic Senate, graduation exercises, and football rallies.

On the steep grassy slope above the Greek, a few hundred coeds huddled together in the darkness, bound by a sense of curiosity and disgust at the unfolding primitive male behavior, unaware of the irony that a woman, the architect of the Hearst Castle at San Simeon, supervised the construction of this bastion of male bonding.

"The Pajamarino Bonfire Rally is one of the biggest traditions of the football season," explained Casey Lee. "When the fire burns low, there will be a call for more wood, and all freshmen must step forward and feed the blaze."

The Dormies, one hundred strong, had marched up Bancroft Way with lighted candles, dressed in a variety of sleeping attire: pajamas, nightshirts, T-shirts and shorts, and bathrobes.

Ollie Punch wore only a jock strap, an athletic supporter, for modesty, he claimed.

"Hey! I sleep in the buff. Want me to embarrass you straight arrow Dormies by being busted for indecent exposure?" he had barked.

The Dormie procession slowed near the juncture of Piedmont Avenue and Gayley Road, joining hundreds pouring out of houses along Fraternity Row. As they neared the Greek Theater, the chanting of "BEAT SC!" filled the night air, growing to an earsplitting roar.

Entering the Greek, the Dormies took the remaining seats high up on the upper rim of the concrete pavilion, sharing the body heat of the unseen audience packed together in the darkness.

A blinding flash, as an incendiary bomb exploded in the middle of a stack of wood piled 10 feet high on the floor of the Greek, the soaring orange flames illuminating the all-male Cal marching band leading the football team and coaches, cheerleaders, pom girls, and Oski onto the elevated stage.

"This team doesn't have a prayer," said Butch, pointing to the team members in street clothes. "Mo and that P U, Chip Fist, are the only big guys on the squad. The rest are shrimps!"

Jonathan thought of Casey Lee's pre-rally talk on the moral superiority of Cal students, wondering if the dorm president had not exaggerated imaginary reasons for supporting a football team with such a long history of losing.

As the flames subsided, the chant they had been expecting erupted, "FRESHMEN, MORE WOOD!"

"Ok, Dormies, show 'em how to stoke a fire," shouted Royal French, waving the freshmen on.

"Junior, let's go," said Butch, pulling Jonathan into the horde of freshmen streaming down the concrete aisles toward railroad ties stacked neatly near the bonfire.

With the heaving of each log into the blazing pyre, the crowds of upper classmen continued to chant,

FRESHMEN, MORE WOOD! FRESHMEN, MORE WOOD!

165

Several hundred freshmen packed into the surging line, waiting to feed the bonfire. Each new step brought more heat, more light. Perspiring profusely, Jonathan felt a lump in his throat, remembering that fateful night.

Flames! Smoke! Heat! Death! All came flooding back.

February 3, 1959.

Unable to eat the early dinner prepared by Cokie, the Aldon maid, Jonathan anxiously paced the front porch, excitement knotting a ball in his stomach.

Hurry, Ziggy, he said to himself.

Show time was eight p.m., and radio station K-HOG had predicted a record sellout of all 1,100 tickets, fans streaming in from Mason City, Garner, and as far away as Meservey and Solberg, seating on a first-come basis only.

The Surf Ballroom was an easy walk from Four Winds Drive, but Jonathan and Ziggy needed to park the Packard near the Surf to set Part 2 of their scheme into action.

Part one had gone smoothly. Jonathan had already paid Mike Limm, son of an Aldon Farms employee, two dollars to save their places at the front of the line.

By the time the two parked the Packard off Main Street, noisy teenagers stretched all the way around the block, the crowd cheerful and orderly, issuing a chorus of good natured "no crowding" and "wait your turn in line." Claiming their spots at the front of the line, the duo tipped their stand-in extra two bucks.

When the Surf Ballroom opened promptly at seven p.m., Jonathan and Ziggy grabbed seats front and center ahead of the surging crowd.

J.P. Richardson, better known as The Big Bopper, opened the show with his hit, "Chantilly Lace," the crowd rising to its feet, joining him in the happy chorus.

Ritchie Valens followed with a medley of hits, including the haunting "Donna" and the raucous "La Bamba."

The crowd was all revved up when Buddy Holly and The Crickets appeared. Pressing against the foot of the stage, The Amazing Double A's sang along with Buddy's hits, "Peggy Sue"and "True Love Ways." In the back, fans danced the be-bop to "Oh, Boy," "It Don't Matter Anymore," and "That'll Be the Day."

For an encore, The Big Bopper and Ritchie Valens joined

Buddy and the Crickets for several rousing choruses of "Not Fade Away."

When the curtain descended, the crowd rushed forward, restrained by the five members of the Clear Lake Police Department. Ducking out the side door, Jonathan and Ziggy resumed the rest of their plan.

As they drove, a light snowfall swirling in the winter wind dusted the hood of the wheezing Packard with a thin coat of powder. The boys devoured juicy cheeseburgers and shakes, Ziggy gerry rigging a heating duct from the engine through the floor of the passenger side into a plastic basket to keep the golden fries crispy and warm.

The two arrived at the Quonset hut bearing the hand-painted sign, *Clear Lake Municipal Airfield.*

Inside they found a balding, middle-aged man reading a copy of <u>Popular Mechanics</u> beneath a single bare bulb illuminating the ancient structure. A horizontal patch on his bomber jacket read, *F Majestic Aero Charter Services.* A small floor heater glowed orange beneath his feet.

"Ain't here yet," said the man, without looking up. "Better get here soon. Gotta get outta here before the snow kicks up."

A small rusted wall clock ticked off the seconds, as the two boys paced back and forth impatiently.

Suddenly, there was a squeal of brakes and slamming doors, as a blast of cold air ushered the trio dashing into the Quonset hut.

"Jeez, it's cold," said the tallest of the three. The other two nodded in agreement, rubbing their hands for instant warmth."Maybe we should have gone on the bus with the band," said the shortest blowing air into a clenched fist.

"Let's get the hell out of here," said the pilot. "Couple of autograph hounds," he said, motioning toward Jonathan and Ziggy. "Don't take too long, boys."

The Amazing Double A's pressed forward with their concert programs. Away from the stage, in the dimness of the Quonset hut, the rock and roll stars seemed quite ordinary. The Big Bopper, soft spoken; Ritchie Valens, chubby and childlike; Buddy Holly, almost frail. The Big Bopper and Ritchie Valens quickly scrawled their names and marched quickly out the back door to the Beechcraft belching and coughing on the short barren runway.

Wiping the steam from his black hornrimmed glasses, Buddy

Holly listened patiently to the instructions of his two fans, writing slowly and legibly,

To my Buddies, Jonathan and Ziggy,
The Amazing Double A's - Buddy Holly, 2/3/59

The Amazing Double A's skipped through the swirling eddies of snow to the Packard, congratulating each other on the success of their plan. As the Packard lurched leisurely toward Clear Lake, the boys could see the Beechcraft still parked, its small wing lights gleaming, its engine gaining resonance. They recounted the sequence of the concert songs, singing the lyrics they had memorized long ago.

"Big storm comin' in," Ziggy interjected. "Goin' home none too soon."

They heard the sputtering of the plane before they saw it, their chorus of "That'll Be the Day" interrupted by a thunderous boom in the flat farmland to their right, followed by a brilliant fireball, no more than a hundred yards away. Ziggy slammed the brakes, skidding the Packard off the road.

Placing a hankie over his face, Jonathan tiptoed gingerly across the frozen corn field, Ziggy following, his hand over his nose. They approached the burning wreckage of a small light plane, its tail section visible through the flames.

No one could have survived the crash, thought Jonathan, the crackling sounds of melting metal and glass filled the air. Smoke billowing from the engine, choked the two.

Jonathan circled to the right side of the plane, advancing until the heat singed the hankie. Turning to retreat, he saw it a dozen paces ahead.

"No," he shouted, his cry muffled by the smoldering hankie. He stared at the black hornrimmed glasses lying in the snow.

There had to be a million others in the world! Not Buddy's!

"Johnny-boy, let's get out of here," yelled Ziggy. "That thing's gonna blow!"

Jonathan crawled on his hands and knees across the patina of snow, the heat intense and stifling. The glasses were hot, but not yet melting. Reversing his path, he stood up to run when a deafening explosion shook the earth, slamming him to the ground, stealing his breath, taking his consciousness.

Blurry images of flashing red lights, a cold, sticky wetness coated Jonathan's face, his ears still ringing with the echo of the explosion. His breath labored, gagging, he coughed, expelling acrid smoke.

He awoke to the comforting voice of Ziggy."Johnny-boy, speak to me. Are you ok? Can you hear me?" he asked, cradling him in his arms.

Squinting, Jonathan was blinded by the flashing of emergency equipment.

"Let him be, son. He's in shock, but he'll be all right," said a stranger's voice. Forcing his eyes open, Jonathan saw Ziggy's frightened face hovering over him. Hunched over Ziggy was a fireman, his yellow slicker read *Clear Lake Fire Department.*

Turning, Jonathan saw a few curls of smoke from the remains of the small plane, the site illuminated by the headlights of fire trucks.

"Worst crash I remember in these parts," said the fireman. Most people killed too."

His throat parched, Jonathan croaked, "that wasn't Buddy's plane, Ziggy?"

"Bad news, Johnny-boy," said Ziggy softly. "The Big Bopper, Richie Valens, Buddy, the pilot, all of 'em, gone."

Jonathan felt tears that did not flow, his face caked with smoke, dirt, and snow. Trembling, partly in sadness, partly in guilt, his hand still clutching the black hornrimmed glasses, he motioned to Ziggy.

"I got 'em, Ziggy. Buddy's glasses!" he whispered, slipping into unconsciousness.

"JUNIOR! What's the matter?"

It was Butch's voice bringing Jonathan back to the line near the bonfire rally. "Jeez, it's hotter than hell," he shouted, perspiration streaming down his face. "Grab your end," said Butch nodding at a railroad tie on top of the pile.

Staggering under the weight of the heavy lumber, the two swung their wooden sacrifice underhanded onto the fireball, scattering sparks into the night sky, amid the continuing chants of "FRESHMEN, MORE WOOD*!"*

Illuminated by the giant bonfire's flames, Jonathan promised himself. *Someday, I'll do something with Buddy's glasses that will honor his music, something eternal that will not fade away. And that'll really be the day!*

30

WISH YOU WERE HERE

9/28/59
  Ziggy,
  How's your bod?
  Here are pix taken at Fisherman's Wharf last "weak end." We crowded into one of those twenty five-cent booths where you can take four photos on a strip. (Had to hustle to get the whole gang in without tipping the photo booth over!)
  In the top frame, yers trooly with a shit-eating grin (great Calif. expression) and my Brooklyn buddy, Butch Tanenbloom, flipping a double bird at the camera.
  In the next, the guy picking his nose with his little finger is our Dorm Pres, Casey Lee, along with our varsity football player, Mo McCart pretending he's strangling himself. (Note the size of his hands and his bald head!)
  The third one is Ollie Punch staring at you with his wandering eye, next to Hunch Hitowski's bare ass pointing straight at the camera! (Note that Hunch's humpback is bigger than his rear.)
  In the bottom shot, the older guy wearing a beret is Royal French, next to Ruby Lips (our Dormie fairy) who is about to stick his tongue into Royal's ear. A second later, Royal was so p.o.'d, he almost destroyed the booth, kicking Ruby out!
  Such craziness and fun!
  We went to The City (nobody calls it Frisco here) to celebrate our second place in the Big C Sirkus. Casey Lee's grandmother

arranged a Chinese dinner in a fancy restaurant on Grant Avenue. You wouldn't believe what we ate! Nothing like the chop suey we used to order with Mike and Pearl at that little Ding How Café in Minneapolis.

First course, bird's nest soup made from dried upchucking of some Oriental bird. (Royal said he saw a live one when he was in Indo-China.) Chewy, petrified Jello!

Then bowls of steaming snails. Not pastry rolls. The kind in your backyard! The creepy crawlers were cooked in spicy, black bean sauce. Casey showed us how to suck the juice out of the shell and spear the critter's foot with a toothpick. (You only eat the foot, not the rest of the body) Peppery, rubber bands?

Then a whole roast pig hacked into strips of crisp skin and melt-in-your-mouth meat! Yum! I filled everyone in on how we process hogs at Aldon Farms. (Didn't seem to dampen any appetites, 'tho)

A huge steamed fish (I think it was called rock cod) was served on a silver platter with its head and tail intact--deboned in ten seconds by a waiter using two spoons in one hand. Casey ate the fish cheeks, and Royal downed the eyeballs! Gross!

Next, a delicious roast duck served with all its innards, head, beak, claws and tail! (Casey said serving all the parts prove the customer got everything he paid for.)

The best dish was cracked, curried Dungeness crab (caught right in San Francisco Bay). We sucked all the gravy from the shells and picked out the tender meat with tiny forks. My nails still smell of curry.

There was a weird dessert called Lichee nuts that weren't nuts at all, but white fruit balls floating in ice. The taste and smell reminded me of some of Mother's French perfume!

Last were long, Chinese spaghetti called longevity noodles for a long life. (Butch interpreted that to mean stiff boners forever!) Somehow we found room to scarf down all the noodles. (Later, Butch complained the noodles gave him a hard-on for 48 hours.) Casey said we now know why Marco Polo brought noodles back from China!

Lotsa things hop, hop, hop-pening. Classes started, but tough concentrating. Competition is rough. Everybody at Cal, including jocks like Mo was an A student in high school.

Got an invite to a P U rush party. Don't tell Father I didn't go.

171

(Told you how the P U's and the Dormies are mortal enemies.)
Haven't attended service at the campus Methodist Church either.
Guess I'll deal with The Three Promises later.

Football season started. Mo sez Cal hasn't had a winning
season for a long time, but the student section is always sold out!
Don't understand this weird loyalty. Casey Lee gave a pep talk to
the Dooch freshmen about Cal's superiority over the other
schools of the Pacific Eight Conference. Cal's won 3 and lost 27
the past three seasons, but we're superior? Weird tradition!

Haven't met any girls from that boarding house you read
about in Playboy (Yearning Arms). "Sleep Walk" by Santo and
Johnny, number one on the Top 40 here. What's big on K-HOG
these days?

Gotta run. More soon. Best to all at A.F. and Clear Lake.
-The other half of those still Amazing Double A's
-Jonathan
P.S. Shit STILL flies both ways!

Jonathan signed the handwritten letter with a flourish, folding the bulky document neatly into thirds, wondering whether Ziggy would see through the exaggerated cheerfulness, sensing the essence of his childhood chum's emotional toe-zone.

Jonathan carefully sealed the envelope and hefted the bulging letter. *Less than three ounces*, he guessed, affixing three, four cent stamps, more than enough postage for first class mail.

In truth, the victory dinner in The City had been dampened by the discovery of how much money had been stolen from the sale of Kerrs. Dick Phuncque and the fifth floor weenie-wimp Eng-ineers had been particularly crushed, blaming themselves for the lapse in security during the wild celebration at the Big C Sirkus.

"We Eng-ineers ARE weenie-wimps," Phuncque had moaned, banging his slide rule on the side of his balding head.

Casey Lee and Royal French had maintained brave public faces. Casey had been philosophical, Royal defiant, reminding the Dormies that the semester was long and there would be other opportunities to recoup their financial losses. But even as they feasted on their Chinese banquet, a curtain of gloom descended on the Dormies. How could the Dormies ever recoup the stolen money, much less replace the one-hundred dollar entry fee for the Big C Sirkus?

172

It was a simple matter of student economics. Room and board at Dooch for the semester was expensive, five-hundred dollars, books were another twenty-five or thirty-dollars. Most Dormies got by on ten bucks a week for incidentals, and only a few with special skills like the Waz, as campus parking control officer, or Ruby Lips, as assistant to Gifted Florence, the fortune teller, had part-time jobs.

The social program would have to be cut Casey said. By giving up four beer busts after football games, there could still be enough for one big party or two smaller ones. The lesson from the debacle was clear: The Dormies had paid a terrible price for their moment in the sun.

Since the Chinese dinner, Jonathan had struggled with a difficult decision. In his heart, he knew what must be done. His new friends must be helped. But a tiny voice asked, *should I risk alienating my parents?* Another, louder voice asked *how would they ever find out?*

He reread Mother's most recent letter. In her familiar, perfectly, neat penmanship, she had written,
September 22, 1959

Dear Jonathan,

We received your letter describing your first three weeks on campus. You really should write at least once a week! Your father and I are pleased that things seem to be going well. Everyone at church has been inquiring whether you've met any Beat-hicks yet, but I've assured them you're too busy being a student to be loitering the streets of San Francisco!

Your classmates sound a bit odd, not exactly the kind of people I would like you to associate with, although I assume this is well beyond your control until you join Pi Upsilon fraternity.

Father has taken the liberty of contacting an influential P U alumnus in the San Francisco area, a Mr. Dirk Krum, II (a rather imposing name, wouldn't you say?), whose son is the President of the Berkeley chapter. Mr. Krum assures us that the P U's are the very best fraternity on campus and that, as a courtesy to a fellow P U alum, he will have his son, Dirk Krum III, invite you to a rush function soon.

We want you to make the best possible impression, so we expect you to dress appropriately when you attend a P U social. We wouldn't want anyone concluding you are a simple farm boy just because you were raised in Clear Lake!

Curious your letter did not describe church services at the campus Methodist Church. Your uncle Leonard did some checking and learned that only the creme de la creme of the student body are members of the congregation. We all pray you will meet more suitable students at church and are comforted that, even in faraway California, the Lord's hand guides your destiny.

We miss you and pray for your success and swift return home.

With all our love,

Mother and Father.

P S Hope you treated yourself to something special with the hundred-dollar bill we gave you!

Jonathan folded the letter back into its envelope, placing it in a small strongbox in the closet. From the strong box, he examined Buddy Holly's glasses and reread the message Crunchy Munchy had scrawled, in pencil, on a popsicle stick when he returned the glasses after the Big C Sirkus.

Not Fade Away - Crunchy Munchy

The alarm clock read 1:30 a.m.. Clicking off the desk lamp, Jonathan inhaled the panorama of his breathtaking view, of the carpet of lights stretching from Dooch Hall down to San Francisco Bay, his eyes following the luminous necklace of the Bay Bridge, past Treasure Island, to The City glowing in the darkness.

Casey Lee had told him how the fog disappeared in September, and Jonathan could see the gigantic billboard of the *Sherman Williams* can splashing colors over the neon globe. Gently closing his door, Jonathan padded down the corridor, toward the fire escape and the outdoor stairway at the end of the hall.

As Jonathan passed the bathroom, he could hear the muffled voice of the All Pro crooning an Eddie Fisher favorite, as he shaved.

"Oh, my P-a-p-a, to me he was s-o W-O-N-D-E-R-F-U-L!"

Strange, he thought, *it did not bother All Pro that he was the only upper classman on the frosh floor, despite all the needling from the freshmen!*

"Rock 'n roll's only a fad. Here today, gone tomorrow," the All Pro had predicted repeatedly, standing before the twenty-foot bathroom mirror, during his many daily shaves with a straight edge razor, "but my hero, the ONE AND ONLY, EDDIE FISHER, the gentleman with the silky sounds, will LAST FOREVER!" All Pro's frequent pronouncements were greeted with multiple flushes of the commodes and urinals and a lusty chorus of good-natured boo's.

Jonathan charged up the steps of the outside stairwell three at a time, encountering a cool evening breeze, the All Pro's warbling of "Oh, My Papa" still ringing in his ears.

Reaching the eighth floor, Jonathan carefully slipped through the fire escape door, tiptoeing down the hallway, winded by his sprint up the fire escape.

He was startled by a sudden shriek as he passed room 804. Stopping, he placed an ear to the door, hearing Royal French's sleepy voice barking commands in an exotic Oriental language.

What did Royal do in Indo-China that triggered such nightmares?

He padded to Casey Lee's door and stopped, holding his breath, praying that the Dooch Pres would be asleep.

No sound.

Relieved, Jonathan removed the empty envelope from his back pocket. Lifting up the flap, he moistened the inside edge. He paused one last time, reviewing the words typed across the front of the envelope, still confident about his decision.

It read: *Casey Lee - President of Dooch Hall Hope this helps - The Phantom*

Jonathan plucked the neatly folded one-hundred dollar bill from his pocket and quickly sealed it in the envelope. Kneeling, he used his left index finger to flick the envelope under Casey's door.

He then raced as fast as he could down the hallway, through the fire escape door, leaping down the outside stairwell one flight at a time, until he reached the safety of the third floor where the muted voice of the All Pro still groaned "Oh, My Papa."

"*Treat yourself to something special,*" Jonathan recalled Father saying, as he handed him the hundred-dollar bill.

Jonathan closed his door, bid his view of San Francisco good night, and curled into bed, satisfied that he had indeed treated himself to *something special.*

31

MEN OF TROY

The slaughter would soon begin, the chieftain thought.

His name was Tommy, claiming his proud lineage from the ancient Phrygian city of Troy, home of the Trojan warrior. Wearing a golden helmet topped with crimson plumage, a gold breastplate, and a white toga, the muscular, bearded warrior sat poised on his magnificent white stallion, Traveler, waiting for his battle-tested army to humble yet another hapless enemy.

Today, the foe would be the weak, fuzzy headed clan known as the Bear people.

A crowd of sixty thousand gathered to watch the spectacle in the large, oval stadium, located in a deep canyon of the eastern foothills, once filled with wild strawberries. Tommy anticipated the celebration of another Trojan triumph by galloping around the perimeter of the alien coliseum, brandishing his sword and shield at the roaring crowd.

An army of foot soldiers, dressed in blood colored tunics and golden helmets, trumpets blaring their victory song, "Tribute," signaled the arrival of the Men of Troy. On every side, winsome females twirled batons and waved golden standards. Twenty-thousand Trojan loyalists dressed in red and gold had journeyed from the Land of Eternal Sunshine to witness the carnage. As the Trojan phalanxes practiced maneuvers on the field of battle, the red and gold partisans thrust two fingers skyward in the sign of a V in rhythm to the music of their favorite song, "Tribute."

"Incredible," said Butch. "Those costumes are leftovers from an old Cecil B. De Mille movie!"

"Lots of kids from my high school go to SC," said Fart-ing."They think those outfits are classy."

"Lesson number one, frosh," interjected Ollie Punch, his wandering left eyeball spinning lazily, "is that flashy LA money has nothing to do with class. Cal and SC symbolize the cultural chasm between Northern and Southern California. To us, SC represents the worst of crass LA *nouveau riche*, the world of Hollywood and Disneyland. To Trojans, we're irrelevant, cultured snobs of the Golden Gate, in love with ourselves, clinging to dreams of the past."

Below, the SC band, in mass formation over the entire football field, played Elvis's "Money Honey."

Casey Lee chimed in. "The rivalry between Northern and Southern California spills over into college athletics. SC has great athletic teams, because they recruit dumb jocks, party animals who graduate without having to worry about grades. We field teams of intelligent, student athletes busting their academic asses along side campus eggheads. Frankly, I don't know how Mo and other Cal jocks compete in the classroom while spending so much time on the practice field."

"And not playing particularly well at that," Ollie Punch mumbled.

"Hey, fatso, cut the crap," said Butch. "Brilliant neo-Renaissance guys like me are the wave of the future. Have no fear, Butch is here!"

Casey Lee continued. "The Trojans beat us up on the playing field; but in our hearts, Cal fans know we are intellectually and morally superior."

"Our superior attitude drives Trojan fans nuts," said Ollie. "They come up here every other year, cheer their team to victory, blow a lot of dough celebrating in The City and get pissed off when we treat them as barbarians."

"But I thought Stanford is Cal's big rival," said Jonathan.

"It is, and it isn't," said Casey. "The Cal-Stanford rivalry is old but friendly and respectful. Stanford may be a snotty private school for rich kids, but both Cal and Stanford hate SC because Trojans are committed more to partying and sports than to education."

"Amen," said Ollie.

On the gridiron, the SC band now formed a large dollar sign as it played "I Found a Million Dollar Baby."

"But UCLA is in LA too," said Tubbins

"Yes," said Casey, "but UCLA is our public school cousin. A lot of their kids are like us, middle-class kids, trying to get a college degree."

"But why does UCLA have better football teams than Cal?"asked Fart-ing.

"It's as simple as black and white," said Casey. "UCLA recruits outstanding Negro student-athletes, like Jackie Robinson and Rafer Johnson. Cal hasn't done that in the past, but there may be changes soon."

The Trojan band scurried off the field as Cal rooters chanted, "Rubber Band! Rubber Band!"

The Dormies sat high up in the middle of the Cal all men's rooting section along the sunny side of Memorial Stadium. Twelve-thousand strong, the men's rooting section occupied the seats between the 40 yard line stripes, the bottom rows reserved for the 200 members of the all-male Cal Marching Band. Two all-female sections, a thousand each, flanked each side of the men's section.

"Freshmen, turn the blue side of your rooter's cap out," barked Royal French.

No student rooter, male or female, was admitted to the rooting sections without a white shirt, and more important, the omnipresent, reversible dark blue and gold baseball cap. The two-sided, blue and gold caps had an aesthetic, as well as practical function. The seats in the rooting section were painted dark blue with a gold block "C" around the perimeter. In the first half, student rooters sitting on the seats painted with the block C displayed the gold side of their caps, while rooters sitting on the blue seats exposed the blue side of the caps, the gold caps forming a C against a sea of the blue. In the second half, Cal rooters reversed their caps so that a blue block C was formed against a field of gold.

"Who are all the people on the hill," asked Jonathan, noticing hundreds sitting above Memorial Stadium.

"Tightwad Hill," said Ollie, "the best seats to watch a game."

Above the rim of Memorial Stadium, thrifty Cal football fans, especially young families, dotted the dense grove of eucalyptus trees, watching the game admission free. When a big name or traditional rival visited Memorial Stadium, the numbers on Tightwad Hill swelled. Today, several-hundred occupied the slope of Tightwad Hill to see the number one ranked, mighty University of Southern California Trojans.

Several rows below the Dormies sat the P U's, the two living groups observing a temporary truce during the football game. As Casey Lee explained, "While the P U's are chugging their pre-game beers, we get to the stadium early and stake out the high ground. Food fights break out when Cal gets too far behind, so we have the advantage of elevation when the garbage starts flying."

Royal French distributed paper cups of a frozen orange drink called Gremlins.

"Gosh, these Gremlins hit the spot," said Tubbins, slurping the melting juice.

"They're tastier when you add a little of this," said the Waz, pouring from a bottle hidden in a brown paper bag. The campus Meter Mel splashed a measure of clear liquid into the Gremlin cups of the freshmen around him. "A touch of vodka adds a little kick."

The freshmen gingerly sipped the concoction. "Gosh, never tried vodka before," said Tubbins, "doesn't seem to have much taste." He took a bigger sip.

"Don't worry about tasting vodka. You'll be feeling it!" The Waz gave a knowing wink to Casey Lee. "If SC really pounds our butts, you'll want more to make it to the end of the game."

"If we're losing badly, why would we stay?" asked Fart-ing.

"Being a loyal Cal rooter is NEVER leaving a game early, even in a blowout," said Ollie, slurping down another vodka Gremlin.

"It's part of another old Cal tradition," said Casey."Before a game, we bravely harbor false hopes that we can beat big name teams like SC, Michigan, and Notre Dame. But the truth is we rarely have a prayer."

The dorm President leaned forward, explaining,"What we're really doing is supporting the school, affirming our intellectual superiority by backing the team through all the endless losses. Look around the stadium. See all that blue and gold? That's part of the Cal tradition, too. It's called Showing the Colors. There are forty-thousand Old Blues, alums who turn out for football knowing full well Cal's going to lose. Being a loyal Cal fan means more than just winning games. It's celebrating a great campus, honoring its academic tradition, reaffirming a memorable student experience, renewing social ties with old friends. As strange as it sounds, winning the game is not the meat of this experience, it's the gravy."

"Gosh, but isn't winning better than losing?" said Tubbins.

"Of course," said Casey. "But long-suffering and overcoming adversity are a part of the Cal tradition. Of course, when we do win, Cal fans go absolutely bonkers. Losing so often, we savor victory more than any other University, except possibly . . . Northwestern or Rutgers."

With a drum roll and fanfare of trumpets, Tommy Trojan and Traveler began a lap around Memorial Stadium. Horse and rider circled a football stadium after each Trojan score, but a gratuitous pre-game insult was always justified when it came to the Cal Bears. Traveler pranced slowly past the cheering SC section, the red and yellow partisans still thrusting their fingers in a V for victory sign while the Trojan band continued to play endless repetitious choruses of Tribute.

"Get your Gremlins ready," Royal French ordered.

Choruses of boo's rained down on Tommy and Traveler as they trotted toward the Cal rooting section. Pausing, Tommy raised his sword haughtily at the Cal rooters. The boo's now deafening, the entire Cal rooting section rose to greet the hated symbols of Trojan athletic superiority.

"One, two, three, FIRE!" shouted Royal French.

One-hundred Dormies rained salvos of Gremlin cups, rotten fruit, and breakfast leftovers. The P U's launched several oranges with their slingshot Rubbers. Most of the debris fell harmlessly around the targets, but a few missiles hit their mark: a soft-boiled egg striking Tommy Trojan's sword, a full Gremlin cup scoring a direct hit on Tommy's breastplate, and a rotten banana splattering sticky goo on his golden shield.

Rising high on his hind legs, Traveler whinnied as Tommy Trojan flipped a defiant middle finger at the Cal rooting section. It was at that precise moment that a carefully aimed water balloon by Butch Tanenbloom struck Tommy squarely on the helmet, showering the horse's snow white coat with a patina of Cal blue

180

dye.

Cheers, howls, applause erupted from the Cal rooting section, as Tommy and Traveler retreated to the safety of the Trojan side of the field amid chants of,

"SC SUCKS! SC SUCKS! SC SUCKS!"

The P U's glanced up at the Dormies, nodding in begrudging approval.

A new chant emanated from somewhere near the all-male Cal Marching Band, gaining in intensity as the Cal rooting section discovered the provocation.

"Take off that RED shirt! Take off that RED shirt!"

An SC fan, dressed in a crimson hat and polo shirt and gold pants, had staggered in front of the Cal rooting section during the bombardment and was taunting Cal rooters with a SC pennant and swigging from a bottle in a brown bag, oblivious to the command of the Cal rooting section to "Take off that RED shirt."

"We don't allow any red in the rooting section," Royal shouted. "Red is a Stanford color."

Creeping up behind the drunk, Oski, the Cal bear mascot, ripped away the paper bag, inserted a straw into the bottle of booze, swiftly draining the contents through one of his eye holes. As the Trojan fan sought vainly to retrieve the bottle, Oski pushed him into the waiting arms of the Cal Band.

"ROLL HIM UP! ROLL HIM UP!" the rooting section shouted, rising to its feet.

"What's happening?" Jonathan shouted, standing on his seat

"This is great, Junior," Butch said. "They're passing that SC guy up the rooting section!"

Chants of "Roll him up! Roll him up!" accompanied a human form floating toward the Dormies, lifted upward by a sea of upraised hands. By the time the SC fan reached the P U's, the crimson cap was gone, remnants of red polo shirt clinging from his paunchy frame, his belt ripped from the gold pants, shoes missing. For a moment, the hapless Trojan fan disappeared among the P U's, who grabbing the victim by his wrists and ankles, heaved him high up into the air toward the Dormies.

"Oh, shit," yelled Butch. "Catch him!"

The flying body landed in a sea of outstretched arms, collapsing the Dormies into a pile, but saving the intruder from certain injury. Nearby, Jonathan caught a whiff of the drunk's putrid breath.

"Where's my booze?" the SC rooter shouted, flailing his hands wildly. "Give it back!"

Amid more choruses of "Roll him up," the partially clad SC fan was passed up hand-over-hand toward the top of the all male rooting section.

Below, at midfield, the trumpet section of the SC band began the national anthem. As the crimson and gold clad rooters sang, "Oh, say can you see . . . ," the Cal rooting section hummed "America, The Beautiful."

When the SC fans sang the words, ". . .and the rockets'. . . ," the next word, "red"was drowned out by the Cal rooters shouting "BLUE!"

The Cal rooters finished humming America, The Beautiful, by adding a Cal phonetic twist to the last five words, singing, "FROM C TO SHINING C!"

Moments later, as the SC fans reached the last line of the Star Spangled Banner, . . . and the home of the . . .," the last word, "brave," could not be heard, as both the Cal men's and women's rooting sections yelled a deafening "BEARS!"

At the top of the rooting section, the SC fan disappeared over the rim of Memorial Stadium, landing gently like a rag doll amid jeering families clustered on the dusty slope of Tightwad Hill. Nearby, the Cal cannon mounted on a tall wooden platform discharged a white cloud of smoke, rousting the SC fan from his sotted stupor, signaling the arrival of the Bear and Trojan football teams.

Now the game could begin!

32

FATEBALL

The 1959 Cal-USC game would be described by Sports Illustrated as *one of the wackiest college football games in history*. SC rooters would cry "foul," while Cal Bears would smugly retort "brains over brawn." In the prior games of the decade, SC had won all nine by a combined total of 387 to 45. In the previous year, SC won 61 to 0, leaving in its first team until the final minutes of the fourth quarter, a SC tradition in improving its position in the national rankings by running up the score.

The game began as expected, with USC taking the opening kickoff and marching methodically down the field for a score. The Bears salvaged a small measure of success when Mo McCart and Chip Fist squirmed through to block the point after.

Trojans: 6-0.

On the Bear's first possession, the massive SC line smothered Cal's first two offensive plays for losses, knocking the quarterback out of the game. Enter Joe L. Capp, a tall, lanky, freshman whose primary responsibility was holding the ball for field goals and points after. As Cal's starting quarterback was removed from the gridiron by stretcher, Capp quickly designed a trick play he had used at McClatchy High in Sacramento.

Anticipating SC would bring an all-out blitz to rattle him, Capp set his two halfbacks and two ends in tandem wide to the right, next to the sideline, leaving only the fullback behind him to block, the unorthodox formation suggesting a quick screen pass to the right. SC countered and positioned their fastest defenders in front of the wedge far away from the ball.

At the snap, Cal's four receivers streaked straight down the sidelines, taking SC defenders with them. The Bear linemen blocked to the right, as Mo McCart lowering his head, plowed off tackle, appearing to take a handoff from Capp.

"Quick opener," shouted the massive SC line closing the small gap, burying Mo for no gain.

Unnoticed by SC was that, prior to faking the handoff to Mo, Capp had placed the ball on the ground behind his center. While Mo was being tackled by a host of Trojans, the right guard had scooped up the loose ball and sprinted to the left, away from the action.

As the gloating SC tacklers untangled themselves from the pile, they realized too late that Mo did not have the ball! On the far right side of the field, the four Cal decoys shouted encouragement as the Bear lineman lumbered untouched into the end zone!

Confusion! Pandemonium! The Cal cannon on Tightwad Hill exploding! Cal fans wildly cheering a mystery touchdown, SC players and coaches protesting angrily, officials in animated discussion.

Decision: the play was legal. Touchdown, Bears!

Kick for the point after. Receiving the snap in a kneeling position, Capp placed the ball on end, spinning its laces toward the goal post. Stepping forward toward the ball, the Cal kicker suddenly bolted to his left around a horde of Trojans rushing to block the kick. Jumping up, Capp floated a pass into the waiting arms of the kicker alone in the end zone. A two point conversion!

Bears lead 8-6!

An aroused Bear team, suffused with the frenzied support of the Cal rooting section's chants of "Go Bears!" held off four Trojan drives with spirited goal line stands.

Halftime score: Cal 8 SC 6.

"Bitch-in," said Butch. "But this is like the Alamo. How long can the Bears hold out?"

"Who cares," replied Royal. "Look at how quiet the SC rooting section is. If they don't get the lead back soon, they'll boo their own team. They can't accept anything less than a rout."

Storming the field, the all-male Cal Marching Band put on a dazzling half-time show of intricate formations and choreographed dance steps, while the Cal rooting sections performed card stunts, forming words and pictures poking fun at the Trojans

When the SC band took the field, the P U's, using their Rubbers, bombarded the SC musicians with Trojan brand prophylactics filled with shaving cream. as the Cal rooting section taunted,

"RUBBER BAND! RUBBER BAND!"

and

"TOUGH AS AN APE! STRONG AS AN OX!
THREE FOR A QUARTER! IN A LITTLE TIN BOX!"

"Frosh, reverse your caps for the second half," reminded Royal.

"At least we won the halftime show," said Jonathan, noting the surly mood of the SC players returning to the field.

"Let's not give up yet," said Casey. "This freshman quarterback, Joe L. Capp, may have other tricks up his sleeves."

On the kickoff, the SC behemoths swarmed down the field to crush the puny upstarts. At the goal line, the Cal kick returner fumbled the ball forward into the arms of Chip Fist who lurched forward to the fifteen-yard line. Swarmed by several Trojans, Fist pitched the ball sideways to Capp, running toward the right sideline. Hemmed in at the twenty-five, Capp launched an overhand lateral to a Cal player in the middle of the field. Gathering an escort of blockers, the new ball carrier moved to the fifty-yard line where he was tackled.

Before his knee touched the ground, the Cal player flipped the ball sideways to Mo McCart who lumbered down to the SC 30 yard line where he was tripped up by the SC kicker. Falling in slow motion like a felled tree, Mo shoveled the ball sideways to Capp who had caught up with the play at the 25-yard line. Capp sprinted untouched into the end zone.

Touchdown, Cal!

The Cal cannon on Tightwad Hill exploded for a second time!

Five different Bears had touched the ball in what generations of Cal fans would fondly recall as The Play.

Point after kick: Good!

Bears now led 15 to 6.

In the fourth quarter, SC's physical superiority took its toll, as the Trojans marched for two TD's against the tired Cal defense.

SC 20 Cal 15.

Two minutes left.

Fourth down, Cal punting. Rejuvenated SC fans thrusting their fingers in their V for victory sign, the Trojan band playing endless choruses of Tribute. Late afternoon on a beautiful fall day in Strawberry Canyon. Rays of the setting sun illuminated the cyclotron above the stadium in an ethereal glow. Flocks of seagulls circled Memorial Stadium, paying their usual fourth quarter visit. Campanile carillons sounded 4 p.m..

"Well, shit," sighed Royal. "At least, we got a moral victory. No blowout. We fought the good fight."

"There's still time for one more miracle," said Casey.

"Can't bear to look," said Super Sleuth.

The Cal punt spiraled lazily down to the SC 20-yard line. Press accounts would note that there was room for a SC punt return, as the Cal team labored down field under the kick. It was at that precise moment, when the backpedaling Trojan punt receiver opened his arms to catch the ball, that a low flying seagull unloaded a large orb of bird shit. The white turd scored a direct hit on the Trojan's face, blinding him, a split second before the football arrived. The pigskin careened crazily off his arms. Fumble!

Players wildly diving, clawing, scrambling for the loose ball, the slippery pigskin squirting, popping from arm to arm toward the SC goal line, disappearing into a gigantic pile of writhing bodies at the 5-yard line. Officials untangled the mass of humanity, players on both teams milling about, pointing toward their respective goals, claiming possession of the ball. On the bottom, beneath two SC Neanderthals, clutching the ball to his chest, Mo McCart. Cal ball!

The following excerpt is from the actual tape of the play-by-play coverage, called by the All Pro for Cal radio KALX:

"ONLY 80 seconds left! Pitch out right gains only a yard to the four. OH, NO! Cal ball carrier didn't go out of bounds! Clock ticking down. Less than a minute. Cal calls time out."

"Capp fakes a handoff into the middle, bootlegs left, ball hidden on his hip. He's got room to score, but, NO! SC safety made a BRILLIANT open field tackle, bringing down Capp on the 2-yard line."

"Another Cal time out. Third down. ONLY 20 seconds left.

Capp rolling right, throwing into back corner of the end zone to the tight end."

"Caught! Touchdown! Cal fans GOING CRAZY!"

"Wait! NO GOOD! Cal receiver came down out of bounds!"

"Fourth down, LAST CHANCE. 10 SECONDS LEFT. Ball on the Trojan 2. Sixty-thousand fans on their feet, CROWD NOISE DEAFENING!. Capp feverishly diagraming a play in the huddle."

"SPREAD FORMATION! All receivers left. No one in the backfield. Capp fades back, looking left, looking over the middle, back to the left. HE'S GONNA BE SACKED! Capp throws right. No one there. WAIT! Tackle Eligible! Ball tipped. HE'S GOT IT. TOUCHDOWN, BEARS!"

"CAL WINS! CAL WINS! CAL WINS! 21-20!"

"For you Cal fans listening at home, here's what happened.

Mo McCart lined up as a tackle and pretended to fall down while pass blocking. Capp looked as if he had thrown the ball away. Leaping up, McCart stretched, dove, and tipped the ball straight up into the air, as he fell into the end zone."

"THEN AS IF IN SLOW MOTION, McCart twisted onto his back, watched and waited, as the ball tumbled end-over-end into his arms!"

The entire Cal rooting section spilled onto the field, a sea of white engulfing Capp, Mo, and the Bear team, the Cal Marching Band playing "Palms of Victory." The Cal cannon fired an extra salvo. SC fans sat in stunned silence, shock. Tommy Trojan slumped down on Traveler, the Trojan band no longer playing choruses of Tribute.

"Operation Red Foxtrot!" shouted Royal, standing tall above the Dormies."Let's grab a souvenir for Mo."

One-hundred Dooch Dormies, locking arms, oozed like a giant amoeba against the tide of humanity to the nearby goal posts.

Royal French had designed this RF for the Dormies a year ago, waiting for a rare, special Cal victory. The Dormies engulfed the north goal posts like a human tidal wave, rocking the wooden uprights, ripping them from their supports, tearing away the crossbar. Gripping the three pieces tightly under their arms, the Dormies jogged away with their booty, aiming them like battering rams through the milling throng.

From Tightwad Hill, the sight of the Dormies carting off the goal posts resembled a swarm of ants carrying away three long, white twigs. For years, the goal posts were displayed in the Dooch library, with the names of Operation Red Foxtrot, along with the historic score:

1959: Cal Bears 21 - SC Rubbers 20

Trotting alongside Butch, Jonathan tightened his grip along the sheared end of the cross bar, suffused with the joy and hysteria of the improbable win. A Bear upset of the mighty Trojans with a timely assist from nature! *Shit flies both ways!* he thought.

33

BEST LAID PLANS OF RATS

"As an academician, it would be wrong to condone violence." The words were spoken wistfully in a deep, distinctively Teutonic accent. Professor Werner Von Seller drew deeply from the Gaulois smoldering in the sterling silver cigarette holder.

The plan had a certain simplistic appeal, Von Seller thought. If it succeeded, his atomic research program would reap the rewards of increased public funding, and he would become the most influential member of the University of California faculty. And if it failed, he could easily distance himself from the two conspirators sitting before him.

"Think of it as an issue of free speech, not violence," responded Clayborn Muck. "It will look like the rantings of the campus left-wing protesting the HUAC hearings; but when things get out of hand, there will be a tremendous outpouring of support for our patriotic causes," said Muck, smiling at the attentive young man sitting at his side.

"And television will be our unwitting ally," Muck continued. "Can you see what coverage of student riots broadcast into millions of homes across America will do for us?" His voice rose with excitement.

Muck had already rehearsed the angry responses he would give on the evening news to Chet Huntley, David Brinkley, and Walter Cronkite.

Dirk Krum sat mesmerized by the magnitude of the moment,

189

basking in the glory of the patriotic Congressman and the famous atomic scientist.

The three sat in the burnished splendor of the Morrison Library, a small, elegant reading room tucked away in the northwest corner of the massive Doe Library. Within its dark, carved oak walls, the sanctuary contained a Library of Congress catalogue, a sampling of newspapers and magazines from around the world, easy access to stacks of popular books, and a mezzanine where 33 1/3 rpm LP record albums of classical music were enjoyed in the privacy of headphones.

Scattered about the cork flooring were eleven intricately patterned Karastan rugs with groupings of three and four high-back leather chairs to facilitate significant discourse. Suspended from the carved, molded plaster ceiling were six antique brass chandeliers which, when illuminated, gave the room an ethereal glow, highlighting the splendid earth tones of the crushed velvet, silk screen Fortuny tapestry dominating the western wall.

On this evening, the Morrison was dark, except for the dim light of a solitary brass floor lamp illuminating the trio sitting in luxurious leather chairs, awaiting the arrival of a fourth for significant discourse of an exotic nature.

The Campanile carillons announced midnight, one hour after the closing of the popular campus reading room.

"Are you sure liberals will be blamed?" asked Von Seller, the Prussian Penguin, adjusting his monocle.

"Positive," said Krum with enthusiasm. "Every campus group has its own style of dress. The P U's will dress like Beatniks. We'll wear fake beards, long-haired wigs, and black berets. Real Beatniks won't be able to tell the difference."

Leaning into the arc of light, Muck said, "I will call a press conference immediately after the meeting of the Academic Senate where Professor Von Seller will make an impassioned appeal for support, even though HUAC will be condemned by the left-wing leadership of the Academic Senate." Muck nodded deferentially to the atomic scientist.

"But of course," said the Prussian Penguin releasing another stream of Gaulois smoke toward the darkened ceiling of the Morrison. "It is my patriotic duty to speak out on issues of national security. After all, that is my expertise."

Muck continued, "At the press conference, Dirk's fraternity

boys, posing as Beatnik protesters, will shout us down and assault us with missiles."

"We'll throw raw eggs and stink bombs," explained Krum, borrowing the idea from the Dooch counterattack on the P U house. "It'll be messy, but you won't be seriously hurt."

"Ingenious," said Von Seller, thinking that he should remember to wear his darkest suit, the better to show off the evidence of the attack. "Young man, with your audacity and fierce sense of competition, you should go far in the business world."

An insistent rapping drew the trio's attention to the entrance of the reading room.

"Ah, my Chief Investigator," said Muck waving in Seymour Graft through the brass and glass doors.

Hasty introductions followed.

Von Seller studied the narrow set eyes and the twitching nose of Seymour Graft.

This is Congressman Muck's trusted assistant, the heart and soul of HUAC's investigative force?

He dismissed the thought of acknowledging this creature in the light of day.

Yes, I will reap the benefit of HUAC's hearings, but the sooner HUAC does its dirty work and leaves the Bay Area, the better off I will be, Von Seller concluded.

"Gaulois?" asked Graft. "I can spot them a mile away! Bum one from you, Professor Von Seller?"

Before Muck could overrule the request, Krum chimed in, "May I try one too? I've never smoked a French cigarette."

God, thought Muck. *Three Gaulois smokers! I must end this meeting soon.*

"Boss, do I have some great photos for you." Seymour Graft produced a stack of enlarged photos, carefully sliding away the bottom few, nude pictures of Anna Zarzana emerging from the shower.

For my personal collection, he smiled.

Increasing the illumination of the floor lamp, Muck studied Graft's latest work. "Wonderful! Fabulous!" he murmured. "Professor, would you like to see the evidence?" he asked, passing the photos to Von Seller.

A Gaulois dangling from his lip, Graft twirled his wispy moustache, pleased with the results of his assignment. How

Seymour loved his private time with Anna. In the evenings he had shinnied up the tall, black walnut tree next to her room at the I-House. There, hidden from view by the thick branches, he had spent hours peering into her bathroom window, photographing her voluptuous, young body with those magnificent proud breasts and that dark soft triangle of her nether hair!

Unseen, yet omnipresent, Graft felt he controlled this beautiful girl's destiny, the knowledge stirring him, exciting him.

She's mine, all mine, he thought, thrilling to the vicarious power he exercised over her.

The beautiful young woman did have one disturbing habit, the weekly rendezvous with Professor Aristotle Scott. Everything seemingly on the up and up, meeting only in public places, no secret hotel trysts. The obvious rapport and genuine affection between them inspired jealousy in Graft. He could not wait until Muck and HUAC destroyed the middle-aged suitor's career!

"My, my," Von Seller intoned with approval, adjusting his monocle. "The photos incriminating Professor Ari Scott are wonderful, but these showing Anna Zarzana enjoying happy moments with Scott and my nemesis, Garrick Nelquist, are truly stupendous!" said the Prussian Penguin, studying the enlargements.

"Well done, Mr. Graft. Perhaps another Gaulois?"

For his part, Krum could barely conceal his joy. All the pieces of his scheme were falling into place. Soon Professors Scott and Nelquist would be disgraced and gone, leaving the Dormies without support among the faculty. Then he would have this year and his Senior year to seek his revenge on Casey Lee.

Yes, time was now on his side. Time for Kate Howell to learn that her destiny is with me! Time for her to realize that her sessions with Casey Lee were misguided and morally wrong!

As the four gloated, their every word was being carefully noted by Super Sleuth, from the dark recesses of the mezzanine above.

Marty Silverstein had been nicknamed Super Sleuth by Royal French for his uncanny ability to be unnoticed in crowds. A shy, soft-spoken, freckle-faced red head, Marty spent his spare time following and ogling five percenters around campus. To avoid detection, he learned to use window reflections, walk backwards, and tie his shoestrings often. According to Royal, the quality that made Marty invisible was his habit of walking with both hands in his front jean pockets, a posture that enabled Super Sleuth to glide like a shadow.

It had been two weeks ago that Super Sleuth had spotted the small, weasel looking man in the large brimmed hat and tan trench coat following the luscious, voluptuous coed. Super Sleuth had added her to his list of regulars; and, although he knew she lived at I-House, he had not yet learned her name. Whomever she was, she certainly had powerful connections within the faculty.

The weekends with Professor Ari Scott were shocking. An affair? Possibly, but probably not, he concluded.

Despite the obvious attraction between the two, he noted that Professor Scott never touched the dark-haired beauty in an intimate manner.

Not the way I'd be all over her if she gave me any of those endearing gazes, he thought.

Intrigued by her beauty, Super Sleuth had broken his own rule against tailing any girl beyond the immediate area of the campus. Last week, he had followed Professor Scott and the girl onto the ferry to San Francisco, keeping them in view from a comfortable distance from the upper deck.

During the short, choppy ride across the Bay, he caught sight of the weasel, cigarette dangling from the corner of his mouth, staring intently at the couple from a few feet away. The swirling Bay breeze wafted the pungent scent of the weasel's smoldering cigarette.

French Gaulois cigarettes, Super Sleuth noted.

A few minutes later, he was startled when he noted the weasel using a miniature camera to photograph Professor Scott and the beautiful coed.

Was he imagining it? Was he projecting his own secretive hobby onto a harmless stranger?

There was only one way to find out.

As the ferry gently bobbed against the quay, awaiting the tie down by stevedores, Super Sleuth jostled through the noisy throng of disembarking passengers. Dashing out onto the gangway, he took a position near the line of passengers waiting to board the return trip to the East Bay.

Craning his neck over debarking passengers, Super Sleuth soon saw the two exiting leisurely, strolling arm in arm along the pier. For a moment, he thought his suspicion was ill founded. But in a few moments, the weasel appeared, abandoning all pretense of what he was doing.

Super Sleuth followed, amazed at the indiscreet manner the weasel kept his subjects in sight. Staying a block behind the couple, he watched as the weasel darted, stoop shouldered, from right to left in a zigzag pattern, provoking the curious stares from approaching pedestrians. The parade serpentined along the abandoned docks, passing Fisherman's Wharf to the foot of Hyde Street where cable cars picked up tourists for the return to downtown San Francisco.

The weasel is getting tired, thought Super Sleuth, watching his quarry remove his wide brimmed hat to fan his perspiring face.

At the front of the Buena Vista Café, Professor Scott waved at someone inside.

The couple entered, and soon the perspiring weasel followed. The BV was jammed with its normal weekend crowd of tourists and locals, all clamoring for the BV's famous Irish Coffee.

Fast-moving barkeeps splashed rows of special tulip-shaped glasses with scalding hot water. On receiving an order, the hot water was quickly discarded. Two cubes of sugar were tumbled into the glass followed by dark, rich coffee topped by an ounce-and-a-half of Irish whiskey. After a quick swizzle of the liquid, a layer of fresh cream was spooned over the swirling concoction.

Super Sleuth positioned himself at the far end of the bar, noting how the weasel pretended to be a tourist photographing the cable cars against the beautiful vista of San Francisco Bay, but was, instead, focusing on the table next to the window where Professor Scott and the girl had joined Professor Nelquist.

The past week, Super Sleuth had concentrated on the beautiful young woman, hoping that what he had observed was an isolated incident. He lengthened his distance while tailing her and; without fail, the weasel appeared, smoking his pungent Gaulois cigarettes, twirling his wispy moustache, stalking her between I-House and campus.

Super Sleuth learned that, after the weasel tracked her back to I-House, he usually went to the late show at the T & D Theater, dubbed the "Tough and Dirty," to see X-rated flicks such as "The Immoral Mr. Tea's" before retiring to a small room at the Dumphy, a seedy hotel on Shattuck Avenue near campus.

At 11:30 p.m. tonight, Super Sleuth had hit the jackpot.

Picking up the weasel as he left his cubby hole at the Dumphy, Super Sleuth noted his quarry veering from his usual habit of trekking up Bancroft to I-House, boosting himself up into the crook of the giant black walnut tree, and snapping photos through the girl's open bathroom.

A real pervert, Super Sleuth had concluded.

From the Dumphy, the weasel had moved northwest across campus, staying in the shadows of campus landmarks. As he passed the base of the Campanile, it was obvious the weasel was heading for the Doe Library.

How would he get in?

The library had closed at 11 p.m. Behind the gigantic Grecian urn on the northern portico of the library, Super Sleuth watched with amazement as the weasel produced a metal ring filled with keys, beginning the tedious process of finding the exact key that would admit him.

Searching his mental inventory of secret entrances to campus buildings, Super Sleuth remembered the abandoned custodian's entrance beneath the portico.

Preoccupied, the weasel did not notice Super Sleuth tiptoing past him, scurrying down to the basement level hidden by decades of undergrowth, admitting himself into the bowels of Doe Library. He felt his way along the darkened basement, emerging at the foot of the grand staircase across from the entrance where the weasel admitted himself. From his vantage, he saw the weasel hurrying toward the entrance to the Morrison glowing dimly from an interior light.

Whom could he be meeting? Who would have access to the Morrison this time of the night? Someone very influential, to be sure, he thought.

Recalling a rear exit to the upstairs mezzanine of the Morrison, Super Sleuth quietly bounded up the grand staircase.

What luck! The rear exit to the mezzanine was unlocked!

Quietly admitting himself and crouching, Super Sleuth crawled to the spindled railing and hunkered down on all fours, avoiding detection from below.

Super Sleuth recognized the familiar whining voice of Clayborn Muck from his many television pronouncements about HUAC.

He heard Muck say, "During my televised press conference, when I shout the slogan 'Save the University From Subversives,' that will be the signal, Dirk, for all of your P U's, hidden in the moving van, to begin your anti-HUAC riot attack on Professor Von Seller and me. We will get our dramatic television coverage; and you boys will escape before the police arrive."

Professor Werner Von Seller, the Prussian Penguin and Dirk Krum, the P U President? Super Sleuth said to himself.

"You do realize," said Von Seller, "if any of you fraternity boys are arrested, the entire plan will fail."

And I shall deny any knowledge of this intrigue, he thought.

"It's foolproof," wheezed the fourth voice. "I'll ask the FBI to have Broadway cleared so the moving van can make its getaway."

That must be the weasel, thought Super Sleuth.

"Gentlemen, it's late," said Von Seller, snuffing out the burning remnant of the Gaulois and sliding his sterling silver cigarette holder into the breast pocket of his jacket, "and I have an atomic research program to run at the cyclotron."

As the quartet rose, exchanging handshakes, they heard the unmistakable sound of rustling newspaper above.

"What the hell was that?" said Muck.

"Follow me," said Krum, motioning to Graft.

Upstairs, the Super Sleuth swore to himself, *oh, shit!*

In his haste to leave, he had backed into a newspaper rack. Silently opening the mezzanine exit, he eased effortlessly into the darkness of the hallway.

Sprinting up the small staircase, Krum and Graft reached the mezzanine. Graft flicked on a flashlight he carried in his trench coat, the circular beam arcing around the dark, cozy enclave, resting on a copy of the New York Times crumpled on the floor.

"Nothing, Boss," whispered Graft, leaning over the balcony. "Newspaper fell off a rack."

"Yeah, nothing," Krum echoed.

And yet . . . .

34

KEEPING UP WITH THE JONESES

"What time did you get in last night, Junior?" asked Butch, the two freshmen following the crush of students surging into old South Hall. High above in the Campanile, Hunch Hitowski banged out a sprightly version of Kurt Weill's "September Song."

"Came by your room a few times to go over our English 1A assignment," said Butch, "but gave up around eleven."

"Didn't get in until midnight," said Jonathan sheepishly, "Guess I'll catch up on the reading assignments some other time."

"Don't get too far behind," said Butch. "Competition's gonna be tough in Professor Aural's class."

"No sweat, Butch, I can do it," said Jonathan remembering, how easy it had been getting straight A's high school.

Besides, he thought, savoring the memory, *yesterday was more memorable than any English 1A assignment. What a fabulous adventure!*

It began a few days ago when a hand-delivered letter appeared at the dorm, addressed to

Master Jonathan Aldon, c/o Dooch Hall, University of California, Berkeley 4, California.

The missive piqued the interest of Ollie Punch, Hunch Hitowski, and the All Pro who found the envelope on the lobby desk. A few feet away, in a corner by the ten-cent Coke machine, Royal French, Casey Lee, Mo McCart, and Ruby Lips, betting pennies, played cards at a square Formica table.

Holding the sealed envelope up to the light of the chandelier, Ollie attempted to decipher the contents, his left eye spinning feverishly.

"Shouldn't nosy into other people's mail, Ollie," admonished Royal, dealing a game of Hearts.

"Didn't Special Forces teach you how to open sealed envelopes with steam or something?" inquired Ollie.

"Why don't you ask Gifted Florence to consult with her crystal ball, Munch-kin," teased Ruby, referring to his part-time job as assistant female psychic. "For a lousy buck, she will see all and tell all."

"Screw you," snapped Ollie. "Aldon gets personal mail from a celebrity, and you don't have an ounce of curiosity in finding out what this is all about? For shame, Ruby."

It was at that moment Jonathan, Butch, Fart-ing, and Tubbins sauntered through Dooch's double glass doors.

Hunch jabbed Ollie with an elbow, uttering an "ahem."

"Told you so," Royal muttered behind a fan of cards spread before his face.

"Jeez, Aldon," said Ollie sheepishly. "Do you really know Reverend Ike?" There was a tone of wonder in his voice, as he gingerly tendered the envelope to the freshman.

Jonathan paused, noting the elegant, flowery handwriting bearing the return address, *Reverend Isaac Jones, Negro Baptist Church.*

Reverend Ike, Aunt Pearl's cousin.

"You've heard of Reverend Ike?" asked Jonathan.

"Are you kidding?" said Hunch. "Reverend Ike's the most popular radio evangelist in the whole Bay Area! Fiery sermons! Great gospel music! A religious icon! Many Dormies get their only religion from Reverend Ike."

Casey elaborated. "Last year the Cal administration decided to broaden our experiences by exposing us to Negro culture. Since there are very few Negroes on campus, the next best thing is broadcasting Reverend Ike's Sunday sermons on KALX."

"I personally wired Reverend Ike's pulpit for sound," the All Pro added proudly.

"Gosh, Jonathan, how do you know him?" asked Tubbins.

"We're related. My uncle Mike is married to Reverend Ike's cousin, Pearl."

198

"You've gotta be joking," said Fart-ing.

"No big deal," said Butch, "Thomas Jefferson had a bunch of kids by his favorite slave, Sally Hemmings. Besides, Fart-ing, it's almost 1960 for crying out loud. Live and let live."

"Yeah," said Fart-ing, "but screwing slaves and marrying a Negro are two different things."

"Shut your fucking mouths up," snapped Jonathan, feeling a rush of anger, surprising himself with the use of profanity. "My uncle is no slave master, and my aunt is no slave. You guys have something to say, keep it to your Goddamned selves."

Ollie Punch tried to ease the tension. "Anyway, your famous relative is the cat's meow, celebrating God with Joy, Hope, Passion, and Music! Not the usual preachy bull shit you get at church."

As Jonathan carefully broke the seal of the envelope, Ollie, Hunch, and the All Pro raised their hands, chanting in unison,

"Hallelujah! Praise The Lord! Sing and Ye Shall Be Free!"

The letter read:

Greetings, Brother Aldon (or should I say, Cousin Jonathan), Cousin Pearl wrote us of your recent enrollment at Cal. Mrs. Jones and I would like to invite you to Sunday supper before you get bogged down by studies. Our three sons would enjoy meeting you too.

Please dial TH3-5673 (The-Lord) for directions to our humble home.

Yours in Jesus Christ,
Reverend Isaac Jones.

Earlier Sunday morning, Jonathan had crowded into Ollie's room to listen to KALX's broadcast of Reverend Ike's service filled with impassioned sermons, underscored by uplifting, gospel songs. Periodically, the room of Dormies raised their hands to heaven, shouting aloud Reverend Ike's famous motto, "Hallelujah! Praise The Lord! Sing and Ye Shall Be Free!"

Handing Jonathan a stack of index cards, Ollie said, "Aldon, Reverend Ike's autograph, please."

In the afternoon, Jonathan, wearing slacks, white shirt, tie, and dark blue blazer, the same outfit he had worn on the CAT flight from Minneapolis, boarded the No. 7 bus at the corner Channing and Telly, eastbound for Oakland

The bus driver, a portly, red-faced man, wearing a name badge,

Stanley Ray, asked for his destination.

"99th Street," Jonathan said, dropping a dime into the fare box.

"End of the line?" asked Ray with a look of disbelief.

"Sure," said Jonathan. Reverend Ike's instructions had been simple.

> *No. 7 bus from Telly to 99th Street.*
> *Three blocks east, left on Heavenly*
> *Court, fourth house from the corner.*

The East Bay Transit bus lurched along the wide streets of Berkeley, leisurely accepting and disgorging riders. At 66th Street, Jonathan saw a rusted street sign announcing, *Oakland City Limits.*

"This is the farthest I go, young man," said Ray. The front door hissed as it opened. "99th Street, eh? Not too late to hop a ride back with me to campus," he said, picking up his lunch pail.

Jonathan shook his head politely.

If this is 66th, 99th Street *couldn't be too far away,* he thought.

Pausing on the exit landing, Ray whispered to his replacement, a thin, silver-haired Negro, with a bulging, rumpled brown paper sack in his hand.

"Hope you're not lost, boy," said the new bus driver, speaking to Jonathan's reflection in the rearview mirror. His name badge read *Otis McCoy.* "White folks don't go all the way down to 99th." He beamed a smile of flashing teeth.

"Positive," said Jonathan, nodding at McCoy's reflection in the mirror, thinking,

If McCoy only knew how lost the Aldon family would have been without the money Grandfather Aldon made from Bones Washington's dice game.

Within the next few stops, the No.7 was crowded with passengers, all Negroes, some Sunday churchgoers, others sweat-soaked workers from the Alameda shipping yards.

Jonathan yielded his seat to an ancient Negro woman wearing a black eye patch, standing instead in the crowded aisle next to McCoy, his hand tightly gripping the overhead strap against the side sway of the bus moving at a snail's pace.

Above the polite, neighborly chatter, Jonathan heard the whispered question, "Where that white boy going?" He breathed deeply, pretending to be calm, nonchalant; but with each new fare, another pair of eyes stared at him, raising the hackles on the back of his neck. For the first time in his life, Jonathan wished he were invisible like the radio hero, "The Shadow." He imagined how grandfather Aldon must have felt as the only white person at Bones Washington's Oh Shit games.

"99th Street, boy," announced Otis McCoy. "Hope you find what you're lookin' for," he said, flashing another toothy grin. "Last bus to Berkeley leaves at 11:00 p.m. sharp. Don't be late. Boss won't let me wait."

Exiting, Jonathan waved good-bye to McCoy turning the bus around for the return to Berkeley. Across the street, standing beneath a weathered street sign, eyeing him intently, were three Negro boys, about his age, all dressed in shoddy, black high top sneakers, faded black slacks, and black berets. Empty bandoleers slung over their shoulders partially obscured logos of black cats emblazoned on white T-shirts.

Jonathan squinted down 99th Street, a double row of small, dilapidated houses devoid of TV antennas, each with front yards of parched hardpan scattered with broken toys. A few rusted cars dotted the street, their tires flat, hoods raised, crying for help. Not a soul in sight.

He reread the directions.

Three blocks east, left on Heavenly
Court, fourth house from the corner.

Jonathan began the trek to Heavenly Court, the only sound, the crunching chips of broken sidewalk, his silhouette casting a solitary shadow along the potholed street. But soon there was another sound, footsteps behind him. Glancing over his shoulder, Jonathan saw the three Negro boys following, matching him stride for stride, two houses behind.

As if alerted by a silent code, people in the homes appeared in windows, on squeaking porches, along broken driveways watching the progress of Jonathan and his entourage. Recalling his neighbors' curiosity in Aunt Pearl's visit to Four Winds Drive, he now appreciated how gracefully she had handled that moment, hoping he would respond as well.

At the end of the first block, Jonathan picked up his pace, crossing to the other side of the street. The trio followed, keeping their distance. The impromptu parade continued for two more blocks, Jonathan anxiously scanning for a sign of Heavenly Court. *There! At the next corner!*

The sense of relief was short-lived, as Jonathan noted two more Negro boys, similarly dressed, emerging from Heavenly Court, waiting along the sidewalk.

As Jonathan swerved out onto the street, avoiding the human obstacles, one of the two new arrivals stepped directly into his path, blocking him. He was in his early twenties with a handsome, ebony face marred by a diagonal, keloid scar slashing across his neck. His expression was stern, his dark eyes boring through Jonathan. Unlike the trio that had been following Jonathan, this Negro carried real bullets in his bandoleer. On his black beret was stitched the name, *Huey.*

Up close, Jonathan saw the ferocious black cat on the T-shirt, underscored by the name, *Oakland Black Panthers.*

The three young Panthers stopped behind him, surrounding him. Up close, they were even younger, in their early teens.

"My, my, lookie here at the nice threads Whitey's wearin'. Jest my size," said one of the three.

Jonathan tensed, feeling a hand picking a piece of lint from the collar of his blazer.

"You must be lost, Honkie," said Huey, hissing spittle onto Jonathan's shoes. "We don't see many Fuller Brush men in this neighborhood," he sneered.

"Reverend Isaac Jones," stammered Jonathan. "I'm having dinner at Reverend Ike's. Doesn't he live on Heavenly Court?" A tightness gripped his throat.

"Shee-it, man," said one of the young boys, "and I'm eatin' at Ozzie and Harriet's." As the others laughed, Jonathan detected a smile on Huey's face.

"What say, Reggie?" said Huey, turning toward the fifth member of the group, a boy about Jonathan's age, arms folded, leaning up against the street sign of Heavenly Court.

"Wup his white ass or let him go?" asked Huey with a mischievous grin.

Reggie eyed Jonathan thoughtfully, then gave a curt nod of the head.

"Must be your lucky day," Huey whispered. "But in this here neighborhood, we don't count on luck." Pointing, he said,

"Reverend Ike's house is the nice, big one 'round the corner. Better get your lily white butt down there before my man, Reggic, changes his mind."

Jonathan did not tarry, sprinting onto Heavenly Court. Behind him the quintet of Negro boys hooted and chortled.

Reverend Ike's house was the largest on Heavenly Court, a freshly painted two story home with a large white cross beside a small TV antenna. Bouncing up the solid stairway, Jonathan pressed the doorbell, resounding with the first few notes of "Nearer, My God, To Thee."

A petite Negro woman, hair flecked with traces of gray, greeted him with a warm handshake, and a dazzling smile. "You must be Jonathan. Please come in. I'm Mrs. Jones. Please call me Doris."

Jonathan entered a large, comfortable living room filled with well-worn leather chairs. In the corner was a black and white TV larger than the one in his parents' den.

"A very generous gift from the congregation," said Doris, reading his mind.

The kitchen door opened, the sharp smell of food trailing after a short, rotund Negro man with big brown eyes and snow white hair, a white collar peeking over a full-length apron.

"Welcome, welcome to our humble home, Jonathan," said Reverend Ike, wiping his hands across the chest of the apron, then firmly grasping Jonathan's right hand with both of his. "I see you found the way to Heavenly Court."

Based on Reverend Ike's deep, booming radio voice, Jonathan had expected much larger man, but then radio voices can be quite deceiving, he thought, remembering how Rooster Face, the All Pro, had such a romantic sounding voice on the air.

"I had a little help from some of your neighbors," said Jonathan.

"Doris cooks during the week, but I like to do Sunday supper," said Reverend Ike, beaming. "Keeping in touch with the work of the Lord on Sunday mornings, keeping in touch with the work of this family Sunday evenings."

He winked at his wife. "Let's get acquainted in the kitchen while I finish cooking."

They entered a small kitchen, dominated by a large stove with a double oven filled with golden pieces of chicken sizzling, a honey-cured ham baking. Pots and pans gurgling, hissing symphonically, as Reverend Ike, a whirling gastronomic maestro, tasted exotic dishes foreign to the Aldon household.

All this food from such a small kitchen, Jonathan marveled, thinking that even Cokie, working in Mother's modern kitchen, could not match this prodigious output!

Jonathan helped move platters of piping hot food to a large, dignified dining room paneled in rich dark wood. There, on a long, sturdy wooden table covered with lace doilies, were place settings for six. Picking up a small silver bell, Doris Jones rang it delicately three times.

Jonathan heard steps bounding heavily down a staircase, two teenage boys materializing, identically dressed in dark slacks and white shirts. Both resembled Doris, one tall and lanky, the other muscular, powerfully built.

"Our two younger sons," said Reverend Ike proudly. "Our budding musician, Maurice Jackson Jones, known as MJ, a member of a local rhythm and blues band, 'Big Berry and the Blackouts,' and our aspiring athlete, Alonzo Jackson Jones, or AJ, who hopes to play college football someday. SC wants him badly, but we want AJ to get a real education by attending Cal. Our other son, RJ, is at a meeting and will join us later."

"All our boys have my maiden name, Jackson, as their middle name," said Doris. "In our home, male and female, parents and children are treated equally. It is God's will."

Reverend Ike offered Grace, asking the Lord's blessing, in his deep, sonorous voice, for their home, the love of friends and family, God's work through the church, and especially for their guest, their cousin from Iowa, concluding with an "Amen!" followed by the entire family chanting in unison,

"Hallelujah! Praise The Lord! Sing and Ye Shall Be Free!"

Jonathan found the fried chicken and ham tender, juicy, and delicious, in stark contrast to Cokie's well done, bland, dry cooking in the Aldon home. He was intrigued by the exotic vegetables of collard greens, grits, and black-eyed peas

"What is that, Reverend Ike? It's very tasty," said Jonathan, pointing to a dish of deep-fried meat with an unusual texture.

"With your family's prominence in the hog farming industry, we thought you'd enjoy some chitlins."

"Chitlins?" said Jonathan. "Never heard of it."

"Hmmm," Reverend Ike cleared his throat, winking at Doris. "The anatomical name for chitlins is the hog's small intestine."

Gulping, Jonathan struggled to regain his composure, as the Joneses chuckled.

Doris Jones piled high Jonathan's plate with seconds, as Reverend Ike introduced the late arrival.

"Cousin Jonathan, may I introduce our eldest son, RJ, Reginald Jackson Jones, our social revolutionary."

"'Cousin Jonathan' and I have met," said a soft, firm voice.

Jonathan's eyes grew wide in shock, recognizing the face of the quiet Black Panther leaning against the street sign of Heavenly Court.

Reggie, the Black Panther who rescued him!

RJ had shed the black beret and Panther T-shirt for dress shirt and slacks. Although he was considerably taller than his father, Jonathan noted the strong resemblance, sensing Reverend's charisma had been passed to his eldest son.

During dessert, MJ whispered, "Dad and RJ are going to have another argument about the old and new way of doing things."

"What's the difference?" said Jonathan, puzzled.

MJ explained as Reverend Ike and RJ's voices grew louder, "Dad firmly supports the nonviolent tactics of the NAACP, but RJ and the Panthers believe in violent, revolutionary struggle to throw off the shackles of the white man. The disagreement is tearing the two apart."

As the argument between Reverend Ike and his son RJ continued, Jonathan remembered Grandfather Aldon's annual bequest of $5,000 to the NAACP in honor of Bones Washington.

"This will go on all night long," said MJ. "Since you play a little guitar, let's slip out to the garage and join Big Berry and The Blackouts."

Big Berry and The Blackouts? Jonathan wondered, *Do they play Buddy Holly's music?*

35

LOUIE, LOUIE

Behind Reverend Ike's home, a two-car garage and loft had been converted into a small auditorium. An audience of twenty teenagers, including young Negro girls and the Black Panthers who had terrorized Jonathan earlier, sat in folding chairs along the front of a raised stage where musicians were tuning up. From the rafters, a handmade sign proclaimed, *Home of Big Berry and the Blackouts.* MJ, who played lead guitar, introduced Jonathan to the band leader, Big Berry, a large, round Negro man in his twenties, wearing dark glasses and a white Navy Admiral's cap with scrambled eggs braiding on its bill.

"Cal college boy, eh?" said Big Berry. "Love to get some gigs up there on campus. We could make some real money instead of playing for fun."

Placing a hand on MJ's shoulder, Big Berry said, "We gotta learn some white music to go with our regular shit."

"White music?" asked Jonathan.

"You know," said Big Berry. "White music. Nat King Cole, Johnny Mathis, stuff like that."

Jonathan picked up a spare bass guitar, as the band plugged into electrical outlets, noting that most of the instruments had been patched together from spare parts, some bound with duct tape. The speakers were tattered; the drum heads were cracked; the keyboard gouged and chipped. Thinking of his own pristine guitars, Jonathan felt a pang of guilt.

The Blackouts began with an infectious, syncopated rhythmic riff that sounded almost Latin. Picking tentatively at the bass, Jonathan tried to duplicate the tricky beat:

DUH (Pause)

Duh-duh-duh. Duh-duh-duh. Duh-duh-duh.

The band's bass player came to Jonathan's rescue, showing the exact pattern of the rhythm. "Man, don't just play it, feel it," he encouraged.

After a few frustrating attempts, Jonathan closed his eyes, beginning to feel the catchy rhythm. Smiling at his small success, Jonathan plucked away on the bass guitar with newfound confidence as Big Berry sang the lyrics to his own composition.

Louie, Louie, me gotta go!

The audience cheered, rising to dance to the hypnotic rhythm. Big Berry repeated:

Louie, Louie, me gotta go!

MJ yelled, "C'mon, Cuz, sing the chorus!" Rocking comfortably from side-to-side, Jonathan sang.

Louie, Louie, me gotta go!

The earsplitting sounds of the electronic instruments muddled the lyrics to *Louie, Louie*, rendering them incoherent. As the verses were repeated between raucous choruses of *Louie, Louie*, Jonathan learned that the song was about a sailor telling somebody named Louie about his girlfriend in Jamaica.

"What's he saying?" said Jonathan, shouting to MJ.

Maurice shrugged his shoulders, flashing a devilish grin

Straining to decipher the words of the verses, Jonathan thought to himself,

Is it my imagination, or are there dirty words in the song? Can't wait to tell Ziggy about these lyrics!

Jonathan surveyed the swaying crowd of dancers, now swelling to more than fifty, undulating happily to dance moves he had never seen. He recalled that, at the age of twelve, Mother had enrolled him in aunt Claudia Frump's social ballroom classes, sessions he hated, reluctantly learning the correct way to hold a girl while dancing the fox trot, waltz, and rhumba.

"You'll need social graces when you start dating," Mother had said sternly. "A smooth dancer is hard to find."

Jonathan noted that in this free form style of dancing, it was impossible to determine who was dancing with whom. Sometimes the dancers were solo, sometimes dancing with a partner, other times joining lines snaking across the floor.

Bitchin, absolutely bitchin, he thought, using the new California slang.

As the energy of the dancers and the raucous sound of the band reached a fevered pitch, the garage was engulfed in sudden darkness.

"Damn," MJ swore, leaving the stage amid groans from the dance floor.

"What happened?" asked Jonathan. "Just when the place was really rocking."

"Blew a fuse," said Big Berry. "That's how we named the band. Happens all the time."

A few moments later, the garage lights flickered back on, the band resuming *Louie, Louie,* jump starting the energy of the crowd.

Jonathan saw two teen-age girls at the foot of the stage whispering, eyeing him. Holding hands they hopped to his side.

"You got pretty good rhythm," said Angela, the taller of the two.

"For a white boy," added the other.

"No use wasting it up here," said the taller girl, "C'mon down and dance with us."

Jonathan glanced at MJ who gave him an encouraging wink, pointing to the dance floor.

"Why not?" shouted Jonathan, unfastening the guitar strap, peeling off his tie "But you gotta teach me."

"With your moves, Sugar, this gonna be easy," said the shorter girl.

The gyrating crowd gave way to the trio, Jonathan, an albino in a sea of ebony. Up close, Jonathan noted there were distinct patterns or steps in the way Negroes danced, not just some innate rhythm. The difference, it seemed, was that unlike Caucasians who were judged by the way their feet moved, Negroes used their entire bodies, swaying and bobbing to the beat.

The line dance was the easiest, with definite patterns of steps, pirouettes, and hand clapping. It was the individual style that was difficult. As he mimicked the arm gestures of his two partners, the two young girls giggled hysterically at his spasmodic efforts.

"Just keep your hands off my baby sis, Honkie," shouted a male voice into his left ear.

Startled, Jonathan turned to see the scowling face of Huey, the Black Panther leader who had confronted him at the entrance to Heavenly Court.

"Bug off, Huey," laughed the taller girl, Angela, waving her brother away.

They danced through two more power blackouts, with *Louie, Louie* played every third number until Reverend Ike and Doris Jones signaled the end of the session by flicking the garage lights

Perspiring profusely, Jonathan rejoined Big Berry and the Blackouts for one rousing encore of *Louie, Louie*.

"Jonathan, you've got soul," said Big Berry. "You can jam with the Blackouts anytime you feel moved by the spirit."

Exiting, each dancer shook his hand, the Black Panthers gripping him in a strange handshake, their fingers wrapped around his thumb.

"Oh, oh," said Jonathan, looking at a wall clock. "I've missed the 11 o'clock bus!"

"Don't sweat it," said RJ matter-of-factly. "Take your time. The Panther Brothers have taken care of everything."

After securing the flowery autographs of Reverend Ike on the index cards he had brought, Jonathan bid them good-bye. The senior Joneses sent their Clear Lake cousin on his way with affectionate hugs. Stopping in the middle of the street, Jonathan took a last look at this remarkable household on Heavenly Court. Above them, the cross on the roof glowed, illuminated by the full moon of September 1959.

"It's a special paint," explained AJ, "makes the cross glow in the dark. With no street lights, Daddy makes it easy for his flock to find him anytime, day or night."

The four arrived 25 minutes late for the 11:00 p.m. bus, but true to RJ's word, Otis McCoy and the No. 7 bus to Berkeley were still waiting. Before Jonathan boarded, each of the Jones brothers gave Jonathan a firm handshake

"You got some mighty influential friends, boy," shouted McCoy, the front door of the bus hissing shut.

From his seat, Jonathan waved at his cousins, the three sons of Reverend Ike Jones.

209

Maurice Jackson Jones.
Alonzo Jackson Jones
Reginald Jackson Jones.
MJ, AJ, RJ.
Musician, Athlete, Revolutionary.

36

SHOWING YOUR COLORS

Dressed in billowing black gowns, the faculty of the Berkeley campus of the University of California marched in close formation along the winding curve of Gayley Road, then hiked uphill through the camphor-scented, old growth eucalyptus grove. The academic foot soldiers serpentined into the sunlit bowl of the Greek Theater, filled with spectators, their arrival heralded by the familiar strains of "Pomp and Circumstance, " performed by the University orchestra seated in risers to the rear of the elevated stage.

Among the ten-thousand in attendance, rival factions battled with a war of words.

A plethora of hand scrawled signs dotted the throng.

No! To Loyalty Oaths
Academic Freedom, Yes! Academic Fascism, No!
Down With HUAC Witch Hunts
Commie Hunters, Move to the USSR

In a corner of the Greek Theater, one-hundred Beatniks dressed students held up a large banner demanding *Fair Play for Cuba* and several smaller ones of *Fidel Si!*

In an opposite corner of the outdoor amphitheater, a rival faction of ROT-C cadets dressed in military uniforms held neatly printed signs proclaiming

Fire Disloyal Profs
HUAC = Help Us Annihilate Commies

Down With Fidel and Commie Puppets
President Clayborn Muck -1964

Cadet chants of "Commies Out! Commies Out!" were greeted by the deafening roar of students shouting, "CAL PROFS GREAT! CAL PROFS GREAT! CAL PROFS GREAT!"

The members of the Academic Senate advanced resolutely, warriors ready for battle. Jacob Aural and his dog Sandy D were followed by Garrick Nelquist, the two professors wearing the pure white hood of Cal's largest department, Humanities. A cocky Werner Von Seller, the Prussian Penguin, adorned in the golden yellow hood of Science, strutted at the front of the school's second largest faculty. Aristotle Scott, in the dark blue hood of his discipline, led the stoic members of Philosophy.

Cheers greeted each new phalanx of the processional, each department bearing its own symbolic color emblazoned on ceremonial hoods draped across the shoulders of its members like battle insignia earned from academic campaigns in exotic, distant wars.

The fiery crimson of Journalism. The dignified brown of Fine Arts. The royal purple of Law. The burnished copper of Economics. The pastel pink of Music. The sky blue of Education. The bright orange of Engineering. More than one-hundred academic departments, present and accounted for.

On the grassy lawn above the Greek Theater, banks of media cameras and the Bay Area press dutifully recorded the panoramic spectacle of this extraordinary, emergency meeting of the Cal Academic Senate.

Above the din, the Campanile carillons solemnly announced the time: *Gong. Gong. Gong. Gong.*

As the members of the Academic Senate seated themselves among the one-thousand chairs crowded onto the circular floor of the Greek Theater, Chancellor Roger Haynes made the introductions.

"It is with pleasure, respect, honor, and affection that I introduce your new Chairman of the Academic Senate for the school year 1959-1960, the distinguished, renowned and popular Professor of English, Jacob B. Aural."

A long, sustained standing ovation engulfed Professor Aural and Sandy D.

"Colleagues, ladies and gentlemen, friends of California,"

212

began the blind professor. "We meet here today in the beauty of this glorious fall day, 1959, to debate a burning contemporary issue. In my view, this discussion goes to the core of the purpose of a great university."

"We are here to elicit a collective opinion for or against the upcoming hearings of HUAC, the House Un-American Activities Committee, and, in doing so, the Academic Senate will be taking a position on the suggestion that members of our faculty sign loyalty oaths or be fired."

"Speaking in favor of loyalty oaths and supporting the HUAC hearings, our world expert on atomic research, the acknowledged Father of the atomic bomb, Professor Werner Von Seller."

A mixture of boos and applause greeted the Prussian Penguin as he waddled slowly side-to-side to the podium. Adjusting his monocle, Von Seller spoke in his slightly accented voice.

"You do me great honor, Professor Aural, by permitting me to speak to this august body."

Filled with rotten Communists, Von Seller said to himself.

Von Seller read from a prepared text. "As educators, we must never forget that, as much as we would like to be intellectually chaste and pure, that the life blood of our chosen profession is money, government money."

Hisses emitted from the Beatnik dressed students.

"Without money, we scientists could not perform our important research for the welfare of our marvelous government. Without money there would be no salaries for you humanitarians committed to the pursuit of your so-called Truth."

A barrage of pennies bombarded the stage. Von Seller paused, allowing the protest to dissipate, smiling for the cluster of newspaper photographers at the foot of the stage.

"We ARE an integral part of the military-industrial complex President Eisenhower spoke of, but unlike our ex-president, I find nothing offensive, nothing morally wrong, about our great University playing an important role in that relationship."

Pointing toward the Big C on the crest of the hill above the Greek Theatre, Von Seller said, "The Big C not only stands for our great university, it also stands for our glorious cyclotron and atomic research!" The Prussian Penguin was referring to the huge atom smashing lab above the Greek Theatre.

"We must be the first to harness all the secrets of atomic

research! Yes, colleagues, C FOR CYCLOTRON!"

Von Seller shouted over a chorus of boos. "All around the world, the evil forces of Communism threaten our very existence. The Russians are poised to beat us in the race to outer space. Their surrogates in Cuba, led by that demagogue, Fidel Castro, are only ninety-miles off the coast of Florida. Their minions in Indo-China will soon threaten our strategic interests in Southeast Asia. Our pathetic, weak leadership in Washington has learned very little from our humiliating defeat in Korea."

Laughter greeted Von Seller's list of enemies.

In this fall of 1959, it was smugly assumed by the American public that the initial successes of Russia's 1957 satellites, Sputnik I and II, would be soon surpassed by a revitalized United States space program.

The overthrow of the Cuban dictator Batista by the folk hero Fidel Castro was viewed by liberal college students as merely Cuba's version of the American War of Independence. A poster of Castro's moody second in command, Che Guevara, was a best seller on the Berkeley campus.

Aside from Royal English and the few members of the Department of Oriental Studies, few at the Greek Theater had ever heard of Indo-China, the country which would eventually become Vietnam.

Von Seller removed his monocle and scowled, "What possible harm would come from signing a loyalty oath? Unless there are among us a few real Communists who should never be permitted to contaminate the minds of our best and brightest students!" he shouted, pounding the podium for emphasis.

First, boos and hisses, then more pennies raining down on Von Seller from the Fair Play for Cuba supporters.

Reinserting his monocle, Von Seller thought, *wonderful*! He paused, watching the television cameras filming close-ups of his detractors making utter fools of themselves.

Soon, he told himself, *you misguided dolts, you unwitting pawns, Muck and HUAC will expose your fair-haired heroes, Garrick Nelquist, Aristotle Scott, and even that pious, little Jacob Aural, as leftist Commie sympathizers.*

It will be left to the true patriots like me to save this University from ruin by ensuring that governmental research dollars continue to flow into Cal's coffers to support the inane activities of frivolous departments like Humanities.

Professor Aural interceded, grabbing the microphone "Please! Please!" Sandy barked for emphasis. "Show respect for free speech. Some of you may not like the thoughts expressed by our speakers, but as members of this academic community, you have the obligation, if not duty, to allow them to be expressed. Please allow Professor Von Seller to continue."

Sustained applause from the faculty greeted Professor Aural's admonition, silencing the Fair Play for Cuba group.

"Mark my words," Von Seller warned, "history will prove that the survival of this great institution rested on enthusiastic support for HUAC and loyalty oaths. To paraphrase President Franklin D. Roosevelt, 'we have nothing to fear but fear itself.' "

"Let us surrender our petty intellectual conceits to mature pragmatic concerns," said Von Seller, leaning forward across the podium so his good side, the one with the monocle, that would be clearly seen and photographed.

"Let us sign loyalty oaths and get on with our great work of research and educating our students to the importance of defeating worldwide Communism!"

Raising both his arms and shaking his fists, Von Seller said, "GOD BLESS, HUAC and the PATRIOTIC WORK OF CONGRESSMAN CLAYBORN MUCK!"

The ROT-C cadets rose as one, cheering wildly while new choruses of boos from the Fair Play for Cuba supporters.

In his suite at the Claremont Hotel, Congressman Clayborn Muck paced before the large bay window, listening intently to radio coverage of the meeting of the Academic Senate. In a corner, HUAC's Chief Investigator, Seymour Graft, slouched in a leather chair, feet propped up on a coffee table. Nose twitching, Graft salivated over his most recent photographs of Anna Zarzana.

"Perfect," Muck said aloud. "Yes, more hisses, louder boos, larger coins, you Commie dupes."

I can always count on liberals to ruin wonderful opportunities for public support by behaving like uncivilized boors. Von Seller had done his part splendidly, used the right amount of sympathy for academic pursuits without appearing to be a money groveling researcher, Muck thought.

Muck listened as Von Seller's position was endorsed by brigadier General Hank Rank, Commander of the Cal ROT-C, who was greeted by even more vociferous jeers, boos, and a rain of rotten fruit by the Fair Play for Cuba group, before being silenced by another appeal from Professor Aural.

"Music to the ears, Seymour," crowed Muck. "By tomorrow morning, media coverage of the Academic Senate meeting will focus on the rowdy acts of those left-wing students. The message of HUAC's enemies will be lost in the public outrage against those Beatniks demanding Free Speech for their stupid little causes!"

"Yes, our plan is working to perfection. Public sympathy will grow for us. I can hardly wait for our news conference to be interrupted by Commie sympathizers!"

From the corner of the suite, Seymour Graft applauded, a freshly lit Gaulois dangling from the corner of his mouth.

"Great, Boss. That kid Krum's phony baloney riot will be the frosting on the cake!" he said, pooching a circle into the air, hissing a stream of smoke through its center.

"Seymour," Muck snapped. "Dammit. I've told you not to smoke that foreign crap." Unrolling a limp dollar bill, he said, "Buy a pack of patriotic American cigarettes, like Pall Mall."

As General Rank concluded his remarks, Professor Aural assumed the podium, quieting down the crowd. "Speaking against HUAC and loyalty oaths is our distinguished colleague, Professor Garrick Nelquist."

Enthusiastic applause greeted the Political Scientist.

"Ladies, gentlemen, colleagues," said Garrick Nelquist. "History teaches us another profound lesson, one that we should never forget. The first act of any dictatorship is to shackle its educational system, making it an organ for government propaganda. This country was founded on the fundamental notion that the right of all citizens to speak freely is inviolate. Without the freedom for all Americans to express themselves, our educational system, and ultimately our form of government, would be meaningless."

"Professor Von Seller asks the question, 'What harm would there be in signing a little loyalty oath as a condition of employment?' Sounds innocuous, seems innocent enough. But what constitutes disloyal conduct? Will waving a sign today, asking for Fair Play for Cuba be considered disloyal five years from now when some of you Fidel fans seek employment at Cal?"

Applause emitted from the ranks of the ROT-C cadets.

216

"And what about you ROTC officers? What if someone in power decides that participating in a college military program, such as the ROTC mandatory of all Cal undergraduate men, is disloyal to the educational process?"

The ROT-C cadets grew silent.

Nelquist continued, "Even if reasonably intelligent people could agree on a definition of disloyalty, who is going to decide what conduct is or is not loyal? The FBI? HUAC? Government bureaucrats appointed by the Governor? Administrators? Faculty members? Students?"

"History also teaches us that invariably it is government that assumes this role. We are blessed with the best judicial system the world has ever known, sworn to protect both the interests of government and the rights of the individual. However, I fear that our wonderful system of checks and balances will be skewed in favor of unwarranted government intrusion into academic free speech and thought if loyalty oaths are required."

"No, Professor Von Seller. Loyalty oaths are not harmless pieces of paper. They are, in essence, the antithesis of our great university and the American system of government. I say, NO to loyalty oaths! NO to HUAC's witch hunts, and NO to demagogues like Clayborn Muck!"

"Let's send a clear message to our elected officials, our citizens, and surely to our students to whom we owe a sacred trust. That education cannot be a true instrument of society, unless it remains free from government control!"

In his suite at the Claremont Hotel, Congressman Clayborn Muck listened to sustained ovations interrupting Professor Nelquist's talk. "Nelquist," he said aloud, "you have sealed your own fate."

"He sure has, Boss," said Seymour Graft, slipping nude photos of Anna Zarzana into the secret pocket of his trench coat.

"You pious sonuvabitch," Muck said to the radio. "Do you think the American public believes that education should be placed on some damned pedestal just because you fuzzy, Commie leaning profs say so? You're about to find out what true patriotism is all about, Nelquist. And when HUAC is through, you're going to regret you challenged Clayborn Muck," the Congressman snarled.

When Garrick Nelquist concluded, Ari Scott spoke, supporting his best friend's views by delivering a short version of his famous lecture on *Higher Truth.*

The vote of the Academic Senate was a foregone conclusion. One-hundred forty-two voted in favor of HUAC and loyal oaths, the other eight-hundred sixty-nine members of the Cal Academic Senate voted a resounding "NO!"

"Perfect," said Muck, smiling at Seymour Graft. "Those liberal professors have painted themselves into a corner. When the anti-HUAC demonstrations get ugly, they will be tarred with their stupid, unpatriotic stand."

Graft nodded approvingly, blowing smoke rings from a Pall Mall.

American ciggies taste awful, he thought.

37

WHO YOU ARE, WHAT YOU REPRESENT

"Nice to have my little sis as partner," said Muffy Peachwick, batting her long eyelashes at the perky, blond freshman across the table. Some Gee Dees were assigned new freshman pledges as "little sisters," and Muffy's little sister was Dandy Cane.

Muffy was short with dark flashing eyes and wore her brunette hair in a standard page boy. Muffy's most noticeable qualities were her long, Minnie Mouse eyelashes and, more importantly, a busty profile that was prominent, despite the modesty of the Gee Dee standard, campus uniform. Joan Dildeaux had described both of Muffy's physical attributes - her eyelashes and her bust - as "gravity defying." Knowledgeable fraternity boys referred to Muffy as a "Treasure Chest," something worth digging for.

Although she was on the Dean's academic list, Muffy had learned, growing up in Pacific Palisades, that the currency of the social marketplace was not her brains, but her bust line.

Dandy Cane bore a striking resemblance to her elder sister, Candy, the stewardess, Jonathan and Butch had met on their flight to San Francisco. She had the same honey-colored hair, bright blue eyes, dazzling, white teeth and a deep tan from her summer job as a Zuma Beach lifeguard.

The Gee Dees had entrusted Dandy's welfare to Muffy because of concern that Dandy's physical charms and naive personality would create the kind of salivating interest among fraternity boys that could compromise the virginal image of the House of Beauty.

Although Muffy was sexually provocative, she was skillful in upholding the high standards of Gee Dee public decorum.

"You're so full of it, Muffy-kins," said Joan Dildeaux, crisply shuffling the well-worn deck of cards. "This is probably a setup, and Dandy's another one of your ringers. You'd stoop to anything to win."

"La-dee-dah, Dildeaux, we shall see," said Muffy, sticking out her tongue and flipping her opponent an extended middle finger.

"One spade," Kate said, opening bid.

The foursome, casually dressed in sweatshirts and Bermuda shorts, sat around a square table in the large, spacious room, known as the Pink Palace with its commanding view of the rear courtyard where lovesick boys often serenaded the House of Beauty. In the privacy of this setting, the girls enjoyed the luxury of wearing glasses to play bridge.

In the background, Little Brenda Lee lamented,

. . . *All alone am I, ever since your good-bye,*
All alone with just the beat of my heart . . .

It was ironic that the favorite singer of the House of Beauty was Little Brenda Lee, a teenager who sang passionately of unrequited love and romance lost, her deep nasal twang filling the sorority house with emotional pronouncements such as "You Always Hurt the One You Love," "I'm Sorry," and "I Want to Be Wanted."

While Dandy Cane contemplated her bid, Kate Howell savored her victory at the house meeting earlier that evening. It had been a highly charged session, with emotions running high, but in the end, with the help of Joan, Muffy, Dandy, and especially, Miss Haversham, she had prevailed.

"Two hearts," said the freshman tentatively.

"Three spades," said Joan, following Kate's lead.

"Four clubs," Muffy said boldly, batting her eyelashes.

Casey Lee had suggested the shocking idea during a recent meeting in his room on the eighth floor of Dooch Hall.

"It's the same old thing, year in year out," she had complained. "Same boring freshman ritual, at the same boring Presents party, with the same boring orchestra. It's supposed to be the most exciting evening for a new pledge, but it's more like somebody's funeral," said Kate, waving her hands in frustration. "All that is expected of those poor freshman girls is to look beautiful hoping

220

to meet their Prince Charming. Yuck!"

"You're not worried about a lack of Prince Charmings, are you?" Casey had said teasingly.

Ignoring the affectionate dig, Kate said, "Just tired of remembering who I am and what I represent," referring to the motto of the House of Beauty.

"Are you thinking about something symbolic or something truly radical?" asked Casey, a gleam in his slightly almond eyes.

Kate beamed the famous smile that melted the hearts of men.

"For Gee Dees, either would do," she said. "I'd love to do something unique, fun, and memorable for the '59 Presents."

"What about hiring a rock and roll band?" said Casey. He was joking, of course, as the only kind of music acceptable for sorority Presents was a San Francisco society orchestra performing traditional ballroom music performed under a suspended, spinning mirrored globe.

"I could get the votes for that," said Kate, warming to the thought.

"And if you were really gutsy," said Casey, "you'd hire a Negro rock and roll band."

What a daring idea, she had thought. *With a Negro band, the 1959 Gee Dee Presents would be talk of the Greek system.*

"But how would we find a Negro band?" said Kate, her excitement waning. "I wouldn't know where to begin."

"How about Reverend Ike?" said Casey. "The All Pro produces his Sunday radio sermon for KALX. He'd be happy to arrange a meeting with the Reverend."

"A Negro rock and roll band! Fabulous!" said Joan Dildeaux on learning of Kate's daring idea.

"A super fine shocker," agreed Muffy Peachwick, joining the conspiracy.

Muffy was the expert on Negro music, owning the largest collection of Fats Domino and Little Richard records within the House of Beauty, as well as a bootleg copy of "Gee" by The Crows, a 1954 song banned by Los Angeles radio stations because of its "dirty colored lyrics."

At Casey's request, the All Pro had arranged an audience for the three Gee Dees with Reverend Ike at his office in the Oakland Negro Baptist Church.

Reverend Ike smiled at the delegation of college girls seated around the well-worn desk of his Spartan office. He listened intently, allowing the trio to elaborate on their plan. *Intriguing*, he thought. Unlike his son RJ's radical ideas about social revolution, this proposal was the perfect opportunity for improving racial harmony peacefully, through rock and roll music.

"I have just the group in mind," he said, a hint of pride in his voice. "It's a very popular band in East Oakland known as Big Berry and The Blackouts."

"Perfect," said Kate, unable to conceal her joy. "Quite a catchy name, too," she added, envisioning the engraved Presents invitation reading,

Music by Big Berry and The Black Outs

The campus will be buzzing with the question, who are Big Berry and The Blackouts? Of course, there would be rumors and leaks; and by the time of Presents, they would be mobbed by the curious. Standing room only!

Leaning forward, his hands clasped, Reverend Ike said, "Young ladies, if it would not be an imposition, Mrs. Jones and I would like to attend your Presents party. You see, our son Maurice plays with the band."

"Great," squealed Joan. "We'll announce a special appearance by the one and only, Reverend Ike!"

"With due respect, young lady, I don't want to steal the band's thunder. We'll just keep our visit hush-hush, ok?" he winked.

. "Then it's a deal?" Reverend Ike extended his hand to seal the arrangement.

"Well, not quite," said Kate. "All the girls in the sorority will have to vote on the proposal first." A tinge of embarrassment blushed her finely, chiseled cheeks. "I'll call you right after our next house meeting." The three glanced at each other, sharing the unspoken knowledge that getting a majority vote for Big Berry and The Blackouts would not be easy.

"Your bid, Kate," said Muffy, interrupting Kate's reverie.

"Four spades," said Kate, winking at Joan.

The Gee Dees had voted overwhelmingly in favor Kate's motion to hire Big Berry and The Blackouts.

Only the graduating Seniors dissented. "Remember who we are and what we represent," they had pleaded, raising the fear that the Gee Dees would harm their social station.

"We're entering the 1960's for chrissakes," said Joan Dildeaux,

"Let's move beyond the Dark Ages."

"Who do we listen to on the radio every day?" added Muffy, "Half of all the rock and roll singers are Negro. Why not hire the Real Thing?"

Mrs. Dee Bee McCormick, President of the Gee Dee Alumnae Club, was aghast, "A Negro band? Unheard of! Impossible! What is wrong with Ernie Heckler's Nob Hill Orchestra?"

Mrs. McCormick cast an emphatic, "NO!"

Under sorority house bylaws, Mrs. McCormick's veto was equal to the membership vote. The tie breaker would be made by Miss Willa Haversham, the Gee Dee housemother.

Anticipating Mrs. McCormick's veto, Kate, Joan, and Muffy had met with Miss Haversham secretly to plead their case. In the girls' eyes, Willa Haversham saw the passion and fire of youth that she had once known as a Gee Dee four decades ago.

That old feeling, that faded memory she had neatly swept away so long ago, suffused her.

If only I had been so brave, she mused. *If only I had followed my heart.*

Now, as she was about to cast the deciding vote, Willa Haversham looked out over the eager faces of her young charges. For the second time in her life, she had a chance to do something daring, a gesture to atone for that regrettable decision made so long ago.

In the hushed silence of the Gee Dee living room, Miss Willa Haversham, tears in her eye, cast her vote in a firm, clear voice, "I vote YES for Big Berry and The Blackouts!"

And by doing so, history was about to be made.

"Pass," said Dandy Cane tentatively, hoping she was correctly following Muffy's lead.

"I'm passing too," said Joan.

Muffy hesitated. Batting her eyelashes again at Joan, she said, "What the hell, six clubs."

"Pass," said Kate.

"I better pass," Dandy said gulping. *Six clubs*?

"Pass. Muff, dah-ling," said Joan, winking at Kate. "Let's see what you've really got."

* * *

In her apartment below the Pink Palace, Willa Haversham sat

223

before the vanity staring at the image in the mirror. She wore her silver hair in a severe bun and rarely applied makeup to her ruddy complexion, but the prominent cheek bones and flashing blue eyes hinted of the beauty of her youth.

The muted laughter from the upstairs bridge game floated down to the sanctuary of her apartment. So did the sorrowful words of Little Brenda Lee from the phonograph.

People all around, but I don't hear a sound.
Just the lonely beating of my heart.

Willa Haversham took a discreet sip from the sterling silver chalice filled with the whiskey her distant cousin in Tennessee manufactured, an obscure, sour mash bourbon bottled in a square bottle with a black label, the smooth brown alcohol inducing a familiar warmth and lightheadedness.

The Gee Dees, as well as the alumnae, knew Willa drank alcohol in the privacy of her apartment. But the success of her thirteen-years as Gee Dee housemother commanded respect, and no one questioned her daily toddy of Jack Daniels.

Gazing intently into the mirror, Willa Haversham smoothed the tiny filigree of wrinkles of her face, wiping away the years.

And she remembered.

It was the innocent, giddy era before the First World War.

His name was A. Juan Valdez, a dashing, South American exchange student whom she affectionately called my "Juan and only." With darkly, handsome features, jet black hair and deep brown eyes, Juan had immediately swept the young Willa off her feet. They would marry and move to his family's farm in Brazil. It had seemed so romantic, so right.

When her Gee Dee sorority sisters learned that Willa had fallen in love with a dark-skinned foreigner, they informed her parents, prominent Sacramento tomato ranchers who threatened to remove Willa from Cal if she did not end her romance. It was mere infatuation, her parents said.

The choice seemed so simple, so clear then.

"Remember who you are and what you represent," reminded her sorority sisters.

Bowing to the pressure of family and peers, Willa broke the engagement.

Willa Haversham never married. She dedicated herself to a nursing career, serving with distinction in both World Wars before retiring, accepting the position of Gee Dee housemother.

Over the years, Willa saw Juan twice.

Once at a Saturday movie matinee, she saw him interviewed in a black and white footage of the *Movietone News*, extolling the virtues of his family's coffee bean crop. The second time was his triumphant return to Cal in 1952 to accept the Walter and Elise Haas Medal as Cal's Distinguished Foreign Alumnus of the Year. A. Juan Valdez had become the world's largest coffee bean grower.

Willa had sat mesmerized, like an infatuated school girl sitting in the first row of the Greek Theater, as Juan, still handsome and dashing at the age of sixty, accepted his award, giving a nostalgic, acceptance speech about his Cal student days. She gasped when he referred to "leaving a piece of my heart on this beautiful campus." For a fleeting moment, Juan seemed to pause, smiling briefly, almost recognizing the silver-haired old maid with tears in her eyes. As he took a courtly bow to a standing ovation, the present merged with the past and, in her heart of hearts, she knew he was still her Juan and only.

Little Brenda Lee's plaintive verse interrupted Willa Haversham's reverie.

The words we used to whisper low
No other love can ever bring again.

Picking up the silver chalice, she offered a silent toast to the image in the mirror.

Here's to you, Willa Haversham, whoever you are, and whatever you represent.

She drank deeply of the Jack Daniels.

225

38

CLUES IN THE NIGHT

Consciousness came to Sam Paean in bits and pieces. The warmth of the sun on his back hinted it was almost noon. The hair of the dog on the roof of his mouth said his body was severely dehydrated. His pounding head warned this would be a long day.

Paean stood up, supporting himself on the antique brass headboard. He staggered to the master bath of the spacious flat he had affectionately called "The Pleasure Pad." Unable to relieve himself, he swore aloud, confirming the growing suspicion that he had exceeded the limits of even his own legendary drinking capacity.

Better get some fluids or I'll be hurting all day.

Paean stumbled into the formal bar, the throbbing pain in his head in rhythm to every tortured step. He passed the etched Victorian mirror depicting a cavorting Bacchus. In the lower right-hand corner of the reflecting mural, in flowery handwriting, was a message scrawled in flaming red Max Factor lipstick.

7:30 a.m.
Thanks for the lovely evening, Sam.
Call me at the gallery sometime.
JU 5-6838. - Leslie Colly

After hours of smoking and drinking, she had followed him home, following his fish-tailed Cadillac convertible in her red MG sports car, like a guppy chasing a whale, up the winding streets of Russian Hill. She had evidently stayed the night, but the question of whether he had scored was lost in the blurry haze of martinis and cigarettes.

He mixed a Bloody Mary, topping off the cocktail with drops of a new Louisiana spice called *Tabasco,* a reader had sent him. The tiny bottle contained a fiery red pepper sauce. Paean found that, by adding six to eight drops of the potion to the vodka and tomato juice, the Bloody Mary masked the pounding pain of a hangover.

Relief was only a few sips away.

His innards caught fire, as the elixir worked its magic. Quickly, Paean mixed another, then another.

Paean carried the third Mary to the den commanding a sweeping vista of San Francisco Bay. To the east, the Campanile was a glistening white needle on this glorious fall day. A seductive, gentle zephyr meandered through the open window beckoning Paean back to bed, but the stronger tug of the Column called him to the portable Royal typewriter.

Scraps of paper lay strewn about the Royal, hastily scribbled tidbits of gossip collected from last week's round of bars and restaurants. Most were the usual: plugs for businesses, society gossip, and "aw shucks" tales about Good Samaritans.

One intriguing eyetem was neatly printed on the remnant of a BV cocktail napkin: that a certain popular Cal Philosophy professor was dating a voluptuous younger woman, not his wife.

Tickling the keys of the Royal, Paean typed:

That handsome, distinguished Cal prof squiring that shapely young damsel may think his tete-a-tetes are secret. BUT THE SHADOW KNOWS

Then Paean saw it, a grey piece of paper stuck to the back of a book of matches from the Taddich Grill. Gingerly, he separated the scrap, unfolding the missive. It read:

Check out Leavenworth 42586. Major scandal could blow up HUAC's effort to smear Cal.

He reviewed the clues. Leavenworth was the name of a street

in The City, also a San Francisco telephone exchange. What kind of scandal could derail that demagogue, Clayborn Muck and his HUAC witch hunt?

Better get my trusty research assistant, E Lyn Chamberlin, on this immediately, he thought.

* * *

Gertrude Aldon leaned against the railing of the back porch of the Tudor, gazing at the placid waters of Clear Lake, now empty of the summer throngs. In the coolness of the late October air, a formation of Canadian geese, the vanguard of thousands to come, honked over the small, whale-shaped lake.

The queasy feeling had set in on that fateful day Mike and his wife had come to dinner.

What had possessed Jonathan to be an accomplice to the scandalous visit of her brother-in-law Mike and that woman?

Reverend Leonard Granger's efforts to depict his sister's ordeal as an example of a brave Modern Methodist Mother had failed to provide the solace she craved.

From her upstairs bedroom window, she had secretly watched Jonathan load his suitcases into Mike's green Edsel. Her son's obvious excitement unsettled her.

I raised my son to be God fearing and respectful. Where had Jonathan acquired this stubborn streak of contrariness? It had to be the evil influence of his uncle. If only he had enrolled at an Ivy League school, he would be safe; and she would be free of this gnawing fear.

Jonathan had written every other week, each letter filled with cheerful assurances that school and college life were stimulating and enjoyable. But there were the disturbing bits of news.

Jonathan's Berkeley friends seemed to be a strange, unsavory lot. He was spending a lot of time around that boy from Brooklyn, the one with the Jewish name. How could her son befriend someone of a religion that did not eat pork? And then there were the others with the strange nicknames: the Polish-Mexican hunchback dwarf, a fat boy with the wandering eye, the boy with a girl's name, the bald football player, a Super Sleuth, and the radio disc jockey he described as Rooster Face.

Children can be so cruel in their teasing!

And that Oriental boy, Casey Lee.

228

How could the Dormies elect a Chinese president of the dorm? Casey Lee must have a wholesome, friendly, all-American personality like Charlie Chan's number two son!

The only normal, All-American boys seemed to be Jerry Farthing whose father had also been a member of P U, Tommy Tubbins, the wholesome boy whose favorite expression was "gosh," and that older, patriotic, ex-Army man, Royal French.

Also, that awful business of going to dinner at that Negro minister's home. From the tone of his letter, it sounded as if Jonathan had actually enjoyed himself!

The most unsettling news came in two letters received the past week, one to her husband, Murle, from the president of the Cal P U Alumni Club, the other to her brother, Reverend Leonard Granger, from the minister of the Campus Methodist Church.

According to the first letter, Jonathan had declined several personal invitations to attend P U rush parties. The P U alumni president, Mr. Krum, II, made it clear that such an honor could not be extended indefinitely in light of the acrimonious relationship between the P U's and the Dormies.

Why would anyone have ill feelings about the P U's, Gertrude wondered, *when the P U motto "Brotherhood, Fellowship, and Loyalty" was a noble goal of well-rounded college men? Surely, Jonathan would find common interests with the young men of Pi Upsilon, even if it was that awful rock and roll music!*

The second letter responded to a letter from her brother Reverend Leonard Granger sent on her behalf, inquiring if Jonathan had become a member of the congregation. Shockingly, the minister of the campus Methodist Church had not yet met a Jonathan Aldon. Gertrude shuddered at the thought of her son living in a strange land without the moral guidance of the church.

"A penny for your thoughts, dearest." It was Murle's calm, reassuring voice. Behind him, Cokie, the Aldon family cook, clattered about the spacious modern kitchen preparing dinner.

"I'm really worried about Jonathan, Murle."

"All mothers worry about their children away at college," he said softly. "My mother was a nervous wreck when I left Clear Lake for the Ivy League."

"It's a different situation," said Gertrude. "Attending the Ivy League was safe and proper. Your family didn't worry about temptation or the lack of moral guidance."

"That's because I met you, dearest," he said with a broad smile.

"Who knows what evil influences surround Jonathan? I really don't think he's strong enough to deal with temptations," Gertrude said.

"Now, now. I'm sure there's nothing to worry about," Murle took his wife into his arms, comforting her.

"I should never have let him go to California." Her nose began to twitch. "It was Mike and that woman who poisoned his mind."

He felt her shaking with anger.

"We must do something to make sure he hasn't been led astray, that he's all right," Gertrude sobbed.

"And what might that be?" he asked. In his heart, he already knew his wife's answer.

"We could fly to California, see first hand what kind of life he's living," said Gertrude. "Find out why he's not keeping The Three Promises. We can organize his life for him, as we always have, making sure he's doing all the proper things, introduce him to the minister of the campus Methodist Church, march him right over to the P U house where he belongs."

Her tone perked up. "Harry Senior and Ziggy can run things for a week. Mike can even come down from Minneapolis to help, but," she added, "that woman should not come with him. What would the neighbors think?"

"Shouldn't we tell Jonathan we're coming?" Murle asked.

"No, we'll keep it a secret," said Gertrude, pursing her lips into a thin smile, "and make it a lovely surprise. Jonathan will be thrilled to see us. He's probably terribly homesick by now."

Down the shoreline, from the juke box of the Blue Horizon Inn, Connie Francis sang "My Heart Has a Mind of Its Own."

* * *

"No such address as 42586 Leavenworth, Sam." There was a tone of frustration in the voice of E Lyn Chamberlin, a tall, thin woman in her mid-thirties, dressed modestly in a gray suit and black heels. She was Paean's trusty researcher, the person he affectionately called "Ace" for her dogged and unerring efforts in uncovering tidbits of important information. "Only four digits are used in the street addresses of The City," she sighed. "This

230

number has five."

E Lyn had been a Library Science major at Cal. After marrying and divorcing a staid chemical researcher for Bonnstetter Oil, she had dedicated her life to Paean's research projects, challenges that filled a gnawing void in her life. If the truth were known, she was madly in love with Paean, an unrequited love that would never be reciprocated. She accepted the fact that, despite his notorious womanizing and boozing, the only thing Sam Paean truly loved was the Column.

And in some small way, it gave her great satisfaction to be his right arm, his intellectual soul mate in scoops du jour, punsmanship, and eyetems.

"How about a telephone number, Ace?" said Paean, placing a Lucky Strike in the crook of his ear.

"Another blank, Sam." E Lyn was already ahead of him. "I checked with Bruno Broons, your inside man with the telephone company; and he confirmed that the Leavenworth exchange only begins with the number 7. It's impossible LE 4-2586 is a San Francisco telephone number."

Leavenworth? Possibly a misspelling. What rhymes with Leavenworth? Heavensworth? Seven worth? The clue made no sense at all. Yet, it was so clear and unequivocal "Leavenworth 42586."

"Maybe we're being too provincial," said E Lyn, peering down at Paean, her glasses perched precariously close to the end of her well-defined nose. "Leavenworth may not have anything to do with The City."

Paean mulled over the thought. There were times when he and E Lyn were uncannily on the same wave length. He looked at Ace and for a split second wondered what she would look like if she didn't wear her long hair piled up in that awful bun, if she wore a little makeup, didn't wear those horrible glasses, stopped wearing those Mother Hubbard fashions.

She could be attractive, he thought. *No denying her finely tuned mind and intellect. Forget it, Paean, you're going mad. She's a colleague and friend, not one of your pretty conquests,* pushing the thought out of his mind.

"Any chance Leavenworth's a small town in California?" he asked, switching the Lucky Strike to his other ear.

"Already checked it out, Sam. Drew a blank."

"What about Nevada, Oregon, and Washington?" he asked, remembering that the Sentinel was distributed in neighboring states.

"Beat you to the punch," Ace responded. "Another zero."

There was something obvious to the clue, something gnawingly simple, something staring them right in the face.

"Let's break this down, Ace. We've got a name followed by a five-digit number. Maybe, the numbers are code for something."

"Like letters," Ace interjected. "4-2-5-8-6 could correspond to alphabet letters D-B-E-H-F. No, that doesn't do it."

The light bulb popped on in both their minds simultaneously. Paean yanked the Lucky Strike from his ear, pointing the cigarette at E Lyn, as Ace flipped her glasses off her nose.

"Leavenworth. Leavenworth, Kansas," shouted Paean, feeling a pang of excitement like rising sexual tension.

"The federal prison in Leavenworth, Kansas!" screamed E Lyn.

They embraced, rocking back and forth, sharing the joy of their mutual discovery. They separated awkwardly, realizing that the brief, physical contact had given them a sense of release and pleasure.

"I'll contact the warden at Leavenworth and get the names of all inmates who have ever had the number 42586 and have Senore Millich at the FBI run a background check," said E Lyn, placing her glasses back on the tip of her nose, her cheeks flushed with a glow of embarrassment for their rare show of emotion.

"Perfect," said Paean, patting his loyal Royal typewriter. "Get back to me as soon as possible. Clayborn Muck's called a press conference, and his HUAC hearings aren't far behind."

Paean was now alone in the large closet that served as his office at the Sentinel. The keys to the loyal Royal begged to be tickled, the daily eyetems and sightems of the Column beckoned, but the excitement of tracking the clue to Leavenworth 42586 lingered. A wonderful chance to help his spiritual alma mater, Cal, and the opportunity to expose that demagogue Muck and HUAC for the phony patriotic nonsense they represented.

Yes, his loyalty to Cal stirred very real emotions. And so were these sudden, curious feelings about his trusty researcher, E Lyn Ace Chamberlin.

Must be going daffy in my middle age.

39

PEDRO AND THE ANGEL OF DEATH

From the third-floor study lounge, Jonathan watched the rising October harvest moon bathe the Big C on the eastern foothill in a luminous glow.

The C that stood for Cal now had a different meaning. C, the grade needed to stay in school. C, the difference between getting by and flunking out. C for academic survival.

In high school, Jonathan had taken for granted the ease in which he had maintained a straight A average. At Cal, he learned that all his classmates had enjoyed equally brilliant high school careers and that since every Cal student was expected to perform well, the typical performance of a bright Cal undergraduate student merited only a C. It was only a superior performance that earned a B, and only an exceptional achievement merited an A.

Around the study table, Butch, Tubbins, Fart-ing, and a half-dozen freshmen were hunched shoulder-to-shoulder, the heavy silence punctuated by the rustle of turning pages, the clicking of slide rules, the scratching of scribbling pencils. Professor Jacob Aural's class assignment beckoned, but Jonathan was paralyzed by his pounding heart and his labored breathing. He had become an emotional basket case, his mind reduced to quivering Jello, unnerved by today's sentence from the "Angel of Death."

At noon, hundreds of undergraduates had gathered at Sproul Hall Plaza. In the Campanile, Hunch Hitowski swung among the ropes of the carillons, banging out a funeral dirge, signaling the

233

imminent arrival of the dreaded executioner.

At twelve fifteen, the Angel of Death emerged quietly from between the massive Ionic columns of the Sproul Hall portico. He was a small, thin, middle-aged man with a passive face, a pair of small spectacles perched on his hook nose. He wore a dark suit, starched white shirt, and a thin black tie. In his arms, he carried sheafs of paper that controlled the destiny of undergraduates, the infamous Cinch Notices, the academic death notices to Cal students.

"Doesn't look that creepy," Butch had quipped.

The Angel marched resolutely down the 14 steps of the first flight of steps, the eight steps of the second flight, then the final eight of the third flight, gazing straight ahead, ignoring the restless crowd. Stopping in front of a series of bulletin boards erected like rectangular gallows, the Angel, with an economy of movement honed from years of practice, stabbed the corners of neatly typed sheets of paper with shiny round tacks. Completing his deed in less than fifteen minutes, the Angel of Death paused briefly to view the tidiness of his handiwork and retraced his path, disappearing into the bowels of Sproul Hall, his work complete until the day of his next public execution in the Spring semester of 1960.

Emitting a spontaneous roar, the masses surged toward the bulletin boards bearing the Cinch Notices arranged in alphabetical order.

"Catch ya later, Junior," Butch shouted, pushing against the tide of humanity toward the bulletin board marked with the letters S and T.

Shouts of "Stop pushing! Wait your turn!" filled the air as Jonathan pressed toward the bulletin board marked A and B. Others replied "Hurry up! Move it!" craning their necks, squinting futilely in search of their names. There were a few squeals of relief, but most left, heads downcast, swearing softly.

Jostling to the front of the line, his heart filled with dread, Jonathan found his name on page four of the A's.

Under ALDON, JONATHAN were posted the grim results:

1. English 1A   (3 Units):   "F" (Failing)
2. Poli Sci 1A   (3 Units):   "F" (Failing)
3. Chemistry 1A (5 Units):   "F" (Failing)

4. Rhetoric 10	(3 Units):	"D" (Barely Passing)
5. ROTC	(2 Units):	"D" (Barely Passing)
6. Bus Ad 10	(3 Units):	Dropped

TOTAL DEFICIENCY: 27 UNITS

Minus twenty-seven! Twenty-seven units below a C average!
For a moment, Jonathan felt he was going to vomit, bile
percolating into his mouth, gagging him. He had dropped the Bus
Ad 10 course after the first week of class, finding it difficult, if
not impossible to contend with simple accounting sheet balances.
*How had Ziggy's father, Harry, Sr., maintained the Aldon
Farm books all these years?*
*Failing. Flunking out. How would he explain this to his
parents? To the people of Clear Lake?*
An enormous sense of guilt and shame suffused him.
His friends had fared better. Tubbins had one 3-unit D,
Fart-ing two, three unit D's, and Butch, none at all.

"P-E-D-R-O!"

The distant sound of a long, drawn-out cry from a fraternity
house along Greek row pierced Jonathan's melancholy. A moment
later, the yell was repeated by another unseen voice.

"P-E-D-R-O!"

Soon, P-E-D-R-O was repeated by a third, then a fourth voice.
The cry was taken up by scores, as "P-E-D-R-O! P-E-D-R-O!
P-E-D-R-O!" echoed from living group to living group.
The origin of the Pedro legend is lost in Cal antiquity. The
most popular version was that Pedro was the lost dog of the
University President who promised to cancel exams if the dog
were found.
Another was that Pedro was the handsome lover of the
daughter of Don Jose Domingo Peralta, an early Spanish settler,
who owned all the land in Berkeley. When Pedro disappeared, the
young woman wandered the ranch lands broken-hearted, calling
out his name in vain. On moonlit nights during exams, her ghost
returns and, with the help of students, resumes the search.

A third explanation was that Pedro is the name of a student who dropped dead from the shock of receiving all A's in his exams. In desperation, students call Pedro for help during exams.

"I think the challenge has been hurled, boys. Let's get Pedro out of our system," said Butch, pushing himself away from the study table, opening the sliding glass doors.

Scrambling out onto the third floor balcony, the Dooch freshmen were bombarded by a cacophony of P-E-D-R-O's cascading down Channing Way. The Gee Dees picked it up, and a few moments later several P U's across College Avenue bounced P-E-D-R-O off Dooch Hall.

"Ok, guys, on the count of three," said Butch, "One, Two, Three."

In unison, at the top of their lungs, the Dooch freshmen shouted, in a long, drawn out yell, releasing stress and anxiety of cramming for exams,

"P-E-D-R-O!

W-H-E-R-E T-H-E F-U-C-K

-A-R-E Y-O-U?"

40

LET'S MAKE A DEAL

"Scotty, shouldn't *WE* feed the parrots?" said Cee Cee Chandler Scott. "They sound awfully hungry."

Ari Scott sat amid the lush splendor of the glass conservatory, his mind spinning with the events of the day. Within the indoor jungle of tropical plants and exotic flowers, the blue and gold macaw named Cal squawked, "Go Bears," at the flaming red and white parrot named Stanford, whining, "Polly wants caviar."

The large brown envelope with no return address, marked *Prof. A. Scott - PERSONAL AND CONFIDENTIAL* had been delivered to his office while he offered Brutus breakfast.

As the squirrel scurried away to the ancient Buckeye tree with his booty, Ari unwound the string flap, finding inside three glossy black and white photographs, enlarged to 8 ½ by 11 inches. One was taken on the Berkeley to San Francisco ferry, another at the BV Café, the third at Pinocchio's. In each, Professor Aristotle Scott was captured in animated, enraptured discussion with a stunningly beautiful and radiant Anna Cappuccino Zarzana.

Clipped to the photos was a white index card with a typed message that read:

Meet at O'Wong's at 5pm

Throughout the day, Ari Scott delivered his undergraduate lectures mechanically, like a finely tuned robot, his mind racing with unanswered questions.

Who had been following him? And why? How much did they know about Anna? What did they want?

By 4:30 p.m., he had walked the three blocks along Telly to O'Wong's, the popular campus hangout co-owned by an Irishman who ran the bar and a Chinese immigrant who operated the adjoining cafeteria-style restaurant.

At exactly 5:00 p.m., Ari ordered a Lucky Lager and seated himself in the middle of the restaurant. From the juke box, Elvis sang "It's Now or Never."

My God, he thought. *This is something right out of a B movie plot. Respectable college professor meets sleazy blackmailer*!

Time passed in slow motion, as he scanned the faces of the hungry late, afternoon crush queuing up for the generous mouth-watering platters of food.

Mostly graduate students, a few teaching assistants, and some pseudo-Beatniks, Ari thought. *No one out of the ordinary.*

Ari ordered a second beer and rechecked the time.

5:15 p.m. The mystery photographer was late. He did not notice the lone patron sitting quietly in a darkened corner, puffing a string of smoke rings into the air.

At 5:30 p.m., a busboy delivered a note scrawled on a cocktail napkin.

Professor Scott, join me at the table behind you.

Approaching the darkened corner, Ari squinted at the small form in the darkened corner, most of his face obscured by a wide brimmed hat, smoke swirling around a twitching nose.

"Have a seat, Professor," the man wheezed softly. "Care for a Gaulois?"

Shaking his head, Ari waved away the pungent plumes, now staring at the small, beady eyes beneath the hat.

"Professor, I should congratulate you on your taste in women." The weasel-faced stranger pooched a wobbly ring and hissed a stream of smoke through its center.

"In my professional experience, I've had the pleasure of photographing some mighty pretty girls; but your little Anna is one of the finest pieces of ass I have ever shot."

Angrily, Ari grabbed the stranger by both lapels, jerking him out of his chair. "Listen, you little creep. I don't know who you are or what you want, but you leave her out of this."

"Touchy, touchy, Professor," said Seymour Graft, exhaling

238

smoke through his nose. "People are watching," he said, his tiny eyes flitting from side-to-side. "I'm disappointed. I thought a man of philosophy is ruled by reason, not emotion."

Ari relaxed his grip, allowing Graft to slide back into the shadows. *Control yourself*, Ari thought. *Let's find out what the little weasel wants.*

"I'll make it simple, Professor," said Graft, producing an engraved business card,

Seymour Graft - Chief Investigator
HOUSE UN-AMERICAN ACTIVITIES COMMITTEE

HUAC! The specter of his old Olympic rival, Clayborn Muck, materialized before him.

"As much as the Committee would love to expose your little fling with the daughter of a world famous Commie, Professor, the Committee has bigger fish to catch."

"Who?" said Ari, holding his breath.

"Like your drinking buddy, Garrick Nelquist," said Graft, lighting another Gaulois with a flourish. "A patriotic statement by you at the HUAC hearings, exposing some of Nelquist's Commie activities, and the photos and negatives are yours."

Ari suppressed the urge to throttle the little rodent. "And if I refuse?"

"The choice is totally yours," said Graft, shrugging. "Congressman Muck believes a man of philosophy will know what the Higher Truth will be." He pooched another smoke ring. "So, what's a couple of little white lies compared to," Graft's nose twitched, "having the photos sent to the Missus in a pretty little wrapper?" He paused for dramatic effect. "Or better yet, to her daddy, the esteemed William Randolph Chandler?"

Abruptly grinding the cigarette into an ashtray, Graft said, "Think about it. Philosophize about it, Professor. Let me know. Call me. I'm staying at the Dumphy Hotel."

As Ari fumed, Graft slithered out the rear exit of O'Wong's, a fresh Gaulois dangling from his lips.

At a nearby table, Super Sleuth chugged the rest of his Pabst Blue Ribbon and hurried after Seymour Graft. He had tailed Graft from the Dumphy Hotel, overhearing Graft's threat to blackmail Professor Scott, confirming the elements of the plot he had eavesdropped on at the Morrison Reading Room.

Something has to be done, he thought.

The fates of the beautiful girl and Professor Aristotle Scott hung in the balance.

Better pass the information along to the Dormies, he thought. Yes, leave it in the capable hands of Royal French and Casey Lee to devise a plan to counter Muck and Graft's evil scheme.

41

JACKPOT

"Bingo, Sam! We got it!" said E Lyn Ace Chamberlin, bursting into Sam Paean's office at the San Francisco Sentinel, clutching paper ripped from the teletype. "This just came in from the warden's office at Leavenworth."

For a moment Paean was stunned by the dramatic change in the appearance of his trusty researcher. For the first time in memory, Ace wore makeup, highlighting sparkling eyes he had never noticed before. Gone was the unflattering bun, her hair now styled in a flip that gave definition to her face. A simple black dress and a strand of pearls emphasized her trim figure.

"You look terrific," said Paean, marveling at the dramatic transformation.

"A few tips from Count Edson," said E Lyn, her face blushing. She was referring to the Sentinel's fashion expert whose outspoken opinions commanded a loyal following among the newspaper's female readers.

"What's the scoop?" said Paean, placing an unlit Lucky Strike in the crook of his left ear.

"Dynamite, Sam. Guess who was inmate number 42586 at Leavenworth Federal Penitentiary in 1950?" she asked, holding the teletype against her chest.

"The suspense is killing me," said Paean beaming, enjoying the growing excitement of the new woman before him.

"How about Douglas M. Dufus," she paused, teasing him with

the tidbit. "Dufus served three years for selling pornographic photographs across state lines."

"Dufus?" said Paean racking his memory for a connection. "Dufus doesn't sound familiar."

". . . who is now known as . . . ," "Ace paused, "Seymour Graft!" she shouted. "HUAC's Chief Investigator."

"Holy cow," said Paean, feeling a rush of adrenaline. "Are you sure? Muck's right-hand man, a convicted pornographer?"

"Your buddy, Senore Millich, at the FBI, found this at the courthouse in Topeka," said E Lyn, handing Paean an official looking document. "Douglas M. Dufus had his name formally changed to "Seymour Graft" after leaving Leavenworth, then moved to Pittsburgh where he became a private eye."

"Do you think Muck knows about Graft's past?" In his mind, Paean was already formulating the intro for this blockbuster eyetem for The Column.

"Probably not," Ace replied. "Graft joined Muck's House Re-Election Campaign in 1954, as a political snoop digging up dirt on Muck's opponent. Since then he's ridden on Muck's coat tails, worming his way up to Chief Investigator of HUAC."

"Great work, Ace, said Paean pausing before asking, "I think I owe you for this. How about dinner at Trader Dick's? Seven, tonight?"

"I'd love it, Sam," Ace said, exiting, leaving behind a hint of Chanel No. 5.

What a fine kettle of fish, he thought, envisioning the eyetem for Sam's Paean to The City:

> *. . . A TALE OF TWO STRANGE BEDFELLOWS.*
> *Clayborn Muck, chief accuser for the House Un-*
> *American Activities Committee and self-proclaimed*
> *guardian of America's public morals, will soil his*
> *demagogic pants for keeping on HUAC's payroll*
> *Seymour Graft, once known as Douglas M. Dufus,*
> *an ex-con with a prurient taste for X-rated photos.*
> *Dufus/Graft was once convict number 42586*
> *at Leavenworth Fed Pen for peddling porno pix*
> *across state lines, but The Shadow Knows! Does*
> *this mean Muck believes free speech embraces*
> *pornography but not political dissent? Stay tuned*

as the murky, Muck-y plot thickens . . .

* * *

"What a fucking asshole!" The epithet shattered the dignity of the wood paneled office of the Political Science Department. Tamping tobacco into his meerschaum, Garrick Nelquist held a match over the porcelain bowl and drew three quick puffs. "Haven't been this pissed since I was sucker-punched in the quarter finals of the college boxing championship."

Seated across the massive mahogany desk, Ari Scott felt an enormous sense of relief. He had spent a sleepless night in the glass conservatory, agonizing over the impact of the impending disclosure on his well-ordered life, envisioning the scandalous newspaper headlines,

Cal Prof's Commie Love Child!
Great Scott's Scandalous Past!
William Randolph Chandler's Bastard Grandchild!

Yet, he had concluded there was only one choice to his dilemma.

Ari had come directly to Garrick's office after leaving the note for Seymour Graft at the Dumphy Hotel. The handwritten message had been simple and direct.

The answer is <u>NO</u>!
I refuse to be blackmailed
Damn the consequences.

"Ari, if you had knuckled under, I would have been madder than hell, but I would have understood. You've got a lot of personal shit at stake here."

"Personal shit, bull shit, Garrick." said Ari. "It's all the same. I've got a past I can't escape and a family I'm going to lose."

"Cee Cee's a little high strung, but she wouldn't leave you over Anna," said Garrick with a tone of uncertainty.

"It'll be up to the Old Man," said Ari. "If he thinks a public flap about Anna will harm his gubernatorial campaign, he'll have Cee Cee leave me, hoping to get some political mileage by

243

portraying her as victim of his son-in-law's youthful indiscretion. If public disclosure of Anna's identity generates sympathy, the Old Man will grandstand by accepting Anna into the family but distancing himself from her Communist stepfather, Pablo Zarzana."

"Cynical old fart," said Garrick, puffing furiously on the meerschaum. "Don't know who's worse. Clayborn Muck or William Randolph Chandler."

"Birds of a feather, Garrick. The difference is Muck's hate for me is skewing his judgment. Possibly we can use it to our advantage. The Old Man is a different story. He's driven by political expediency. If he decides I'm a liability, I'll soon be his ex-son-in-law."

Ari cringed at the fallout from Seymour Graft's photos. *What price will I be paying for my Higher Truth?*

42

FOR WHOM THE BELLS TOLD

"Gosh, I'm bushed. How much farther?" Tommy Tubbins' question echoed off the recesses of the dimly lit stairwell, as he struggled to keep up with the single file of boys.

"Halfway there," said Hunch Hitowski, bounding sprightly, two steps at a time, his round hunchback bobbing at the head of the line.

Toting duffel bags, the Frosh quartet had struggled to keep up with the tiny bell ringer, reaching only level five of the bell tower.

They were using the stairwell, rather than the Campanile's public elevator, to avoid detection.

"I'm dying. Can we stop?" said Jerry Fart-ing, slumping down on a landing. He was soon joined by Jonathan and Tubbins.

"Frosh wimps," said Hunch peering over a railing a flight above. "Try doing this every day."

"Shit, this is a real killer,"panted Butch, leaning against a wall, sweat streaming down his face, "tougher than laps the basketball team does up to the Big C."

"Now I know why they call the Campanile, Peder Sather's Greatest Erection," said Jonathan, catching his breath. "Once he got this big thing up, he died of exhaustion."

Their destination was the latest RF from the creative mind of Royal French.

At their last house meeting, the Dormies had voted unanimously to endorse the vote of the Academic Senate and condemn the upcoming HUAC hearings.

"Most Dormies wouldn't be here today if Professors Scott, Nelquist, and Jacobs hadn't pushed through changes in Cal's admissions policy," explained Casey Lee, "and fought for the money to build Dooch, our concrete fish bowl."

As they rested, Hunch rattled off a string of Campanile facts. The tower had been completed in 1915 after the Great San Francisco Earthquake and consisted of 2,808 blocks of California granite embedded with diagonal steel bracing, making the Campanile the safest structure on campus. Modeled after the famous bell tower in Saint Mark's Plaza in Venice, the Campanile was 34 square feet at its base and tapered up to its 30 square foot belfry. Its 31 flights of stairs made the bell tower taller than the length of a football field.

"Jeez, look at all the bones!" said Butch, peering through the window of a door on a landing.

Hunch smiled. "This, you gotta see," said the tiny hunchback, admitting the four freshmen into a large, dimly lit room stacked with large crates of skulls, tusks, and teeth, all neatly numbered and catalogued.

"This bone zoo is one of the surprises of my tours of the Campanile," Hunch said with pride. "Cal's got one of the largest collections of prehistoric bones in the world, 50 tons of the stuff stored here in the middle six floors. Dinosaurs, mastodons, we've got 'em all."

"Perfect," said Butch. "Peder Sather's Greatest Erection is truly the world's biggest boner."

Resuming the climb, the group felt a vibration, a persistent, rhythmic, grinding moan.

"The hands of the clocks ticking off the minutes," Hunch explained. "The tower clocks are the largest in Northern California. Each is 17 feet in diameter with bronze Roman numerals and eight and a half foot wooden hands.

Pointing to a large key protruding from the wall, Hunch said, "like grandfather clocks they're hand wound with huge mother weights hanging down several floors."

At the top of a landing, Hunch opened a lacquered wooden door, ushering the group into the sitting room to a suite of offices.

"The best amenities on campus, including this bitchin view," said Hunch, standing next to a tall, vertical window with a commanding vista of San Francisco Bay.

"We've got a sound proof practice room, a special library filled with volumes of carillon, sheet music, and equipment to tape every performance."

"Jeez," said Butch, marveling at the shower and kitchenette "This is a friggin' high-rise country club."

"Gentlemen," Hunch bowed to the tiny figure. "May I present my mentor and inspiration, the head honcho and real boss of the Campanile, Miss Betty Burdick, chime mistress."

"Oh, Hunch, you make me blush with your nonsense. But at my age, I'll take all the sweet talk I can get."

Miss Burdick was a gaunt wisp of a woman with a shock of white hair and sparkling blue eyes. A Cal graduate of 1899, Miss Burdick had been chime mistress of the Campanile for more than 50 years, banging out tunes on the 12 original bells and now supervising Hunch in playing the new carillons.

"Hunch, about this prank you boys are pulling off, what do you call it? RF? What does RF stand for?"

"Eh," stammered Hunch, grasping for a plausible lie. "RF? RF stands for Riot Function. It's slang like 'cool' or 'daddy-o.'"

The freshmen looked uneasily at their shoes, relieved that they had avoided explaining the literal meaning of the term RF.

"If the campus police ask, I know nothing and certainly saw nothing. With HUAC and all this Commie nonsense, we've got to lighten things up."

Putting her frail arm around Hunch's back, Miss Burdick whispered, "The only thing I ask is, please be careful." She winked. Raising a fist, she shouted, "Go Bears!"

"Go Bears,' the Dormies replied.

As the group approached their destination, the boys counted aloud the final steps to the top, "313 . . . 314 . . . 315 . . . 316."

"We're here," said Hunch, pushing open the door to the belfry, a brisk sea breeze cooling them after their sweaty ascent.

On each side, three arcades, more than 20 feet high, arched above the tops of Corinthian columns, framing breathtaking views of the Bay Area.

"The Farrallons," said Hunch, pointing to several tiny dots beyond the Golden Gate 20 miles away.

"Gosh, people down there look like ants," said Tubbins peering over the railing at pedestrians scurrying through the esplanade.

Hunch described how the ceiling of the belfry and the arches of the arcades were fashioned from curved, solid pieces of California granite and paneled with classical Italian ornamentation of coffers with rosettes. Towering above them, clusters of bells of varying sizes were suspended in orderly rows by an intricate network of braces.

"We've got a five-octave range," said Hunch. "The smallest bell is 29 pounds and has the highest tone. The bigger the size, the lower the tone." Hunch pointed to the largest. "That moose, named Bourdon, is middle C and weighs 4118 pounds."

"The original 12 bells, the rusty looking ones in the corner tiers, were made in France," said Hunch, pointing to a dozen covered with a green patina of oxidation. "The newer ones, the ones that are still bronze colored were cast in England."

"This," said Hunch with pride, "is the playing cabin."

He ushered the quartet into a glass room in the center of the belfry. Inside the cramped enclosure stood a golden oak console, resembling an upright piano with rows of large, wooden batons jutting above a network of 29 foot pedals.

Hunch pointed to clappers inside the bells attached to a web of wires and ropes crisscrossing down to the wooden levers.

"These levers are arranged like the keyboard of an organ. Someone as tiny as Miss Murdock can play the carillons by pushing down on the levers and stepping on the pedals attached to a pulley system with powerful springs that work the clappers inside the bells."

"However, I prefer to play my concerts this way," said Hunch, pressing a button, releasing the wiring apparatus from the wooden levers, freeing the ropes to the clappers, now swinging a few feet above the console. Hopping onto a narrow rampart around the glass siding of the playing cabin, Hunch nimbly swung from rope to rope, banging the bells in deafening, rhythmic flight, shaking the belfry like a musical earthquake.

"Keeps me fit," said Hunch, dropping down to the rampart.

Suddenly, a solitary bell struck twice, shaking the floor of the belfry.

"2:00 p.m., guys," said Hunch. "Time for the afternoon concert." The little hunchback swung into action, beginning his first selection of the afternoon concert.

The quartet watched transfixed, as Hunch deftly flew from bell to bell, swinging like the famous daring young man on a flying trapeze.

Pausing for a moment, Hunch reminded them, "You have only 18 minutes to complete the RF by the time my concert ends at 2:20 p.m."

Hunch resumed his aerobatic concert, swinging gracefully among the carillons, as the freshmen hurriedly emptied coils of ropes and folded swatches of black cloth from the duffel bags.

Butch and Tubbins quickly looped ends of the ropes around the upper railing of the balustrade on the west side of the Campanile, anchoring them to their bodies while Jonathan and Fart-ing carefully secured the other ends snugly around their waists.

"Take it easy, guys. You don't have that far to go," said Butch, patting Jonathan and Fart-ing on the shoulder. "Whatever you do, don't look down!"

Butch and Tubbins gripped the ends of the ropes tightly, bracing their feet along the base of the balustrade, as Jonathan and Fart-ing eased over the railing, inching slowly, step by step, with the black swatches slung over their shoulders.

Earlier, Royal French had explained, "Since the Campanile is visible for miles, we'll turn it into a billboard for our message."

Royal had estimated that the distance from the railing to the face of the Campanile clocks was about 20 feet. When the minute hand was between 2 p.m. and 2:10 p.m., it would be easy for Jonathan and Fart-ing to affix the two larger black swatches outside the perimeter of the clock. The more delicate move would be attempted at 2:15 p.m. when the minute hand was perpendicular, allowing the two to sidestep into the interior of the dial. There, they would attach the two smaller black swatches near the Roman numerals II and X.

The four had practiced the maneuver in the evenings after study hall, lowering themselves out of Royal's eighth floor window, scaling down to the sixth floor and back.

Now, the two freshmen gingerly repelled down to their first stop as a chilly Bay breeze buffeted them, rocking them from side-to-side. Tethered by Butch, Jonathan bobbed along the right side of the clock. Fart-ing, suspended by Tubbins, bounced slowly down the left side.

Using small hammers, the dangling duo carefully attached the larger black swatches to the surface of the Campanile, tacking pitons into the natural cracks and crevices of the granite. The wind hissed insistently beneath the flapping, black swatches, but the pitons held.

"Ready?" Fart-ing shouted, pointing toward the minute hand 2:12 p.m.

Above, Butch and Tubbins waved, slackening their ends of the ropes, dropping their comrades another ten feet. Jonathan gave a thumbs up, and the two Dormies inched in a slow sidestep toward the interior of the clock. They felt the tremor of the low, grinding moan of the clock's internal mechanism, the hand advancing another minute.

2:13 p.m.

Up close, the hands of the clocks were dark green. The sharpened tip of the minute hand was the tapered end of a Sitka spruce milled in Belgium. The log, two feet in diameter, loomed close to Jonathan's waist, blocking his path. He could allow the minute hand to level off to 2:15 p.m.; but if he waited, there wouldn't be enough time to finish the RF and scamper back up to the belfry by the 2:20 p.m. deadline.

Jonathan saw Fart-ing, unimpeded by either of the clock's hands, reach his designated spot inside the Roman numeral X. He had no choice.

Gotta climb onto the minute hand, he told himself.

Jonathan steadied himself on the log. Just then a sudden gust blew him directly toward the pointed tip.

Swinging too fast to stop, he thought. *Gonna crunch my balls!* Jonathan screamed to himself.

Flailing desperately, Jonathan arched his back, thrusting his legs high as possible, his buttocks smashing onto the tip of the minute hand, contact barely missing his groin. He heard the sound of tearing blue jeans, and felt a blast of cold air on his exposed buttocks. Shaking, Jonathan lowered his legs onto the tip of the log. Firmly astride, he scooted on his haunches to the mid point of the minute hand.

2:15 p.m.

Rising slowly, leaning against the side of the tower, Jonathan worked feverishly, tacking up the smaller black swatch as the minute hand droned on, grinding out another minute.

2:16 p.m.

250

Balance was now difficult, the minute hand was beginning its downward tilt. A layer of goose bumps spouted across Jonathan's bare bottom.

"Hurry," Fart-ing shouted, bouncing step by step back to the belfry with the help of Tubbins tugging mightily on the other end of the rope.

There! Done!

Jonathan pushed the hammer into his belt loop. The minute hand moaned, slipping down another notch.

2:17 p.m.

Sliding downward on the angled surface, Jonathan stumbled, then lurched backwards in heady, numbing free fall. Tumbling, he caught a glimpse of South Hall's roof and the brick herringbone pattern of the esplanade rushing up to meet him.

Gonna die, he screamed to himself. The sensation felt like an upside down carnival ride suffusing his body. *Bye, Ziggy*, he thought, squeezing his eyes shut.

Sudden, violent pain to his waist, as air rushed from his lungs, the rope jerking violently, bouncing his body against the surface of the clock. Panting, Jonathan slowly opened his eyes. A few inches in front of him was the Roman numeral V of the clock's dial. Looking up he saw Butch's grinning face, his massive hands firmly clutching the end of the tether.

"Get your bare ass in gear, Junior," shouted Butch.

Within seconds, Tubbins and Fart-ing joined Butch in hoisting Jonathan toward safety. With a mighty tug from all three, he clambered back over the point of the minute hand.

2:18 p.m.

Still time to escape.

Leaping over the railing, Jonathan hugged the trio.

"Don't be such a hero next time," said Fart-ing.

"Gosh, some guys will do anything to avoid those stairs," added Tubbins.

"Lucky you ripped your britches, Junior, or it'd be full of shit," grinned Butch.

The quartet added the final touch to the RF, unfurling a long, white banner over the railing next to their handiwork.

"Get the hell out of here," shouted Hunch, pausing before the final selection of his afternoon concert. "Time to add my musical touch to Royal's Campanile RF."

251

The four commandos dashed through the doorway of the belfry, echoes of their whooping and hollering reverberating through the recesses of the Campanile's steep, narrow stairway.

* * *

In Stephens Hall, Aristotle Scott paced his office in troubled thought. The upcoming confrontation with Muck and HUAC consumed his every waking moment. Anna, Cee Cee, his children, Marc and Monique, the Old Man, and Garrick were all players in a drama spinning crazily out of control.

What would happen to his family? To his career?

The carillons issued a popular child's song. Curious, Ari pushed aside the opaque curtain, gazing up at the Campanile, his face breaking into a broad smile. Uncontrollable laughter gripped him, his body shaking with joy.

Thank God for Cal student humor, he thought, wiping away tears of laughter.

The dial of the Campanile clock had been turned into the face of a popular cartoon mouse. Large, round black circles along the sides of the clock formed the distinctive ears. Inside the clock dial were two black eyes. Fluttering beside the rodent's happy face was a large white banner proclaiming,

HUAC = MICKEY!
CAL = GREAT!

Atop the Campanile, Hunch Hitowski swung effortlessly from bell to bell, ringing out a bouncy rendition of the mouse's popular television theme heard weekly throughout the homes of America.

Ari hummed the familiar tune filling the campus sky. When Hunch launched the Campanile bells into the ten note chorus, Ari spoke the first three letters of the celebrity name aloud, his spirits soaring. He then sang the remaining three letters of the rodent's name, the melody unlocking and releasing the fear he no longer felt. As Hunch banged out the final five notes, Ari shouted slowly, at the top of his lungs.

"M - O - U - S - E!"

43

SURPRISE, SURPRISE

"This is a big day for Pi Upsilon," said Dirk Krum, surveying the living room packed with P U fraternity brothers, snapping their fingers in approval. With the exception of Graduate Advisor, Chauncey Remington, the P U's were dressed in faded blue jeans, black T-shirts, black berets, and dark glasses, their crewcuts hidden beneath long-haired wigs, fake beards and moustaches.

The outside doors of the P U house had been locked, every drape drawn. A large sign in the bay window read,

Fraternity House Meeting-Do Not Disturb.

"By disrupting Congressman Muck's press conference, we'll build public sympathy for HUAC's patriotic cause," said Krum, the P U's snapping their fingers in approval. "And placing the blame on left wing pinkos will go a long way in ridding Cal of undesirable elements. First, fuzzy minded liberal professors, then Dormies!" he shouted, the finger snapping reaching a crescendo.

"At the press conference, aim your rotten eggs at Congressman Muck and Professor Von Seller. We want the newspapers and television cameras to have good closeups of the attack." A cruel sneer crept across Krum's face. "And for good measure, Chip and the upper classmen will set off their stink bombs."

"Bitchin, bitchin," said Fist, unable to control his glee.

Krum continued. "We'll use an old moving van that can't be

traced. HUAC's Chief Investigator, will drive the clunker with a police escort so we can park right next to the press conference and make good our escape." The P U's snapped their fingers wildly.

Krum nodded at their P U graduate advisor. "Chauncey will stay behind to provide us an alibi and cover the house phone."

From the driveway behind the P U house, a deep honk sounded.

"It's here," a pledge shouted. "The van is backing right up to the kitchen door."

"Ok, P U's, let's go!" said Krum, leading the Beatnik looking group out.

"P U's rule!" shouted Fist.

Remington watched the P U's pile into the rear of the ancient moving van, packing the compartment like bearded sardines. He gave a thumbs up to the driver hissing smoke rings from beneath a wide brim hat. Remington noted hornrimmed glasses perched on a large bulbous nose.

Seymour Graft, HUAC's Chief Investigator, is rather youthful looking. Could pass for a college age student, Remington thought.

A few moments later, Fist hoisted the rusty chain, closing shut the rear door of the van. As the engine coughed, then growled to a start, a uniformed officer appeared astride a motor scooter, motioning the driver to follow.

Strange. I thought policemen ride motorcycles, not Vespas, Remington thought.

As the officer turned his head looking for cross traffic, the P U graduate advisor thought he recognized him. *Resembles that Meter Mel who enjoys ticketing fraternity men's sports cars*, he thought. *But no, it can't be,* he concluded.

A few moments after the van and its escort sped out of sight, a yellow cab skidded to a stop in front of the P U driveway. Behind the cab, two uniformed officers balanced themselves on motorcycles. Throwing crumpled dollar bills at the cabbie, a small man hurried up the driveway.

"Got here as fast as I could," he wheezed. "You a P U?"

"Graduate Advisor," Remington replied, looking down on a second man wearing a tan trench coat and a wide brim hat, a Gaulois cigarette dangling from his bottom lip.

"Seymour Graft, Chief Investigator for HUAC," he said, producing a dog-eared business card from the pocket of his trench coat. "Where the hell is Dirk Krum? Got some bad news for you frat boys."

"They just took off," said Remington, describing the arrival, loading up, and departure of the ancient van and its police escort.

"Impossible!" shouted Graft, his nose now twitching, his breathing labored. "Some prick just stole the damned moving van from the lot next to the Dumphy Hotel! The boss will really be pissed about this."

"If you're Seymour Graft, who was the driver of the van?" said Remington, suddenly realizing something was terribly wrong.

* * *

From the eighth floor of Dooch Hall, Casey Lee and Royal French had closely followed the frenzied activity at the P U house through Royal's telescope.

"Congrats, Royal," Casey chuckled, "another brilliant RF in the making. Simple but effective. By the time Dirk and the P U's reach their destination, they'll be in no position to disrupt the HUAC press conference."

"Using Rod Organ, the San Francisco cabby friend of Aldon and Tanenbloom's to double as Seymour Graft was an inspired idea of the two frosh," said Royal."Did you see those God awful Beatnik disguises? Phony as three-dollar bills. They wouldn't have fooled a soul. Looked like discards from a bad Halloween party."

"I thought Super Sleuth was exaggerating in his description of Seymour Graft," said Casey, "but he really does look like a weasel!"

"Yeah," replied Royal, "if I looked that creepy, I'd hide in a trench coat and a big hat too!"

* * *

"Seymour, you incompetent idiot! How could someone steal that fucking van from under your nose?"

Clayborn Muck angrily rustled the morning edition of the San Francisco <u>Sentinel</u> pointing to the banner headline,

SAM PAEAN EXCLUSIVE: PHONY
BEATNIKS INVADE NORTH BEACH

255

On the front page was a large photo capturing the P U's frantic exit from the old, dilapidated moving van. In the foreground, a young man in a beret and dark glasses futilely attempted to put an outstretched hand in front of the camera lens. Despite the wig and moustache, it was the distinct face of Dirk Krum, frozen in a dazed, wide-eyed sneer.

"But Boss, let me explain,"

"Shut up, you fool. There's nothing to explain," said Muck, his voice rising in frustration. "The HUAC press conference was a zero, a bust. Look, it's buried way back here on page four under a tiny headline,

Cool Reception for HUAC

"Without that riot, we didn't generate one ounce of public sympathy!"

"Listen to this disaster," said Professor Werner Von Seller, standing by the bay window of Muck's hotel suite. "It would be almost amusing, if it wasn't so pathetic."

Von Seller read aloud Sam Paean's account of the P U foray, his deep, Teutonic-accented voice calm, almost soothing.

Yesterday, during the busy Friday lunch hour, City police arrested dozens of unidentified young men as they burst from a moving van parked in front of The City Lights Bookstore. Disguised as Beatniks and armed with scores of rotten eggs and stink bombs, the unidentified group surrendered peacefully, surprised by the appearance of the police.

Adjusting his monocle, Von Seller said, "Unfortunately, this incident played right into Sam Paean's putrid, purple writing style," he sighed, continuing to read aloud.

Tipped by an anonymous call about a possible riot on Broadway, police units, supported by attack dogs and firemen, quickly surrounded the vehicle. Paddy wagons whisked the mysterious men to city jail, where all were booked and charged with mayhem and malicious mischief.

The ragtag group was released after socially prominent San Francisco business man, Dirk Krum II, posted fifty-thousand dollars bail. Krum did not return phone calls placed to his office.

Although the motive for the incident remains unclear, police officials speculate the ill-fated assault involved a Cal fraternity

initiation rite. However, Da Shadow Knows that the true story behind the botched scheme involved a sinister plot to muck up a certain Congressional press conference to garner sympathy for that visiting whew-ack trying to stir up a phony Red Scare.

"Where the hell is this newspaper guy, Paean, getting all this stuff on us, Boss?" said Graft, an unlit Gaulois dangling from his lips.

"You're the expert. You tell me."Muck shouted.

Regaining his composure, Muck said, "Make sure Cee Cee Scott gets a set of those photos of her husband cavorting with his young Commie girlfriend. When the Old Man finds out Ari's been cheating on his darling Cee Cee, all hell's gonna break loose," said Muck, savoring the thought of his long awaited revenge on the so-called Great Scott.

"Piece of cake, Boss. I'll slip 'em into the front seat of her Caddy El Dorado."

"I'm warning you, Seymour. One more screw up, one more news leak, and you're fired. Understand?"

"No chance of that happening, Boss."

Across the room, the Prussian Penguin folded the newspaper neatly, gazing intently at Alcatraz, the tiny island prison sitting in the middle of San Francisco Bay.

Yes, he said to himself, *one more mistake, one more embarrassment, and I will have to quickly distance myself from these fools. Supporting Congressman Clayborn Muck and HUAC may not have been the best way to advance the cause of atomic research, after all!*

257

44

TRUTH AND CONSEQUENCES

"Daddy, what should I do?" said Cee Cee Chandler Scott, dabbing away tears. There was something reassuring about the masculine feel of this office with its well-worn leather chairs, its warm glow of Tiffany lamps, the faint hint of Cuban cigar smoke. Cee Cee had spent her early childhood playing with her dolls in the deep piled carpet, while very important people talked to Daddy about very important problems of the world.

Daddy will find a way out of this mess, she thought.

"Some horrible person put these awful photos in my Caddy last night," Cee Cee sniffled. "Ari has been acting strangely lately, and I thought it was the pressure of those HUAC hearings." More tears flowed. "But Daddy, I had no idea he was having an affair!"

She produced a fresh silk handkerchief. "She must be one of his graduate students. She's so young," Cee Cee sobbed, "and so pretty."

"Now, now, honey," said the Old Man, patting his daughter's shoulders awkwardly.

Damn, he swore to himself. He had never been comfortable dealing with female emotions.

Studying the large black and white photographs arranged neatly in a row on his desk, he thought, *at least the conniving bastard has good taste. She is a knockout.*

William Randolph Chandler was a tall, big-boned man with broad shoulders and large hands. A thick shock of silver hair framed a well-chiseled face he enjoyed profiling and deep-set eyes he used to intimidate his many adversaries.

He ran his newspaper, the San Francisco <u>Gazette</u>, with a heavy hand, subjecting readers to his highly opinionated views on issues, causes, and crusades, casting fire and brimstone with the best. For years, he had backed spineless, numbskulled candidates for public office. Now William Randolph Chandler was about to realize his own dream, of becoming Governor of California. The last thing he needed was an embarrassment to the campaign. The Chandlers could not be viewed as condoning infidelity or adultery! No, he had to distance himself from this scandal as quickly as possible.

"No note?" he asked.

"Oh, yes, Daddy." Cee Cee unfolded a crumpled piece of paper from her purse. "I was in such shock, I almost threw this away."

The Old Man had seen extortion notes shared by members of the Pacific Union Club, cheap, clumsy shakedown efforts. A discreet delivery of money somewhere along the Montgomery Street business district, and the black and white negatives would appear in an unmarked envelope. Domestic peace and tranquility bought for a few hundred dollars. Another marriage saved.

He studied the neatly typed message.

What will your father think of the Higher Truth
of your husband's secret?

Odd, he thought. *This one doesn't ask for money. Ari's indiscretion seemed to be aimed more at him than Cee Cee. Why?*

"Honey, you and the children must leave Ari."

"But Daddy, only movie stars get divorced," she wailed. "How can I start a new life without a husband to support me."

"Let's not worry about money," said the Old Man in a soothing voice. "I'll put you on the election committee payroll as an executive secretary. You'll join me on the campaign trail. You'll meet the most eligible bachelors in the state who will fall all over each other for the chance to know the beautiful daughter of the future Governor."

"You'll get over Ari. Soon you'll understand how this little hurt was the best thing that ever happened to you." He jutted the famous profile and said, "I always thought you were too good for a common college professor."

* * *

"My God, Murle, look at all the weirdos!" said Gertrude Aldon, clinging tightly to her husband. During the CAT flight from Minneapolis, an uncontrollable fear had gripped her, of what she would find in California, the kind of uncontrollable dread she felt awaiting the arrival of her brother-in-law Mike and that woman that fateful day in Clear Lake. It was the same terror she experienced in those nightmares about Jonathan bringing home a girl from the cover of National Geographic.

"Should be a limit on foreigners in America, Murle," said Gertrude. Her nose twitched, as she gaped at the noisy hordes dressed in exotic clothing, swirling around them at the San Francisco International Airport.

Wearing her sable mink coat, Gertrude felt vulnerable, almost alien. "Can we get away from this horrible place?"

"Now, now, dearest, there's nothing to worry about," said her husband, patting her hand. "The porter said it's an easy taxi ride to Berkeley."

"Nice of that Mr. Krum II of the P U Alumni to make us reservations near campus," said Murle. "He said that in this day and age, it's getting awfully difficult to find boys of sterling P U quality, especially legacies, like Jonathan. Those were the exact words Mr. Krum II used, dearest, 'of sterling P U quality.'"

He beamed at his wife. "With his help, Jonathan is sure to pledge the P U house."

"And join the Campus Methodist Church," added Gertrude. "Jonathan needs spiritual guidance." She frowned at a group of bald Orientals dressed in flowing orange robes.

"Look over there, dearest," said Murle, pointing at an unusual taxi, an old station wagon with broad, wooden panels trimmed in yellow and chrome, bearing a crudely handwritten sign,

Starving Student Needs Work-Cheap Fares & Tours

"Let's help the young man out, Gertrude."

"I don't know, Murle," said Gertrude, taking stock of the cab driver's torn chinos, long black socks, and tattered T-shirt. "He doesn't look very reputable to me. He could be one of those Beat-hicks."

"We're in 'Frisco, dearest. Let's have a little adventure, go

260

Bohemian." Murle Aldon waved at the skinny cabby sitting on the hood of the woodie reading a <u>Playboy</u> magazine.

"Taxi! Can you take us to the University of California?" he shouted.

"Yes, sir," replied the cabbie, pushing his hornrimmed glasses up onto the bridge of his large bulbous nose.

As he strolled across the street to pick up his fares' bags, Hot Rod Organ thought, *with weird, cold weather clothes like that, they must be out-of-state tourists.*

"Interest you in a quickie tour of San Francisco? Will cost a little more, but you'll love it. Chinatown and North Beach. I'll throw in a cable car too."

"Why not?" said Murle, smiling at his wife. "Give us your very best tour of San Francisco. Let's find out why Mike has such fond memories of his Navy days."

"Disgusting," whispered Gertrude, but secretly she desired a peek at this strange city.

How better to condemn this Philistine society, this Sodom and Gomorrah, than by speaking from first-hand observations, she thought.

"Yes, Murle, but only if you insist," Gertrude replied. She could hardly wait to report to the next meeting of the Clear Lake Daughters of the American Revolution.

"Hope you folks don't mind a little rock and roll," said Rod Organ, flipping on the car radio full blast. Little Richard screamed a chorus of "Tutti Fruiti."

Lord, have mercy on our souls, thought Gertrude, clinging tightly to the felt strap of the cab with both hands.

Peeling out in a cloud of smoke, Rod Organ thought, *the money from these nice folks will make up for the time I lost driving that van load of pseudo-Beats from Cal to Broadway.*

* * *

"Scotty, how could you do this to me?"

Rivulets of tears streamed down Cee Cee's reddened cheeks, dripping a trail of tears across the glossy black and white photos scattered across the Danish modern table. Her sobs mingled with the contrapuntal dissonance of the dueling parrots.

"It's not what you think, Cee Cee," said Ari Scott softly, picking up the enlargement of a photo taken at the BV, marveling at how happy Anna and he appeared.

"The shame. What will our friends at the Piedmont Country Club say?" wailed Cee Cee. "How will I ever face them again?" she said, slumping into the Saarinen "womb" chair.

"I'm sorry, Cee Cee," Ari's whispered, "I should have told you sooner."

"Do you think our marriage is worth breaking up over a middle-age fling with some young girl?" said Cee Cee, jutting her lower jaw. "If you needed an affair, why didn't you just find some discreet call girl like Daddy's friends do?"

Her eyes suddenly brightened. "Are these photos about blackmail? If money is all she wants, we should pay. Lydia Ann Collins's husband had an affair with a cocktail waitress from the Pacific Union Club, and it cost them only a thousand dollars for the negatives of photos taken at the No-tell Motel in Emeryville."

"She's not a gold-digger, Cee Cee," said Ari, anger rising within him. "Anna is a very special person."

"So her name is Anna," Cee Cee said. She stifled her sobbing, examining the photos of the voluptuous, dark-haired, young woman with renewed interest. "She looks Mediterranean. Is she Greek?"

"Italian," Ari replied. "Half Italian," he added proudly.

Why don't I have the courage to tell Cee Cee the truth?

"Daddy told me I should leave you, Ari." Cee Cee dabbed at her tears. "This scandal could harm his campaign."

"How do you feel about it?" said Ari, envisioning the pious self-righteous countenance of the Old Man.

"Daddy's always right, but I don't want a divorce, Scotty. If you just let this Anna go, forget her, pretend she never existed, we can go on with our lives as if your little affair never happened. Please, Scotty." She began to weep again.

"But what if I can't let her go?" said Ari. "Anna's a part of me now, a part of my life."

Cee Cee's voice took on a steely edge. "It's either me or her, Scotty. You can't have both of us."

Ari took a deep breath, swallowing hard. The moment of truth had arrived. He blurted, "What if I told you that long before I ever met you, during the Olympics, I fell in love with a beautiful Italian

262

girl named Sofia Cappuccino, and that we planned to marry but were separated by the War?"

Cee Cee's sobbing stopped, her eyes widening in disbelief.

Ari continued. "I thought Sofia had died, but she had given birth to a daughter, my daughter, Anna, in Palermo Prison, and both had survived the War."

Gaining courage, Ari continued, "Later, Sofia married a charismatic, Italian political leader who adopted Anna and raised her as his own." He paused, "Anna's stepfather is Pablo Zarzana."

Cee Cee's face paled on hearing the name of the Italian Communist, the man her father had denounced many times on the editorial pages of the San Francisco <u>Gazette</u>.

"Anna?" Cee Cee's voice was barely audible. "This Anna is your illegitimate daughter?"

"Yes," Ari replied, holding up a photo of father and daughter in animated conversation. "Anna's a remarkable young woman."

Cee Cee buried her face in both hands, breaking into a low, sustained moan.

"You'll love her, too, Cee Cee. She's really a lovely person."

"How could you," Cee Cee snapped upright with a snarl, "have an illegitimate child?"

"Cee Cee, it was such a long time ago," Ari's voice was soft and tender. "I was young and so much in love."

"Don't talk to me about love," said Cee Cee, now fully jutting her jaw. "I saved my virginity for marriage, for the man of my dreams, for you." She spit the words out like bullets. "You have the nerve to ask me to accept this bastard daughter of yours, this offspring of some Italian slut."

"Sofia Cappuccino is not a slut," said Ari, warm memories of Sofia flooding back. "She was an Olympic swimmer, the daughter of a famous Milanese industrialist."

"SLUT! SLUT! SLUT!" Cee Cee shouted, cupping her ears with her hands. "How will Marc and Monique feel when they learn that their father, the Great Scott, couldn't keep his Thing in his pants? How can we ever trust you again?"

"But facts are facts, Cee Cee. They are reality. We can't stick our heads in the sand, pretending they never happened."

"Don't give me that philosophical nonsense, Scotty. I'm not another one of your wide-eyed, adoring students. I'm your wife. How can I ever forgive you for this humiliation?"

263

"I'm asking for understanding, Cee Cee, not forgiveness."

"NO!" she exploded. "Daddy taught me there are things that can never be forgiven. And this is one of them," she said, shaking with anger. "He warned me about marrying you, about taking in someone beneath my station." Cee Cee's face was red with fury. "I could have had anyone I wanted. There were so many eligible young bachelors who would have been thrilled to marry into the Chandler family."

Ari closed his eyes as her venom continued.

"I thought I could change you, Scotty, turn you into the kind of man Daddy would be proud of. But you never accepted the Chandler family responsibility, did you? Of the duty we have to ourselves, to society, to be special, to be better."

Ari did not respond, could not respond.

"Nothing about our marriage has really mattered to you, has it?" asked Cee Cee, tears no longer filling her eyes. "Not our beautiful home, not our perfect children, not our wonderful friends."

Cee Cee leaned forward, her eyes narrowing, "I'll tell you something, Professor Aristotle Scott. Without the Chandler family, you're nothing."

"But Cee Cee, don't you see Anna won't lessen the quality of our lives. You may feel disappointment now, but you'll learn how wonderful she is." He pleaded, "All I'm asking is to keep an open mind."

"She will never set feet in my home." A look of cold determination swept across her face, her voice now calm, devoid of emotion. "You can stay in the house for a while. The children and I will move in with Daddy in Pacific Heights. When the election is over, we can talk about your visitation rights. Right now, we should keep things quiet, avoid anything that will embarrass Daddy's campaign."

She rose and, with the discipline instilled in graduates of the Anna Bransome Boarding School for Refined Young Girls, Cee Cee Chandler walked out of Ari's life.

Watching her leave, Ari realized that, in a sense, Cee Cee was right. For too long, he had deceived himself, believing his life had been created by his own accomplishments. He had been comfortable, firmly ensconced in the trappings of the Chandler clan.

But, it was also true that he had never been happy, that something essential was missing from his life. It was Anna who had rekindled within him the capacity to love, something vital he had left somewhere along the *toure di amore* so long ago.

Standing before the bay window, he inhaled the familiar vista from the glass conservatory: the Golden Gate peeking above the inbound fog, the Bay Bridge, a glistening necklace of lights, the symphony of fog horns braying in the cool grayness of San Francisco Bay.

He would miss all this and the material comforts that life with Cee Cee and the Chandler family had afforded.

But a Higher Truth awaited, his own Higher Truth.

Of love lost and found. Of loyalty to friends and colleagues. Of honor to his University.

"Yes," he said aloud. "The Higher Truth."

Nearby, Cal, the blue and gold macaw, cooed, "Go Bears."

45

ANTICIPATION

The full moon hovered over the East Bay foothills, draping the Claremont Hotel in a silver patina of light. Completed in 1915, the silver-shingled hostelry was the largest convention resort west of Chicago. During the Big Band Era, the Claremont hosted live radio broadcasts of the Lawrence Welk, Russ Morgan, and Dick Jurgens orchestras from its Garden Room overlooking San Francisco Bay.

Occupying 22 acres of sloping, landscaped gardens of the Berkeley-Oakland foothills, the Mediterranean style resort reflected the timeless grace of a proud, aging dowager, in stark contrast to the modern chrome and glass upstarts sprouting up in the flatlands below her. On this Halloween night, luminous shafts of light circled above, heralding her grandeur as the hostess of the evening's festivities, the 1959 Gamma Delta Presents Ball.

"The spotlights are a nice touch," said Sam Paean, easing his double-finned Cadillac out of the darkness of the Treasure Island tunnel. "This sorority Halloween Ball should be quite an affair, but don't you think my raincoat and the calabash pipe are a bit much?" he asked his passenger, tilting the deerstalker hat crouching on his eyebrows.

He had received a note from that beautiful coed, Kate Howell, who had been a co-judge at the Cal Big C Sirkus. In her sweeping handwriting, she had invited Sam to be Official Chaperone of the Gee Dee Presents Halloween Ball featuring Big Berry and the

Blackouts, the first Negro band to ever play at a Cal event. "Be a sport, Sam," cooed E Lyn Chamberlin. It had been Ace's idea for him to dress like Sherlock Holmes. "You're in the perfect getup for the newspaper scoop of the year. You even look like Basil Rathbone!" Paean winked at his trusty research assistant. *What would I do without her*, he wondered?

E Lynn was dressed in the blue, red, and gold costume of the comic strip heroine Wonder Woman, replcte with knee length boots and a faux diamond tiara. Recently, she had let her hair down from that awful bun and removed her thick glasses. Before the change, Paean had not appreciated how really pretty she was. Glancing at Ace cinched into her scanty costume, he noticed for the first time her long, lovely legs.

Keep your mind on business, he scolded himself.

The chance to witness this historic event on the Cal campus would have been enough to pique his interest, but there was also that tantalizing tip. In his mind, Paean reread the note that came in yesterday's mail.

The identity of the coed Seymour Graft has been tailing holds the key to Clayborn Muck's vendetta against the Cal prof. She too will be attending Gee Dee Presents Party.

Who is the mysterious coed? Why would HUAC have such a strong interest in her? What could Paean learn to help Cal survive the attack of Muck and HUAC?

It would take the skills of a real Sherlock Holmes to find the answers tonight, Paean thought.

* * *

"Why, Miss Scarlett, you look absolutely ravishing," teased Joan Dildeaux, admiring how well the color of Kate Howell's gown matched baby blue eyes.

"Fiddlee-dee, Miss Melanie, you look right fine yourself," said Kate in a mock Southern drawl. "I do declare, all gussied up, you're an entirely different woman." Kate noticed how pretty Joan looked without her thick, coke-bottle glasses.

"But without my eyes on, how will I ever find my Rhett or Ashley, Miss Scarlett?" Joan squinted at her own blurry image in the full-length mirror. From the hi-fi stereo, Little Brenda Lee lamented, "I Want to Be Wanted."

"I swear, Miss Melanie," Kate said coyly, "with the way your lush boobies are popping out of that low cut dress, I don't think boys will have any problems finding their way to your side. Like bees to honey."

The compliment brought a blush to Joan's cheeks. She had never dressed so daringly, but, succumbing to Kate's insistent urging to "strut their stuff," the Gee Dee roommates had dressed themselves as Margaret Mitchell's literary heroines from *Gone With the Wind*, cinching each other tightly into the prisons of their antebellum party gowns.

Presents was the ceremony at which sororities officially presented their new pledges to the campus public. The Ball was normally a formal tuxedo and gown affair with music provided by a San Francisco, Nob Hill, society orchestra.

In reality, Presents was an opportunity for leering fraternity boys to meet new freshman girls for potential dates, an event Joan lamented was nothing more than a "USDA prime meat show."

"Can you believe the crowd coming to our party tonight?" said Kate, unable to control her excitement. "Thanks to your wonderful idea of having a Halloween costume theme, Joanie."

"Because of Big Berry and the Blackouts," said Joan, "we'll have standing room only, more people than the Presents of those snotty Kappas and Thetas combined."

When the Gee Dees announced they had hired a Negro rock and roll band, the decision was greeted with derision by other prominent sororities. "Revolting," sniffed the Kappas. "Bad taste," dismissed the Thetas. But as Presents day approached, initial shock turned to intense curiosity, fueled by a titillating eyetem in Sam's *Paean to The City*.

Paean had reported a near riot during a concert held at San Jose State College, a notorious party school near Stanford, when the infectious music of an obscure East Oakland Negro band, called Big Berry and The Blackouts, had drawn a campus throng exceeding the capacity of the gymnasium, inciting hundreds of students to riot and storm the building.

"Fiddlee-dee, Miss Melanie. You know what I always say.

Girls who can't say a kind word shouldn't say anything at all." Kate gave Joan a knowing wink.

"But thank goodness for the mention in Sam Paean's column and your idea to request Mr. San Francisco to be our Official Chaperone. That was a stroke of genius, roommie," said Joan.

"We needed one," said Kate, "after Mrs. Cee Cee Scott of the Alumnae Club bowed out for personal reasons."

"Fiddlee-dee true, Miss Scarlett," said Joan, thrilled with the unorthodoxy of the Gee Dee break from tradition. "This will be one Presents party I'm really going to enjoy, USDA Prime meat show or not!"

* * *

"Dearest, I haven't had this much fun since our college days," said Murle Aldon, reviewing his handiwork in the mirror."What do you think? Don't I look like Al Jolson in 'The Jazz Singer'? '*M-a-m-m-y*, " he crooned at his reflection.

"And I look like Aunt Jemima," said Gertrude Aldon, frowning at her blackened image. She cringed at the thought of a life as a real Negress, the horrible life her sister-in-law, Pearl, faced every day.

"Dearest, wasn't that cab tour of the City entertaining?" asked Murle, picking up the top hat that completed his costume.

Now I know how San Francisco cast a spell on my brother Mike, he said to himself. *Wonder what would have turned my head had I been here in the Navy*?

Murle dismissed the question before considering an answer.

"Disgusting, if you ask me, " said Gertrude. "And that Chinatown! I've never smelled anything that putrid in my life. How can all those people live so close together in all that stench?

Gertrude recoiled at the memory of the pungent scents and dissonant sounds that enveloped Rod Organ's cab floating through the sea of weekend shoppers and tourists.

"And they look so much alike with their black hair and squinty eyes. And all that public spitting . . . ," her voice trailed off.

"That guy dressed up like a blonde in North Beach," Murle chuckled, "really fooled me. She was cute."

"Murle!' Gertrude shouted. "The Lord created men to be men and women to be women. He said nothing about men dressing up like women," she said with authority.

Gertrude thought, *wait 'til I show the Daughters of the American Revolution pictures I took with my Brownie Hawkeye!*

"And those Beatniks Jonathan is so fond of," said Murle, recalling the motley group assembled near the entrance to the City Lights Bookstore. "They didn't look too bad."

I wonder how I would look in a beard, thought Murle. *Gertrude always said I resemble Ernest Hemingway, and Hemingway wears a beard!*

"Can't they find anything better to do than bang on those bingo drums all day?" asked Gertrude.

"I think they're called bongos, dearest."

"Bingo, bongo, bungo. Whatever they're called, they gave me a headache," said Gertrude, adjusting the red bandana. "And those weirdos playing flutes! Even that rock and roll nonsense sounds better.

"What was the name of Jonathan's favorite singer, the one who died in that plane crash near us last winter? Oh, Murle, you know. The skinny boy with the thick, black glasses? Wasn't it Bucky Hawley?"

"I think his name was Holly, dearest. Nice of young Dirk Krum to invite us to join the P U group for the Presents Party," said Murle, dabbing his chin with the end of a charred piece of cork.

"A marvelous sense of humor," said Gertrude, peering at her darkened image in the mirror. "I'm impressed that there are still young men who know right from wrong. Attending the party in black face to protest the awful idea of hiring a Negro band is just marvelous! The Devil must have possessed those sorority girls!"

"When we get home, I don't think we should talk about this evening," said Gertrude. "No God-fearing person in Clear Lake would ever consider hiring such a band! The crazy thinking of California people!"

"But what a wonderful surprise for Jonathan," said Murle. He was heartened by the news from the elder Krum that Jonathan's name was among the list of the group representing Dooch Hall.

"We'll introduce Jonathan to young Krum and the other P U's, and he'll discover how much they really want him to join their fraternity," Murle said.

Placing the top hat at a jaunty angle, he said. "There, I'm done." He gave Gertrude an affectionate hug. "Let's see how long it will take for Jonathan to recognize his parents."

Gertrude completed her disguise, concealing the bun of her hair in the red bandanna.

Yes, she thought, gazing one last time in the mirror, *I look just like Aunt Jemima.*

* * *

"Jeez, Junior, I'm bushed," said Butch Tanenbloom leaning against a wash basin of the third floor bathroom, scraping away at his five o'clock shadow with a Gillette safety razor.

"Butch, you're our frosh super jock?" asked the All Pro, from beneath mountain of shaving cream. "During my broadcast of the Big Berry and The Blackouts concert, remind me not to embarrass you by asking you how well you're holding up on the dance floor."

Flipping on his electric razor, Jonathan grinned at his image, pleased with the hour long dance lesson he had given the Dormies. With the help of a reel of tape of Big Berry and the Blackouts, performing *Louie, Louie,* Jonathan had demonstrated the intricacies of the line dances and free-form gyrations he had learned at the jam session at the Joneses.

Due to the unprecedented interest in Big Berry's band, the Gee Dees had requested each living group limit its party to a dozen. The Dooch representatives included Casey, Royal, Ollie, Hunch, Super Sleuth, Ruby, Lizard, Mo, and Waz, with Jonathan, Butch, Tubbins, and Fart-ing rounding out the Dooch's baker's dozen.

All Pro had been asked to serve as Master of Ceremonies, representing campus radio station, KALX.

"You sure we're not gonna embarrass ourselves?" Royal French had huffed, contorting his imposing frame like a mating praying mantis.

"Positive," Jonathan had explained. "This is the beauty of dancing this way to Big Berry's music. You can wiggle around any way you want, and the band will feel comfortable, seeing familiar dancing."

"I'm gonna need a chiropractor after this," Ollie Punch had moaned, his left eye spinning wildly to the beat of the music.

"Think of all the girls we'll sign up for Hunch's Campanile tours," said Super Sleuth.

"What about a hunk for me?" said Ruby Lips, undulating like

a serpent. "I can't wait to shake my stuff."

"Be discreet, Ruby," said Mo McCart, staggering like a bald headed, Brahma bull, "I don't want to save you from some pissed-off frat rat whose butt you find attractive."

"You might be surprised, Mo, babe. Maybe, just maybe, some tall, dark, handsome fella will find me irresistible," said Ruby, blowing a kiss into the air.

The Dormies had decided to dress as Meter Mels with old uniforms the Waz had found in storage. In a stroke of artistic genius, the Lizard had sprayed the outfits in psychedelic patterns with a special neon paint, making the Dormie uniforms glow in the dark.

"No one will miss our moves, even with the lights out," the Lizard said proudly, admiring his artistic fashion creation.

"Ya know, dis is how I meet most broads," said the Waz. Pulling out a packet of parking citations, he explained, "Wimmin' love guys in police uniforms. Must be da power of da badge. Whatcha do is screen dates by filling in da boxes on da parking ticket. It's da poifect ice breaker. Yer repartee will tell ya if yer gettin' to foist base."

Demonstrating, the Waz stood with a book of citations in one hand, a ballpoint pen in his other hand.

"My opening line is, 'Lady, somethin' tells me you've been naughty.' She'll be real friendly, hoping to get out of a ticket. So while yer flirtin',' ya fill in all the important info on the ticket."

"Where do I note any Generals?" asked Butch, slipping on his spats.

"Jot it under Miscellaneous," said the Waz. "Butch, dem spats look cool with the uni-form."

"Ha, Ha, Ha. What about bra size?" asked Ollie Punch.

"Fill in da box labeled Make and Model."

"What about sexual experience?" said Royal

"Mark da space Previous Driving Record," said the Waz.

"Waz, what do you do if you get lucky and actually get a date?" asked Casey.

"In da interests of justice, ya tear da friggin' ticket up!"

Jonathan slapped a palm full of Old Spice on his cheeks and thought, *Big Berry & The Blackouts, Louie, Louie, and the Dormies, all at Gee Dee Presents. How much more excitement could there possibly be?*

46

FOLK DANCING

"LIVE! From the Grand Ballroom of the HISTORIC Claremont Hotel, Cal radio station, KALX proudly brings you its exclusive broadcast of the Gee Dee Halloween Presents Ball with your host, the ALL PRO!"

"Yes, guys and gals, there is a SPECIAL MAGIC in the air as this standing room crowd, dressed in WILDLY COLORFUL COSTUMES, anxiously awaits the arrival of the sensational East Oakland band, BIG BERRY AND THE BLACKOUTS!"

The All Pro was dressed as a full-feathered yellow rooster, with webbed feet and claws. With his beady eyes, large hook nose, and fleshy neck folds, Rooster Face, looked realistically fowl even without a mask.

"EVERYONE who is ANYONE is here. Looking at this JAMMED PACKED THRONG, I can tell you the Gee Dees have wisely limited the guest list to ONLY TWELVE per living group. How people will be able to dance among this mob will be anybody's guess! CO-ZY? YES!"

"OH, MY! " the All Pro shouted, "even the CRUNCHY MUNCHY is here!" He waved at the ancient campus ice cream vendor dressed in a tattered black tuxedo, pushing his white cart among the crowd.

"Arriving to applause is Official Chaperone, San Francisco <u>Sentinel</u> columnist, SAM PAEAN, cleverly disguised as Sherlock Holmes and his assistant E Lyn Chamberlin PROVOCATIVELY dressed as Wonder Woman. I see them being warmly greeted by popular Professors ARISTOTLE SCOTT, DRESSED AS A PRIEST, and GARRICK NELQUIST, AS A PREGNANT NUN! Accompanying the two popular professors is a BREATHTAKINGLY GORGEOUS GIRL wearing a 1930's-style swimsuit, in the tricolor of the Italian flag!"

"There is a RUMOR that Congressman Clayborn Muck Chairman of HUAC will drop in on tonight's festivities. It will be VERY INTERESTING to see the confrontation between Congressman Muck and Professors Nelquist and Scott!"

"We've received word the band entourage arrived a few minutes ago, but has dropped from sight. While we await an explanation of this MYSTERIOUS disappearance, let's take a brief time out for a word from our wonderful sponsor, *Burma Shave*. This is the ALL PRO on KALX Radio 69, the exclusive VOICE of the Cal Bears!"

* * *

"Professor, I'm sorry if my eyetem caused you unnecessary grief with the Chandlers," said Sam Paean, admiring the voluptuous young woman poised on Ari Scott's arm.

What a beauty, Paean thought. *I can understand why the Professor would leave Cee Cee Chandler for this luscious babe.*

"Stop drooling, Sam," said E Lyn, whispering in Paean's ear. "It'll ruin your image of Mr. Cool," she said, giving him an affectionate jab to the ribs.

"Please call me Ari, Sam. We should rendezvous at the BV and compare notes on the Old Man's enemy's list," said Ari, shaking Paean's hand. "For years he's hated you for poking fun at the Chandler family and the <u>Gazette</u>."

Turning to the young woman at his side, touching her arm gently, Ari beamed, "May I introduce Anna Zarzana, stepdaughter of Pablo Zarzana."

"Holy cow!" said Paean, stunned by the revelation.

"Does Congressman Muck know you've been seeing the daughter of a famous Communist?" asked Ace, instantly recognizing the danger to Ari Scott.

"Sure," said Ari, winking at Anna. "And he's got pictures to prove it."

274

"But," sputtered Paean, "aren't you worried about what he's going to do to you with this information at the HUAC hearings? Why, he'll tar and . . . ."

Ari cut Paean short. "Sam, I said Anna is Pablo Zarzana's stepdaughter," emphasizing the word stepdaughter. "I'm Anna's real father," said Ari, placing an arm around his daughter, "and frankly, I don't give a damn about what people think."

"And I'm guilty as hell by association," added Nelquist, making the sign of the cross with his meerschaum.

Paean and E Lyn looked at each other in wide-eyed disbelief, the disclosure shocking, both sharing the sudden understanding of Ari and Anna's predicament, the missing piece of the puzzle falling into place.

"Muck was runner-up to you in the metric mile in the '36 Olympics," said Paean, now pulling the fact from the recesses of is memory.

"He was an also ran in another way," said Ari, his mind flooding with images of the *toure di amore*. "He never got to first base with a certain beautiful Italian Olympic swimmer, Anna's mother."

"We must talk soon," said Paean, the curved calabash pipe falling out of his mouth. "On the record, of course. You've got to go public about Anna before Muck can make any Commie hay of this." Paean's mind was spinning with the political ramifications of the eyetem.

"I don't care anymore," said Ari. "I've regained a daughter and a part of my life that is more important to me than anything Clayborn Muck or HUAC can ever do to me."

"I'll follow up," said E Lyn, retrieving the calabash from the floor. "Call you tomorrow?" Once again, her efforts in Paean's service would validate her nickname, Ace.

"Yes, I would like that," said Anna in a low, silky voice that raised the hackles on the back of Paean's neck. "Papa has suffered in silence too long. I would like the chance to straighten the record, as you Americans say."

And I'll be there to make sure Paean doesn't get too goo-goo eyed during the interview, E Lyn said to herself.

In animated discussion, the quintet did not notice the new arrivals, greeted by both hissing and a smattering of applause. The swirling crowd parted for the P U entourage, in black face, escorting Congressman Clayborn Muck and Professor Werner Von Seller dressed in black tuxedos.

"Professor Scott," said Werner Von Seller, tapping Ari sharply on the shoulder. "So good of you to mingle with your students at this marvelous event," he said, a hint of sarcasm in his Teutonic accent. "I believe you and Congressman Muck have met."

"In that black tuxedo, Von Seller does look like a penguin," said E Lyn, whispering to Paean, taking mental notes of the face-to-face meeting between the two old antagonists.

Ignoring the others, Muck said, gritting his teeth in a forced smile, "If my memory is correct, Ari, you were once called the Great Scott."

"Yes, Muck," said Ari, offering a perfunctory handshake, "a very long time ago."

"But I never forget," said Muck, moving his gaze to the young woman at Ari's side. "Nor do I forgive," he added.

"Ah, this must be our beautiful, young Communist, Anna," said Muck, bowing, smirking. "How is your father doing with his part of the Great Communist Conspiracy?" Muck feigned embarrassment. "Please, you don't need to answer that, my child. I suppose it was probably an indelicate question."

Ari tensed, his anger rising. *I could throttle the creep right here and now*, he thought. *But that's exactly what he would like me to do, lose my temper, embarrass myself in front of all these people, show the world that the Great Scott is just another emotional mortal.*

"I know all about your fierce sense of competition, of your need to always have what you want, Congressman," said Anna in her low, silky voice.

"I am flattered you should know so much about me in such a short time," said Muck.

"I've heard about you since my childhood. Mama told me how you pursued her at the 1936 Olympics," she said sweetly, without malice. "And since coming to America, I have learned how your passion for Mama has turned to hate for Papa," said Anna, looking admiringly into her father's eyes, entwining Ari's arm tightly with both of hers.

"Impossible," muttered Muck, the old memories reviving, forging to the forefront of his consciousness.

Sofia, so young, so beautiful, so unattainable. All because of her stupid infatuation with the California Golden Boy, Aristotle Scott!

Staring at the radiant young woman, he saw in her the familiar jet black hair, voluptuous figure, and creamy, smooth skin of Sofia Cappuccino.

Then the sudden revelation! The revulsion welling up in his very being, as he noticed the similarity of the luminous grey eyes of his old nemesis and those of the young woman standing before him!

This Anna, the daughter of Sofia Cappuccino and Ari Scott!

Trembling, tears welling in his eyes, slowly retreating with Von Seller at his side, Muck growled, "Scott, you sonuvabitch. If it's the last thing I ever do, I'll get you for this," he screamed, disappearing in the crowd of partygoers.

Holding tightly to Anna, Aristotle Scott, in his mind, spoke to the love of his life, from across the years and across the miles,

Thank you, Sofia. Thank you for our daughter, Anna.

* * *

"This is totally insulting, humiliating us this way," said Reggie RJ Jones above the clattering din of the Claremont kitchen. Hotel security had herded the group unceremoniously into the large pantry, ordering the group to change into the white uniforms hanging along the wall.

"Now, now, RJ," said the soothing voice of Reverend Ike. "After all, this is a costume party. We don't want to ruin MJ and Big Berry's big night, do we?"

"But," said RJ, his voice rising with anger, "making us wear uniforms of common domestics! Slavery was outlawed almost a hundred years ago!"

The group grew silent. Reverend and Doris Jones, MJ and AJ, Big Berry and The Blackouts, girlfriends of the band members, all were dressed as Claremont Hotel servants, maids, and cooks.

"Cool it, RJ," said Big Berry, "this is the most dough we've ever made for a gig. Shee-it, I'd do it naked if they asked. Let's leave social revolution out in the street tonight and just enjoy."

"Oh, RJ," said Angela, the sister of the Black Panther leader. "I won't tell Huey on you."

"Ok, Big Berry," said RJ, buttoning up the front of a white

chef's jacket. "Just this one time for you and MJ. But I'm not wearing this stupid cook's hat." With a defiant flourish, RJ substituted the chef's toque with a beret of the Black Panthers.

"That's cool, RJ," said Big Berry. "And I'll wear mine," placing at a jaunty angle, his admiral's cap with the scrambled eggs insignia.

"Thank you, son" said Reverend Ike, giving RJ a reassuring hug. "Now, let's go out and show these college kids how to have fun! Hallelujah! Praise The Lord! Sing and Ye Shall Be Free!"

* * *

"Murle, there's Jonathan," said Gertrude Aldon, pointing in the direction of a group of boys passing through the Gee Dee reception line.

"Are you sure, dearest? They're all dressed like police officers, except for that tall boy with the Fred Astaire spats. Maybe we should get a closer look."

"I'm positive," said Gertrude, "but let's wait and watch. We've got all night to spring our little surprise. Besides, I want time to get Congressman Muck's autograph."

"They must be serving food now," said Murle, pointing to a Negro group emerging from the kitchen.

* * *

"Those parking tickets are the hit of the party, Casey," said Kate Howell, surveying the Dormies along the reception line, chatting with the Gee Dee pledges, scribbling notes on citations, then tearing them up.

"Congratulations, ladies. What a turnout!" said Casey, smiling at Kate, Joan Dildeaux, and Muffy Peachwick. "But where are Big Berry and The Blackouts?"

"The All Pro is keeping an eye out for them," said Kate, leaning forward, touching Casey's arm. "You will dance with me later? I'm dying to try those moves you showed me." Casey had demonstrated the dance steps Jonathan had brought back from the jam session at Reverend Ike's.

"Kate, let's not forget who you are and what you represent," said Casey teasingly. "We wouldn't want anyone to think Gee

Dee's do naughty things, would we?"

"Oh, of course not," said Kate sweetly, her face turning slightly crimson.

Across the packed dance floor, Dirk Krum scowled at the tete-a-tete between Kate Howell and the Dormie leader.

Keep your fucking hands off her, he said to himself, shaking angrily.

"Be cool," Chip Fist, had advised, "Kate will come around. In the end, P U's always rule."

But something inside Krum snapped.

Got to save Kate from the evil influence of that Chinaman.

Rushing through the festive throng, Krum pushed to the side of his beloved.

"The first dance is mine, Kate," said Krum with a sneer visible through the black face makeup.

"I really haven't decided, Dirk," said Kate sweetly. "You know Casey, of course?"

"But you personally invited me to this party," snapped Krum.

"Why don't you go through the Presents line, like any other polite human being," said Casey.

"Or is politeness a foreign concept to P U's?" added Joan Dildeaux, batting her lashes.

Wheeling, facing his almond-eyed nemesis, Krum barked, "don't you ever . . . ."

"Why, Miss Kate, Miss Joan, and Miss Muffy, you all do look so lovely tonight," Krum's tirade was cut short by a deep, resonant voice from behind.

"Reverend Ike!" said Kate, shaking the minister's hand. "Where have you been? Everyone's been looking for the band. Why are you wearing those silly outfits?" she said, noticing the Claremont kitchen staff uniforms of the entourage.

"Just a little misunderstanding," said Reverend Ike. "Not a big deal." He gave a jovial wave to Jonathan approaching from the reception line.

Kate made quick introductions. "This is my friend, Casey Lee, and my across the street neighbor, Dirk Krum."

Fuming, Krum thought to himself. *Casey Lee is her friend and I'm only a neighbor?*

Shaking Casey's hand, Reverend Ike turned to Krum, saying, "Any neighbor of Miss Kate is a neighbor of mine, son."

279

Krum refused Reverend Ike's extended hand, thinking, *Neighbor, a Negro neighbor? Never.* The idea appalled him.

"This Honkie's hand not worth shaking," the growling voice belonged to Reverend Ike's son, RJ. "Black faces on white folks went out with Al Jolson. We're no Steppin Fetchits. We don't need to take this crap."

"Don't talk to me, boy, unless I speak to you first," said Krum.

"Don't ever call me boy," said RJ pushing past Reverend Ike.

For what seemed to be an eternity, the two locked eyes. Krum's coal-black eyes burning above his trademark sneer, RJ's eyes fiery red, his fists clenched.

"Let's get the band set up," said Jonathan, stepping between Krum and RJ.

"Great idea," said Casey, pulling Reverend Ike out of harm's way.

"RJ?" asked Reverend Ike, his eyes pleading with his son to turn the other cheek.

"Marvelous idea," echoed Kate Howell, motioning the band members toward the stage.

Later, Krum thought, backing away slowly, yielding to the wishes of his beloved Kate Howell.

Reading Krum's mind, RJ nodded in agreement.

There will be plenty of time in the coming Revolution to teach white trash like you a lesson in respect, he thought.

Turning, RJ escorted Huey's sister, Angela, and the other girls to chairs beside the bandstand.

As the band flipped on their amplifiers and tuned up their instruments, Kate Howell took the microphone from the All Pro.

"On behalf of the Gamma Delta sorority, thank you for this wonderful turnout. We want you boys to have a great time. But remember, there are only so many Gee Dee pledges to go around; so try not to monopolize the girls on the dance floor. There will be plenty of time for everyone to get in a dance or two," Kate said.

"Now to introduce our band, here is the soothing voice of KALX radio, the All Pro."

Bounding up to the microphone, the All Pro said, "LADIES AND GENTLEMEN, boys and girls! I hope you've got your Halloween costumes on tight, 'cause there's gonna be some serious shaking here tonight! You've HEARD about them, you've READ about them, now you're gonna HEAR them. The scintillating, heart arresting, jumping-for-joy, sounds of the INCREDIBLE BIG BERRY AND THE BLACKOUTS!"

Taking the mike, Big Berry said, "Ok, folks, we're gonna start off with some romantic tunes to get your feet in a dancin' mood. Here's our very own MJ Jones, doing his version of the Johnny Mathis hit, "Chances Are."

As MJ crooned, Dirk Krum swept to Kate Howell's side, encircling her tiny waist, leading her to the middle of the dance floor. As they swayed in two step, Kate gave Casey Lee a little wave of her left hand. Following Krum's lead, the P U's rushed forward, pushing aside the ranks of other guests, taking their pick of Gee Dees. The Zates and SAE's followed. Soon, all the Gee Dees, even Joan Dildeaux, had dance partners, swaying to MJ's solo.

Standing at the edge of the dance floor fidgeting, the Dormies watched the frat rats dancing with the Gee Dees, chatting with airs of polished arrogance.

Big Berry and The Blackouts segued from "Chances Are" to Nat King Cole's "When I Fall in Love," as a second wave of fraternity boys invaded the dance floor, cutting in on the dancing Gee Dees.

"Junior, when are they gonna play something wild," said Butch, locking his eyes on a Gee Dee pledge dancing with Student Body President Ralph Van de Kamp. "Hey, isn't that General, the sis of the CAT stew?" Butch pointed, recognizing Dandy Cane.

"Patience, Butch, our time is coming," said Jonathan.

From the far corner of the ballroom, Murle and Gertrude Aldon watched intently.

"See dearest, there's nothing to worry about," said Murle. "A traditional college dance, just like the old days. Would you like a dance, Mrs. Aldon, before we surprise Jonathan?" Murle bowed, taking Gertrude's hand.

Following her husband's lead, Gertrude thought, *yes, this seems to be a normal college dance.*

The ballroom lights dimmed, illuminated only by the shafts of lights glancing off the spinning silver ball suspended from the ceiling. Through the maze of slow-dancing couples, Gertrude Aldon caught sight of Jonathan standing among a group of boys dressed like police officers, their uniforms glowing in a swirl of

281

bright neon colors in the dark.

Why isn't Jonathan dancing, she wondered?

* * *

"Ok, folks," announced Big Berry, "now that you've loosened up those dancin' feet, it's time to do some serious stompin.' The next number is dedicated to the X Ho Fish EE Ho - you college kids know what that fancy word *ex officio* means - member of The Blackouts. He's a Cal student living at your very own Dooch Hall, JONATHAN ALDON! Shake your booty out here! "

As the band lay down the bass intro to *Louie, Louie*, Jonathan shouted, "C'mon, Dormies," waving his friends onto the floor, "let's show them how it's done."

The Dormies formed a single row behind Jonathan. Clapping their hands in unison, Jonathan led them in the line dance he had taught them

> DUH (Pause)
> Duh-duh-duh. Duh-duh-duh. Duh-duh-duh
> Undulating.   (Clap)
> Duh-duh-duh. Duh-duh-duh. Duh-duh-duh
> Serpentining   (Clap)
> Duh-duh-duh. Duh-duh-duh. Duh-duh-duh
> Wiggling.   (Clap)
> Duh-duh-duh. Duh-duh-duh. Duh-duh-duh
> Twirling.   (Clap)
> Duh-duh-duh. Duh-duh-duh. Duh-duh-duh

From the corner of his eye, Jonathan saw fraternity boys laughing, pointing at the strange dance steps. But he also saw the Gee Dees swaying, bouncing, clapping to Big Berry's beat.

As Big Berry launched into the lyrics of *Louie, Louie*, Jonathan felt a female rushing to his side, dancing beside him. It was Angela, the sister of the Black Panther leader, Huey.

"C'mon, sugar," she shouted. "Shake your stuff!"

Breaking ranks, the Dormie dozen danced free form, Angela and Jonathan leading the others in spasmodic gyrations and undulations.

From the center of the mob, crowding in for a closer look at the exotic terpsichore, Murle and Gertrude Aldon strained to see what was happening.

282

"Gertrude," shouted Murle Aldon, lifting his wife up by the waist. "Look, it's Jonathan!"

From her elevated view, Gertrude Aldon saw Jonathan performing obscene body movements with a young Negro girl! Gertrude's mouth dropped, her nostrils twitched and flared. Before her, vividly realized, was her recurring nightmare: Jonathan and the girl from the cover of <u>National Geographic</u>!

Oh, my God, Gertrude said to herself, as she swooned, crumping to the floor, as the Claremont's Grand Ballroom pulsated with the rhythm of *Louie, Louie.*

* * *

Casey waved at Kate to join him. After huddling quickly with Joan, Muffy, and Muffy's little sis, Dandy, the four bridge players sprinted onto the dance floor, lifting the bottoms of their antebellum skirts. Within the circle of dancing Dormies, they gracefully imitated the contortions of Jonathan and Angela. Soon, they were joined by the entire Gee Dee pledge class, as Big Berry began the second chorus of *Louie, Louie.*

The floor was now jammed with dancers, improvising steps to Big Berry and The Blackout's hypnotic beat, suffused with the rhythm and joy of the music.

"I don't know what the hell you guys are doing, but I go where the babes go," shouted Monty Montgomery, bouncing past.

"Easier than pitching pennies," said Jonathan to the fraternity boy he had bested in the coin toss at the Big C Sirkus.

"Almost as fun as chucking Frisbees," yelled T.A. Brewster, hopping and twisting past Casey and Kate. Casey gently slapped the back of the surfer he had beaten in the Frisbee competition.

The music now a fevered pitch with the fourth chorus of *Louie, Louie,* Jonathan danced with a Gee Dee pledge who shouted above the din, "you look just like Tab Hunter." Beside him, Butch towered over and wiggled with the giggling Dandy Cane.

* * *

Dripping with perspiration, Ruby Lips entered the men's room of the Claremont Hotel. *Classy head,* he thought, marveling at the marble, brass, and indirect lighting.

That crazy freshman Aldon had done a great job of breaking the ice of this stuffy party.

Dancing free form had lifted his spirits, allowing him to express himself sensually in a manner he could not do in the structured steps of ballroom dancing.

And all those cute guys wiggling about the floor!

Splashing warm water on his face, Ruby entered the stall at the far end. Only one message was scrawled in pencil on the door.

Do not write graffiti on this door.

Ruby heard the entrance to the men's room open, then silence. *Louie, Louie must have ended,* he thought. *Gotta get out of here. This place will be crawling with sweaty dancers.*

Suddenly, a piece of paper was pushed under the door, then steps tiptoing quickly across the marble floor and out the door. Unfolding a Claremont Hotel cocktail napkin, Ruby read the neatly printed message.

Loved your moves.
Meet you on the hotel veranda?
Gay, too.

Ruby reread the message, his heartbeat quickening.

Impossible! Someone else at Cal unashamed of his sexual orientation! A frat rat? Probably, as the Dormies were the only non-Greeks at Gee Dee Presents.

Exiting the stall, Ruby straightened his tie and primped his hair.

Romance? Mr. Right? Be cool, he told himself. *No harm in a little talk,* he said.

Heading swiftly for the veranda, Ruby Lips passed the entrance of the Grand Ballroom, still rocking with *Louie, Louie.*

* * *

From the bandstand, MJ waved Jonathan up to jam with the band. A spare bass guitar quickly tuned, Jonathan played and sang with The Blackouts.

The crowd, now totally energized and in sync, was driven by the beat of the music. Student President Ralph Van de Kamp, and even the P U's, with the notable exception of Dirk Krum, jumped, wiggled, gyrated, and undulated.

The band completed the last ear splitting chorus of *Louie, Louie.* Jonathan bowed with Big Berry and The Blackouts to cheers and thunderous applause. As Jonathan moved through the sea of smiling faces, he felt a tugging at his elbow. Turning, he saw a middle-age couple with blackened faces, the man carrying a woman in his arms. Despite the makeup, Jonathan immediately recognized the features of Murle and Gertrude Aldon.

"Father! Mother! Jonathan said, shocked by the recognition. "What are you . . . ?"

Gertrude opened her eyes on hearing Jonathan's voice.

"You have disgraced the Aldon name!" Gertrude screeched, her blackened nostrils flaring and twitching.

"Meet us tomorrow morning at 8:00 a.m. in the restaurant of the Durant Hotel," yelled Murle above the din.

Jonathan watched his parents disappear into the cheering crowd of the Claremont's Grand Ballroom. A wave of melancholy enveloped him, at this, his moment of triumph.

Shit flies both ways, he thought sadly.

47

NO PLACE LIKE HOME

Jonathan Aldon stood on the balcony of Dooch Hall and watched the taxi gliding down Channing Way toward the Bay. As the yellow cab braked for jaywalking pedestrians, he glimpsed the couple in the backseat. Instinctively, he fluttered the fingers of his left hand, a minor gesture compared to the last time he had bid good-bye to Clear Lake from the entrance to the CAT Connie on Labor Day.

Was it only sixty-days ago? A lifetime, Jonathan concluded, biting his lower lip, drawing blood, driving away the demon of sadness suffusing him.

Clear Lake. Aldon farms. Father and Mother. Home. Gone.

8:00 a.m. that morning, Jonathan had walked next door to meet his parents at Henry's, the restaurant of the Durant Hotel. Although he had not gone to bed until 4 a.m., he was not tired, still reveling in the excitement of the Presents party. Big Berry and The Blackouts had been a sensation, the deliriously happy crowd calling them back for three encores. Jonathan rejoined the band for a final rendition of *Louie, Louie.*

After the party, MJ and Big Berry had been besieged by offers to play at fraternity parties, insuring their future success on the Cal campus. Reverend Ike and Doris had hugged Jonathan several times, the trio shouting together above the music,

Hallelujah! Praise The Lord! Sing and Ye Shall Be Free!

As he bounded up the stairs of the Durant Hotel, Jonathan

cringed at the ugly consequences of the P U's black face stunt, had the Dormies not interceded. Two images were seared in Jonathan's memory: Dirk Krum's smirking sneer as he insulted RJ and the burning hate in RJ's eyes while Reverend Ike physically restrained him from throttling Dirk.

Dirk and RJ's paths will cross again, he thought, *and the next time there will be blood spilled.*

Since the turn of the century, the venerable Durant had been the traditional hotel of choice for alumni returning to campus. With its six-stories of dark-paneled walls, hardwood floors, shiny, brass accessories, and broad-leafed palm trees, the hotel was a reassuring symbol of gracious leisure, now dwarfed by the gray concrete and glass monolith of its new neighbor, Dooch Hall.

The dark, dimly lit lobby was empty, too early for the Sunday morning brunch crowd. Entering the clubby confines of Henry's, Jonathan saw his parents seated in a corner booth. Behind massive, double swinging doors, kitchen staff clanged a symphony of pots and pans.

Sliding into the bench seat, Jonathan immediately recognized the telltale signs of his parents' anger and disapproval: Gertrude Aldon sitting in stone silence, arms folded, her nose twitching furiously; Murle Aldon withholding his usual hug and handshake.

"Sit down, son," said Murle. It was a command, not an invitation.

"Yes sir," said Jonathan, snapping ramrod straight, a habit he had acquired in moments of childhood scoldings at the Aldon dining table.

"Your mother and I couldn't sleep a wink last night," said Murle. "We wanted to give you a happy surprise visit, but, judging from the shocking things we witnessed . . . ."

"Disgusting, despicable behavior," Gertrude hissed. "You should be ashamed to call yourself an Aldon."

His father continued, "We can't let you stay here in Berkeley any longer."

"You will pack your things immediately," said Gertrude, "and leave this God-forsaken place!"

"Now, now, dearest," Murle patted his wife's hand. "No need to shout. Jonathan understands our feelings."

"Where will I be going?" said Jonathan, already dreading the answer.

"Home to Clear Lake until the end of the year, son," said Murle. "That will give us time to enroll you at an Ivy League school for the spring semester of 1960."

"NO!" said Jonathan, surprising himself with the suddenness of his response. "I can't! I won't," he said, pounding the table.

"Yes, you will, you ingrate," said Gertrude. "For all the things we've done for you, to help you get ahead in the world. For all the expensive things we've given you to make your upbringing superior. What in God's name have we done to deserve this?"

"What is the horrible 'this' that angers you, Mother?"

"Don't play stupid little games with me, Jonathan Aldon. Is this part of the free speech rabble we've been reading about? Is this what you've learned in California? How to be rude and disrespectful to your parents? Don't you ever be insolent to me again. I'm your mother!"

"But . . . ."

"Do not speak until spoken to," Gertrude snapped, "or is that something else you've already forgotten."

"Let me explain, dearest," said Murle in a soothing voice. "Son, it's just a simple matter of not keeping The Three Promises. The Dean's Office informed us you're doing poorly. Mr. Krum II, the P U alumni president, told us you've turned down every rush invitation, and the minister of the Campus Methodist Church told us you haven't attended one service. This is just not acceptable. Promises are meant to be kept."

Jonathan traced clockwise circles on the table with a glass of water. "I'm sorry, Father," he said softly. "I should have explained why I haven't been able to keep The Three Promises."

"Explained what?" said Gertrude. "That you've become crazy, corrupted by evil influences." Tears welled up in her eyes. "I prayed for your soul, prayed that something like this would never happen to my only child. But we should have learned from Mike's Navy days that prayer is not enough to protect God-fearing people from Satan's hand in California," she sobbed.

Jonathan reversed the direction of the circles he traced with the glass of water.

"I know I've disappointed you, but I can't leave Cal," said Jonathan. "I've never been so happy. With my new friends, this wonderful school, the Bay Area, this is the best kind of education for me."

"You're wrong, son," said Murle. "At eighteen, you're young enough to get over your first serious mistake. Believe me, the Ivy League is the best education money can buy and will give you the business contacts you'll need when it's your turn to run Aldon Farms."

"And proper girls to meet," added Gertrude.

Murle continued, "Being here seems so much fun now, but soon you'll soon realize that it is only a short chapter in your life. Think of your two months at Cal as a nice vacation before your real education begins."

Murle leaned forward with a broad smile. "California's like a lot of modern fads that won't last. Just like that Chinese food you like so much. You know what people say. 'Tasty, but in an hour you'll be hungry again.' Trust me, son. After a few days back in Clear Lake, California will be out of your mind like the last Chinese meal you had."

Gertrude's face brightened for the first time. "When you get home, I'll have Cokie learn to cook Chinese. What is that exotic dish that's so popular in Minneapolis?"

"Chop suey, dearest," said Murle.

"Yes, we can have chop suey once-a-week. You can invite Ziggy, and the two of you can be Clear Lake's experts on Chinese food. It will be just like old times."

"But I can't go back to Clear Lake," said Jonathan.

"Why not, son? It's your home," said Murle, removing the glass of water from Jonathan's grip.

"Chop suey's not real Chinese food, and Clear Lake's not my home anymore," said Jonathan.

"But we're still the only family you've got," Gertrude's eye narrowed, her nose twitching.

Jonathan studied the intense expressions on his parents' faces. Home and family. Until Labor Day, Clear Lake and Mother and Father, were the only home and family he had ever known. But now he had a new home and a new family. And a clear sense of destiny that must be fulfilled.

"My future is here. I won't leave."

"But you're failing in your school work," said Murle. "If you drop out of Cal now, you can still enroll in an Ivy League college without a problem. One of the wonderful things about an Ivy League education is that once you're admitted, it's impossible to

289

flunk out."

"I'll knuckle down," Jonathan said bravely, cringing about the task of making up his 27 units of grade point deficiency. "There's still three-months before final exams. I know I can do it."

"Not without money," said Gertrude, playing her trump card. "Your father and I are not going to support a sinful lifestyle among these heathens. God, I prayed that it would not come to this. But I will not let you turn your back on the teachings of our home and church and everything right and good that we raised you to respect."

Her face turning a bright crimson, she hissed, "Jonathan, if you disobey us, you will be disowned, disinherited, a worse outcast than your uncle Mike. Turn your back on us and you turn your back on your future with Aldon Farms. You will no longer be our son!"

From the lobby of the Durant Hotel, the lilting laughter of arriving patrons filtered into Henry's.

Jonathan turned from Gertrude's twitching stare to Murle, eyes downcast, tracing squares with the confiscated glass of water. "Father?"

"Your mother is right," Murle whispered. Jonathan detected the beginning of a tear welling in his father's eye. "Son, you must come home with us."

The restaurant began to fill with patrons. Henry's staff marched from the kitchen in a single file, carrying platters of piping hot breakfast food to the long buffet along the far wall.

In the corner of his eye, Jonathan noticed a college girl and her parents seated at an adjoining table. Movement. The girl at the next table was waving. Returning the wave, he recognized her as the Gee Dee pledge he had danced with at the Presents party, the one who said "you look just like Tab Hunter." She smiled warmly, forming the words *Louie, Louie* with her lips.

Jonathan felt an uncontrollable force slide his body laterally, then levitate him slowly, as if he were a marionette manipulated by invisible strings. Now standing, he felt no sensation in his limbs, only a knot in his throat and a throbbing sadness in his heart. His parents averted eye contact, as he spoke slowly, deliberately.

"I'll always love you, Father, Mother," he said, feeling the force moving his feet resolutely across the restaurant floor. Exiting Henry's, Jonathan did not look back.

Emerging into the bright Sunday morning of November 1, 1959, Jonathan noted the time on the south clock of the Campanile. 8:15 a.m..

Hunch Hitowski was well into his early Sunday morning concert. Squinting up at the bell tower, Jonathan could see the outline of the tiny hunchback swinging freely from one carillon to another, as the bells pealed "I'll Walk Alone."

48

A NEW TOMORROW

What a disaster!

Slipping the monocle from his eye, Professor Werner Von Seller steamed the glass with his Gaulois breath, wiping away debris with a silk handkerchief. Squinting the eyepiece back into place, the Prussian Penguin scanned the shocking, lead article on the front page of the San Francisco <u>Sentinel</u> that proclaimed:

HOUSE UN-AMERICAN COMMITTEE
HEARINGS CANCELED!
Chief Investigator Fired in Wake of Scandal

The parade of bad news had started yesterday with the titillating revelation in Sam Paean's column about Seymour Graft's past as a convicted pornographer, with the prison number of 42586 in Leavenworth Penitentiary.

Now, this. The front page article read,

Just hours before the start of hearings by the House Un-American Activities Committee on alleged Communist activities on the campus of the University of California, the hearings were abruptly terminated. In a prepared statement, Congressman Clayborn Muck, Chairman of the powerful Congressional committee, blamed the distraction of irrelevant, left-wing distortions, and cited the best interests of patriotic citizens of the United States as reasons for the cancellation.

Congressman Muck announced that HUAC would bypass its Bay Area appearance and instead move onto Hollywood where it would conduct hearings on the pervasive Communist influence in the entertainment industry.

Muck's statement listed films such as "Some Like It Hot," "La Dolce Vita," "Psycho," and "The Apartment" as examples of insidious Marxist propaganda corrupting the moral fiber of American youth.

I would have included the musical, "The Sound of Music," thought Von Seller. *That play was much too harsh on Nazis.*

Von Seller fumbled a Gaulois into his sterling silver cigarette holder, his hands still trembling. He could not remember when he had been so disturbed by a sudden turn of events.

It was only a few days ago that he had met with Muck and Graft to review the details of his appearance before HUAC.

"You will be the new star on the academic horizon," Muck had promised, "the leader of the patriotic movement in our universities. With your dramatic testimony denouncing fuzzy thinking, left-wing professors of the Letters and Humanities departments, I can assure you Congress will appropriate millions of dollars for your atomic research."

"All we need is a law requiring a loyalty oath," added Graft, pooching a smoke ring, hissing a stream of Gaulois through its center.

"With your ringing endorsement of a loyalty oath," said Muck, "such a law will be passed in Washington soon. "And," he added, "when our supporter on this issue, William Randolph Chandler, is elected Governor of California, this state will have its own version of the loyalty oath, ridding Cal of such Communist professors as Aristotle Scott and Garrick Nelquist."

Buoyed by Muck's optimism, Von Seller had contemplated releasing to the press an advance copy of his speech to HUAC; but a strange premonition, a vague sense of impending disaster, had changed his mind. Maybe it was the rumor that Scott and Nelquist were planning a spirited public repudiation of HUAC. Or yesterday's tidbit by Sam Paean about Graft's scandalous past.

Somehow, Werner Von Seller had miraculously escaped the humiliation of Muck's about-face.

What luck! He concluded. *All my life, I have been a survivor. Yes, once again, I will escape the forces of ignorance. I will immediately call Chancellor Haynes and confess to an error in judgment in supporting loyalty oaths. I will strenuously reaffirm my support of academic freedom, expressing my undying dedication to Cal's academic reputation by pursuing patriotic, atomic research.*

This is only a minor setback in a long battle, he reminded himself. *I shall retreat momentarily, waiting for the next opportunity to resurface. Yes, there will always be another chance to lead the patriotic movement for greater atomic research!*

Drawing deeply from the sterling silver cigarette holder, the Prussian Penguin thought, *yes, once again, Professor Werner Von Seller will survive and rise again. And next time, I shall prevail!*

49

LIFE AFTER DEATH

"You made a gutsy decision in staying with us, Jonathan," said Casey Lee. "It would have been easier to obey your parents and join the P U's."

"Not really that difficult," mumbled Jonathan, thinking back on his introduction to the P U's, the Dooch retaliatory attack on the fraternity house.

"If you're willing to work your ass off, we'll do our damndest to give you a hand," said Royal French, scrunching his six-foot nine-inch frame into the modern, tulip-shaped chair. "You may not be as dorky looking as the typical Dormie, but we've enjoyed having you around."

Jonathan surveyed the solemn faces of the upperclassmen crowded into the third-floor study for the emergency meeting. On one side of the long Formica table seated next to Casey Lee and Royal French were Ollie Punch, Hunch Hitowski, and Lizard. On the other side of the table sat Super Sleuth, All Pro, Ruby Lips, Mo McCart, and the Waz. A vacant seat had been left at the head of the table.

"The first issue we're going to deal with is the negative units of The Angel of Death's cinch notice," said Casey. "Cal gives you only one chance to make up grade point deficiencies. By the end of the semester, if you don't bring your overall grade point average to a C, you'll wind up at a two-year junior college in the Spring with no hope of coming back."

"Aldon, at 27 units below a C average, you've established a new dorm record for academic incompetence," barked Ollie Punch, his wandering eye spinning dizzily.

"You don't need Gifted Florence's crystal ball to tell you it'll take a major miracle to keep you in school," said Ruby Lips.

"No one will ever accuse you of doing a half-ass job of trying to flunk out," added Super Sleuth, grinning.

"But how can I ever make up that many grade points?" sighed Jonathan, overwhelmed by the enormity of the task.

"There's still enough time between now and finals, but you're going to need help," said Casey, "a lot of help."

"You've got to learn to budget your time and stay focused," offered Mo. "With football practice and travel, I had a helluva time keeping my bald head above water without the help of my mentor." The giant gave Ruby Lips an affectionate nudge with his elbow.

"Jonathan, meet your personal tutor," said Royal. He motioned a new arrival to sit at the empty seat at the head of the table. "Michael Hu, better known as the Living Buddha."

Jonathan shook hands with a stoic, round-faced Oriental with almond eyes so slitted he appeared to be asleep. Michael Hu wore his wavy hair long, combed to one side. As he spoke, his lips did not seem to move.

"So, you are my academic RF project," said the newcomer, his hooded eyes opening slightly to gaze directly at Jonathan. "You don't look as stupid as your grades indicate," said the Living Buddha, speaking with an accent Jonathan could not place.

Definitely not Oriental, Jonathan thought.

"Unfocused might be a diplomatic description of Jonathan's predicament," said Hunch Hitowski, scratching his small, rounded back.

"If you want to stay in school, you must follow my instructions precisely," said the Living Buddha.

"First, you will have to catch up on all your reading assignments. Secondly, since you're not attending your lectures anyway, you will have to buy Phy Bate notes." The Living Buddha was referring to a company that hired students to take lecture notes and then sold summaries and outlines to students who skipped classes.

"You will spend at least five hours of every day at the library,

Sunday through Thursday. "And," said the Living Buddha, smiling for the first time, "you will meet with me from 10:00 p.m. to midnight to review your progress."

"For this plan to work," continued the Living Buddha, "you will sleep only five hours a night, between midnight and 5 a.m. After waking to Mrs. Beerwagen's wonderful breakfast creations, you will spend another two hours in the morning studying."

Jonathan grimaced at the thought of rising at the crack of dawn.

The Living Buddha seemed to read Jonathan's mind. "I will teach you how to get by on little sleep, tricks I learned from the Portuguese when I was growing up in Brazil."

Latin American, thought Jonathan, *the Living Buddha's accent was a dead ringer for the voice of Mother's favorite foreign actor, Cesar Romero.*

"Even if I make up my grades, how will I stay in school without money?" said Jonathan, feeling the reality of his decision to remain at Cal.

"We've come up with several part-time jobs for you," said Casey Lee. "Together, they should earn you the four-hundred dollars for your dorm room and food for the rest of the semester."

"You can earn minimum wage of a buck an hour by scraping the rust off the carillons in the Campanile," said Hunch. "I cleared it with Miss Burdick, but she wants you to be more careful than the last time you visited the Campanile," referring to the Campanile RF. "We don't have sewing kits if you rip your britches again."

"You can also join the crew in the 8th floor photo lab," said Royal, referring to the bustling, new business of producing and selling phony ID's to students under the age of 21. "We're making a killing at five bucks a pop." Counterfeiting documents was another skill Royal had acquired in Army Special Forces.

"Nobody can touch the quality of our fake driver's licenses," Royal added. "The frat rats and Sallies are buying 'em like crazy for weekend dates in the City. Even the P U's are buying. Of course, we charge those assholes double."

"On weekends, you can help me write parking tickets along Telly," said the Waz. "You looked pretty sharp in a Meter Mel's uniform at the Gee Dee Presents."

"And, of course, you can work the front desk setting

appointments and cashiering when I'm fortunetelling at Gifted Florence's," said Ruby Lips, fluttering his long eye lashes at Jonathan. "I won't even ask you to dress in drag."

Jonathan was stunned by the outpouring of support.

"Hog farmers must really love misery," said the Living Buddha, shaking his head. "Are you sure you are willing to do all these things to stay in school?"

Jonathan looked at the earnest faces around him. In only two months, he had been disowned by his parents, become penniless, and teetered on the verge of flunking out of school. Yet, during the same sixty-days, he had been transformed. Something magical about this campus and these wonderful friends suffused him, made him want to survive, to finish his four years, to graduate with a Cal degree.

Instinctively, he whispered, "Shit flies both ways."

"What was that?" asked Casey.

"Shit flies both ways," Jonathan repeated, "a saying I made up as a kid."

"Shit flies both ways. It has philosophical connotations," said the Living Buddha.

"Verbal RF at its best," said Royal, repeating the phrase.

"Gifted Florence may incorporate it in her palm reading," said Ruby Lips. "How does dung doth sail indiscriminately sound?"

"HA! HA! HA! That describes Mrs. Beerwagen's culinary skill in preparing Dorm food," added Ollie Punch.

"We could write a Dorm song with that title," offered Hunch Hitowski. "I could play it in the Campanile."

"I might consider a shitty psychedelic mural," said Lizard

"Yes, I can see it now," said the All Pro intoning with his deep, disc jockey voice.

"KALX presents the NEW NUMBER ONE SONG on campus, sung by the new rock sensations, 'The Doochmen', "Shit Flies Both Ways!'"

The Dormies took up the chant.

"Shit flies both ways!
Shit flies both ways!
Shit flies both ways!
Shit flies both ways!"

For Jonathan Aldon, an eighteen-year-old Pilgrim on the Coast, Clear Lake, Iowa was ancient history.

50

SE CONTINUER

The whispering of the four young women around the bridge table of the Pink Palace was tinged with excitement.

"Where did you get these?" There was a tone of awe in Joan Dildeaux's voice as the four Gee Dees carefully removed the circular containers from small plastic boxes.

They had heard the rumors and read the magazine articles about them, but here in their hands was the real thing, Enovid, The Pill.

"My sis, Candy, the stewardess for CAT Airlines, picked some up in a layover in Boston where the research is being done," said Dandy Cane, a tinge of pride in the freshman pledge's voice.

"But is The Pill safe?" asked Joan Dildeaux. "I've read there can be side effects like depression and weight gain."

"What else is new? Girls have those problems every month anyway," Kate Howell chuckled.

"These little beauties are what I've been praying for," said Muffy Peachwick. "I hate fooling with those damned rubbers. Takes me right me out of the mood." Muffy was the only Gee Dee who admitted to any sexual experience.

"Muffy-kins, spare us the details of your sex life," said Joan, carefully examining the 28 pills, each encased in a circle next to the numbered days of a cycle.

"The way I see it. It's more than just sex. If this thing becomes available, girls will take control of their lives as well as their bodies," said Kate. A tone of determination crept into her voice. "We won't have to worry about being trapped with four kids before we're thirty. We can think about real careers."

"You pseudointellectuals are all alike," said Muffy. "Talk, talk, talk. You talk everything to death. It's simple, girls. We don't have to worry about getting preggers. We can now have as much fun as boys do."

"But if we start putting out instead of waiting for marriage, won't we be considered sluts?" said Joan.

"Use some common sense, Dildeaux," replied Muffy. "You don't have to do it with every Dick. Or for that matter, every Tom and Harry either."

"You could still save it for someone you really care about," said Kate.

"But what about our virginity?" said Joan. "Who's gonna marry used goods?"

"Take it from one who knows," Muffy interrupted. "Losing IT is no Big Deal. In fact, you can always fake the Big Moment," she added, batting her enormous lashes. "Why, I've lost my virginity many times. Dicks, Toms, and Harrys are so into their own gratification they'll always believe the little white lie that they were your first."

The four giggled at the wisdom of Muffy's retort.

"Well, what say we give it a try," said Muffy, eyeing each of her sorority sisters. "Three months left in the semester. In February, we can share Valentine's secrets."

"I don't know," Joan whispered, although a voice within her told her, *Try The Pill, Dildeaux. Nothing to worry about. Who would want to sleep with an ugly legacy anyway?*

"Joanie, you don't have to surrender your virginity. You can treat The Pill as a medical experiment," said Kate.

"I'll do it," said Dandy, "but if anyone asks, I'll deny it."

"All for one, one for all," added Kate. "What we do or don't do is no one's business."

Joan scanned the earnest expressions of the other three."What the hell, count me in," she said.

The quartet held up the dispensers to seal their agreement.

"Here's to three months of freedom," offered Kate.

"To three months of freedom," the other three echoed.

And to three months of anxiety, Joan said to herself.

* * *

The 45 rpm recording of "Scotch and Soda" sung by the Kingston Trio had replayed for a half-hour, but no one in the room cared.

. . . Scotch and soda, mud in your eye.
Baby, do I feel high. oh me, oh my, . . .

High in the penthouse of the P U fraternity house, surrounded by stacks of law school books, outlines, and notes, Chauncey Remington studied the distraught faces of Dirk Krum and Chip Fist. Empty beer cans littered the hardwood floor. The P U Graduate Advisor had patiently listened to the duo relive the distressing events of the Gee Dee Presents Ball.

How sad they look, he thought, pouring another three fingers of Courvoisier into the brandy snifter. *How uncharacteristically P U sad.*

Earlier, he too had been shocked of the news that the House of Beauty had hired a Negro band, but he had expressed reservations about Krum's idea of attending the party in black faces.

"The stunt may backfire," he had warned. The decade of the Fifties was coming to a close, and the winds of change were everywhere. Cal's long history of liberal, political thought was rubbing off on even the staid, conservative Greek system. What would have been considered a clever little joke a few years ago might now be criticized as a breach of good taste. But Dirk had insisted, and the P U's had blindly followed.

More disturbing to Remington was learning how the Gee Dees had enthusiastically joined in the primitive dancing inspired by the Negro band. Obviously, the Dormies had secretly learned the dance steps.

But where?

There were no Negro students in the Dorms; and, other than a few African students at I-House, black faces on campus were rare.

The Kingston Trio sang *Scotch and Soda* on-and-on.

"We've got to put those fucking Dormies out of business before their numbers get too big," said Krum, his hands trembling.

"Let's not panic," said Remington, caressing the snifter. "Cal's

301

got the largest Greek system in the country. No university can match our total of 52 fraternities and 28 sororities."

"Time is on our side," the Graduate Adviser continued. "Once the Dormie leaders graduate, things will return to normal. Casey Lee and Royal English are minor blips in the big picture. It's a fluke that Casey Lee is even a student."

Remington had saved this ironic comment as a retort. "Remember, Dirk, if your family hadn't hired Casey's great-grandfather as a houseboy eighty-years ago, do you think he would have ever been inspired to attend Cal?"

Serves the Krums right, Remington thought. *See what happens when you take foreigners into your house? Soon they start believing they're as good as you.*

He continued, "Dirk, two years from now, they'll be history; and no one will take their places. Let's just mark time and ignore them." Remington took a deep sip from the snifter.

"Turn our cheeks for two years!' Krum shouted. "The wait will drive me insane! Those Dormies are like a disease we've got to cut out before it spreads. Look at the kinds of Dormie assholes who are thumbing their noses at us: that Chink, that half-breed hunchback; that flaming faggot, and all those weenie wimp Engineers wearing slide rules on their belts like sissies."

Krum crushed a beer can and slammed it into the burning fireplace. "They've got to be stopped NOW!"

"Yeah," said Fist, salivating at the thought of violence. "Let's kick some Dormie butt."

"Dirk, don't let the Dormies become martyrs," sighed Remington.

"Benign neglect is the best policy. Cal is big enough for separatism. Remember what happened when our fathers made the Peace Pact with the Jewish fraternities in the Thirties. Some thought that was the end of the Greek system, but look what happened. We ignore them, and they don't cause us any trouble. Those Heebs know better than to fool with our Christian sorority girls." The Graduate Adviser paused to allow Dirk time to think.

"But we can shut them down," said Krum. "I talked to the Director of Research for Dad's oil company, and he can get us a colorless, tasteless chemical that will cause vomiting and diarrhea. If we slip it into their dorm food, there will be mass food poisoning. Chancellor Haynes will have to shut Dooch down for the rest of the semester, send the Dormies to live in the streets until the cause is found. Their lives would be in total chaos."

"I get it," said Fist with an extended burp. "We'll slip something into dorm food and make those assholes sicker than dogs!"

"Dirk," said Remington. "I hate to be tactless, but let's be honest. The only reason you're so mad is this Casey Lee-Kate Howell flirtation."

Remington poured himself another three fingers of Courvoisier. "But you're being a bit irrational. Let's think about this logically."

"The main reason girls attend Cal is to find a suitable husband. Do you think for a minute that any Dormie can really compete with a fraternity man for status and security? True, some sorority whores get a cheap thrill slumming with low lives. But when push comes to shove and they need their MRS degree, they'll come crawling back to fraternity men like they have for generations."

"This deviant behavior by Kate Howell really doesn't amount to a hill of beans. But the more you react, the more time she'll spend with Casey Lee. Ignore her. By the time she's a senior, she'll be back, begging you to take her back."

The Kingston Trio continued to sing another round of "Scotch and Soda."

There's some logic to what Chauncey was saying, Krum thought. *Two years, just two short years, for Kate to understand that Destiny meant her for me.*

"What if those Administration liberals start letting in more minorities, more queers, more . . ." Krum's voice trailed off.

"You forget an important reality of campus life," said Remington. "Greeks control 90% of the campus housing. There's no way the Administration is going to open the flood gates to the poor and middle class if there's no housing for them. Dooch has 100 rooms. Even if the Administration doubles the Dormies per room, that's still only 200 weenie-wimps."

"If the Inter Fraternity Council implements a rule that no new pledge will be accepted if he has ever lived in Dooch, think what that will do to those who wait until their second year to go through fraternity rush. This would force them to rush as a freshman or forever lose their opportunity to be a fraternity man."

"In the meanwhile," Remington smiled, "you can clip your horns with the girls at the Yearning Arms." He stood and drained the last of the brandy. "Excuse me, guys. I have to call my honey in Honolulu." He turned off the stereo as the Kingston Trio sang the last verse to *Scotch and Soda*.

"Jeez, that Chauncey's gets more nookie than Carter's got pills,"said Chip.

Yes Kate, thought Krum, the sneer returning to his handsome face. *Time is on my side. Casey Lee may have had the upper hand on Halloween, but as sure as the Greek system will rule the Cal campus, you'll be mine!*

* * *

High on the eastern foothill above campus, Anna Cappuccino and Ari Scott snuggled arm-in-arm on the edge of the Big C, the 30 by 60-foot concrete letter, encrusted with thousands of layers of paint. For years bands of marauding artists from rival schools -usually Stanford-painted the Big C an offending red. After each raid, Cal students, led by Oski, immediately rushed up the hillside to paint over the crimson insult.

C, thought Ari. *C for Cal. C for Cappuccino.*

Before them the dappled light of San Francisco Bay gleamed in the fall sunset. The three bridges-Bay, Golden Gate, and Richmond-San Rafael-sparkled like strands of holiday lights. Silhouettes of the low rise buildings of the City's financial district cast shadows over the small crowded hills.

"This must be the most beautiful view in the world, Papa."

"Your mother said those same words to me when we looked out over the rooftops of Florence during our *toure* di . . ."Ari's voice trailed off as the old memory came flooding back. "I asked her to marry me there."

"Mama told me how romantic that moment was," Anna said, squeezing Ari's arm. "Whenever she visits Firenze, she walks from the Duomo, past Uffizi, over the Ponte Vecchio, through the Pitti Palace and the Boboli Gardens, up to the wall of Fort Belvedere There, she looks out across the Fiume Arno and remembers."

"Yes," said Ari, feeling a tear well up in his eye. 'We were so young, so foolish then."

"Papa, " said Anna, leaning her head on the shoulder of his tweed jacket. "I must tell you that Mama has always loved you and will love you for the rest of her life. Pablo Zarzana has been so wonderful to us, but he understands that you were the only true love of Mama's life. Nothing will ever change that."

Ari brushed away the trickle of tears streaming down his face. "And I will always love her," he whispered.

A small, radiant star emerged from behind the rising moon, and for a moment, Ari thought it was the Russian satellite, Sputnik. Then he remembered the celestial event of this day, the planet Venus orbiting close to the moon.

"Look at Venus, Anna! Like the planet, you appear but once in my life."

"But we will always have each other, Papa." Anna looked adoringly into Ari's eyes. "Thank you so much for our own *toure di amore* these last few weeks."

"When I have my own children, I will tell them about their handsome, loving American grandpapa. I will name my first son Aristotle, middle name Scott," she said with a wink. "Of course, you will come to Italy to visit your grandchildren, eh?"

Nodding, Ari said, "Thank you, Anna. Thank you for teaching me the Higher Truth."

They held each other in silence, as the burnished sun disappeared into the Pacific beyond the Golden Gate.

* * *

The moon slowly dissolved into the pink translucence of the emerging dawn. Sipping the last of a perfect martini, shaken not stirred, Sam Paean surveyed the familiar sweep of San Francisco Bay from his Russian Hill flat. A nip in the air hinted of winter several weeks away, but for now, free from the cool, grey fog of summer, the magic glow of fall still embraced his beloved Baghdad by the Bay.

He had picked up an early edition of the <u>Sentinel</u> after closing the El Matador, celebrating the exclusive interview he had wangled from Professor Aristotle Scott and his gorgeous daughter, Anna Cappuccino. One week after the Gee Dee's Presents Ball, his trusty assistant, E Lyn Chamberlin, had arranged a journalistic coup.

305

Whadda gal, he thought. Ace had been persistent, cajoling the Cal professor and his now celebrity daughter into granting Paean a frank interview about Scott's youthful romance with Sofia Cappuccino and his recent reunion with Anna.

WARTIME LOVE LOST AND FOUND

Paean's front page coverage had proclaimed.

Over at the rival newspaper, the San Francisco Gazette, the Old Man, William Randolph Chandler, would be furious about the embarrassment to his family and, more important, to this political campaign. Paean fully expected some future act of revenge, as the Old Man would never forgive nor forget this scandalous affront to the Chandler name.

Paean reviewed his interview with Ari and Anna in his mind.

He had asked Ari pointedly,

What impact will this revelation have on your father-in-law, William Randolph Chandler's gubernatorial race?

The love of father and daughter is more important than a family's political gain, said Ari. *This is a Higher Truth to which I am committed.*

Gutsy, Paean had thought. *Scott gave up a cushy lifestyle with his socialite wife to be reunited with his long lost daughter. This act of familial love bodes well for the approaching Sixties.*

What has most impressed you about America? Paean had asked of the voluptuous, dark haired young woman.

Without hesitation, Anna Cappuccino had responded in a low, silky accented voice.

I cannot speak about the entire United States, for my experience is limited to the University of California. But, if Cal is a microcosm of society, then what a wonderful country America must be.

At Cal, there is far more freedom, tolerance, and diversity than I have witnessed anywhere in Europe.

In their own homelands, some of the foreign students living at I-House have seen first-hand the excesses of government and the suppression of dissent. It is sad most Americans do not appreciate what precious rights they enjoy in their freedoms of speech and association.

Hatred and intolerance exist in America, as they do everywhere else in the world. But I do not know of any country, through its laws and public goodwill, that tries harder to

306

minimize the effects of prejudice on its minorities.

America is far from perfect, but, from what I have seen it offers, through educational experiences at its universities, great opportunities for the best and brightest students to develop solutions for lasting peace and prosperity.

I am proud to be an Italian, but I am also pleased that Papa is an American, a Californian, raised in a society where debates are decided by elections, not guns.

This is what I shall always remember about Cal and America.

So long as people of conscience and goodwill care enough to be informed and involved with the running of their government, freedom will always flourish in this great land of America. And so long as great educational institutions, like the University of California, vigilantly dedicate themselves to the public good through excellence and diversity, new generations of student-citizens of the world will carry the torch of Democracy.

Anna's eloquence had brought a lump to his throat. *What a class act*, Paean thought, echoing her remarks on his loyal Royal typewriter.

In her brief time as a Cal graduate student, Anna had already gleaned one of the immutable truths about American society. Paean envisioned a future in which Anna Cappuccino, empowered with the benefits of her Cal education, might become a future leader of Italy!

The rays of the morning sun now slanted over the East Bay foothills, washing brightly over the Big C, illuminating the alabaster of the Campanile. Paean gazed at the gleaming white bell tower, transfixed by the timeliness of Cal's symbol.

In his mind, he heard the familiar tune of the carillons, the daily tribute to California, a golden state of mind.

Paean sang out loud, the closing lyrics of the alma mater of his spiritual, once-and-future university:

> *. . . Stand for right,*
> *Let there be light,*
>
> *California,*
> *Here's to thee!"*

"GO BEARS!" Paean shouted.

51

EPILOGUE

The P U-Dormie rivalry raged for two more years until Dirk Krum, Casey Lee, and Kate Howell graduated with the Cal Class of 1961. The struggle between the two living groups became a footnote to the dramatic changes in the campus demographics. In the mid-1960's, the California legislature approved millions of dollars for the construction of new student housing to accommodate the anticipated influx of Baby Boomers. A dozen high-rise dorms sprouted up on the Cal campus, all identical in design to the prototype, Dooch Hall.

By 1980, the ratio of men to women equalized, forcing the campus administration to convert all the Cal dorms which had been previously segregated by gender, into coeducational living groups with communal bathrooms.

By the year 2000, Dirk Krum's worst fears had been realized, as the influx of middle-class Baby Boomers reached epic proportions. The student population that, in 1959, was 93% White and 7% Other; by the new millennium, had been transformed to 38% Asian, 35% White, 10% African-American, 5% Hispanic, and 12% "None of Your Business."

Spurred by Civil Rights legislation and by the need for survival from dwindling membership, the Greek system at Cal abandoned its policy and practice of discrimination based on race or religion.

Portions of the campus forest were bulldozed in the 1960's

and 1970's making way for the construction of sterile, blocky edifices to accommodate the burgeoning student enrollment. A charmless, modern monolith now towers over the Mining Circle where the Big C Sirkus competition once raged. A library annex replaced the wooden T-Buildings after 50 years of use as "temporary" offices.

Yet, Cal's bucolic charm and traditions have, for the most part, endured the onslaught of modern progress.

Strawberry Creek continues to swirl and gurgle beneath Memorial Stadium, through Faculty Glade, and past the eucalyptus grove. Many descendants of Brutus, the chirpy squirrel, still inhabit the family estate in the Old Buckeye tree next to Stephens Union.

Old South Hall was spared from the wrecking ball; and with its bulky neighbors, Wheeler Hall and Dwinelle Hall, remain the central axis of the Cal campus. Nearby Sather Gate now bares the four nude panels that Mary Sather had removed as an affront to public morals.

The stately, clubby comfort of the Morrison Library reading room remains an island of quiet civility, and the Hearst Mining Building remains a tribute to the timeless beauty of Beaux Arts architecture.

Greek and non-Greek students now gather at the concrete-ringed trees of Dwinelle Plaza, enjoying the daily concerts of the Campanile's carillons.

International House continues its tradition of nurturing future world leaders, infusing foreign students with the spirit of the Cal experience. Like Anna Cappuccino, visiting students have met and mingled at I-House, sharing the youthful vision of goodwill and optimism for a lasting world peace.

The Reserve Officers Training Corps, aka ROT-C, was eliminated as a mandatory class for freshmen and sophomore males because of student demonstrations against the Vietnam War that swept through America's college campuses in the late Sixties. Now voluntary, ROT-C has a co-ed membership for its future military officers.

Telegraph Avenue continues to be the central nervous system of human activity near campus. Telly abounds with Japanese and German tourists, taking photos of bearded and silver-haired, aging street vendors peddling beads and trinkets left over from their psychedelic days of the late Sixties when these same merchants were protesting against America's materialistic, capitalistic society. Many of today's Telly entrepreneurs are college dropouts from USC and Stanford.

On the wall of a small smoke shop, at the corner of Bancroft and Telly, facing campus, a small weather beaten plaque commemorates the half million Eskimo Pie ice creams Crunchy Munchy sold from1946 until his death in 1980.

The insanity and hysteria of mass Reg Lines have been replaced by electronic enrollment by phone and computer. However, during final exams, frantic, forlorn cries for

P-E-D-R-O! P-E-D-R-O!

echo up and down Berkeley's rugged, eastern foothills.

Oski, the Cal Bear mascot, still prowls mischievously about campus, inhaling beer through plastic tubing inserted in his eye hole. The synchronized Cal band-now 50% female- marches to the delight of generations of long suffering Cal football fans who bear witness to the Cal tradition of gridiron futility.

Frozen Gremlins were banned from sale at Cal football games after an incident of mass ptomaine poisoning overtaxed the campus sewer system, the day after the all-men's rooting section was formally integrated by angry females demanding equal seating along the Bear fifty-yard line.

On Tightwad Hill, a new generation of young Cal freeloaders wear T-shirts bearing the genealogical message:

I was conceived on Tightwad Hill
during a boring Cal football game.

The Campanile serenades the campus daily with its 61 carillons, 49 acquired during the long tenure of chime mistress, Betty Burdick. At Ms. Burdick's memorial service, her ashes were scattered from the belfry, as her favorite protégé, Hunch Hitowski, swung among the bells, chiming "Nearer My God to Thee."

For Jonathan Aldon and his extended clan, life made a serendipitous circle.

Under the tutelage of Michael Hu, the Living Buddha, Jonathan survived his freshman year. Graduating with the Class of '63, he joined JFK's Peace Corps. On some enchanted evening in the Fiji Islands, he fell in love with Peng Kai "Pinky" Hwang, a grad student at the University of the South Pacific. The two were married in Hong Kong on the Michael Hu family estate, high on the wind-swept slopes of Victoria Peak. Ziggy, on leave from Viet Nam, served as best man; and Mike and Pearl were the only Aldons who attended the nuptials.

After the Peace Corps, Jonathan remained in Asia for 20 years as a U.S. State Department farming advisor. A daughter, Kelly Ming Aldon, was born in Singapore and educated in American schools, including Cal. The highlight of Jonathan's Far Eastern career was appearing, with Pinky and a group of Chinese hog farmers, on the cover of National Geographic.

When Murle Aldon died of cancer in 1975, Mike and Pearl Aldon and their son Francisco (Frisco) moved from Minneapolis to manage Aldon Farms. Gertrude Aldon dedicated the rest of her widowed life to martyrdom. In 1980, Gertrude suffered a fatal heart attack after seeing Jonathon and Pinky on the cover of National Geographic. She was laid to rest beside Murle in the ornate Aldon mausoleum at the *God Be With You Sanctuary*, once an empty field where Buddy Holly's plane crashed in February 1959.

In 1988, Mike and Pearl Aldon retired from hog farming to spend more time with their son Frisco, now a Minneapolis judge, and their grandchildren. On Mike's urging, Jonathan returned to Clear Lake for the first time in 28 years. He and Pinky moved into the family Tudor along the shores of the small, whale-shaped lake and assumed the management of Aldon Farms.

After a 30 year hiatus, The Amazin' Double A's resumed their musical career on Oldies Night at Buddy's Place (formerly the Blue Horizon Inn) owned by Ziggy and his wife, Zelda. The middle-aged duo's signature song remains Buddy Holly's "That'll Be the Day."

Jonathan's Oakland cousins, the Jones family, answered Destiny's call.

Reverend Ike and Doris retired from their radio ministry after the City of Oakland claimed their home on Heavenly Court, through eminent domain, to construct a coliseum for the new professional football team, the Oakland Raiders.

After starring in football at Cal, AJ graduated with a degree in political science and was elected to consecutive terms in the

California state legislature. In 1968, RJ died in a shootout between the Black Panthers and the Oakland police. MJ pursued a music career, producing 12 Grammy award winning albums under the *Blackouts* label.

From his *Louie, Louie* royalties, Alfonso (Big) Berry acquired controlling interest of a corporation developing cemeteries in upscale communities. One of the company's most profitable units is the *God Be With You Sanctuary* near Clear Lake, Iowa.

The controversy over HUAC and loyalty oaths foreshadowed the unrest that would sweep the Cal campus in the turbulent decades to follow: the Free Speech Movement, anti-Vietnam War sit-ins, People's Park riots, and pro-affirmative action demonstrations.

In the aftermath of HUAC, several Cal professors served the government. Werner Von Seller was Chairman of the Atomic Energy Commission under Lyndon B. Johnson. In 1969, the Prussian Penguin died in a freak accident when he waddled, stumbled, and fell into Cal's atom smasher. His monocle and silver cigarette holder are on display at the Visitor's Center of the Cyclotron.

Governor Ronald Reagan appointed Garrick Nelquist California State Boxing Commissioner. Later, Nelquist returned to Cal before retiring to a small Cotswold cottage near London.

Jacob Aural declined a cabinet position with President John F. Kennedy and continued to teach at Cal. Both he and his loyal dog Sandy passed away in 1985. The two are buried side-by-side on the hillside above the Big C. The inscription on their gravestone reads:

Excellence, Tradition, and Diversity

History has not been kind to political candidates of the late Fifties and early Sixties.

After Congress dismantled HUAC, Clayborn Muck remained active in national politics for three decades. Between 1964 and 1996, Muck was the presidential candidate of the Christian Anti-Communist Party, finishing a dismal last in each of his nine runs for the White House, breaking Harold Stassen's record for futility.

William Randolph Chandler took an opposite tack. After

losing his gubernatorial bid, the embittered Old Man became a recluse, rarely leaving the family compound, *Xanadu*, before his death in 1981.

Cee Cee Chandler Scott, was appointed Society Editor of the San Francisco Gazette. Later, Cee Cee became a born-again Christian and married the multimillionaire, television evangelist, Jimmy Faretheewell.

Muck's henchman, Seymour Graft, reinvented himself and started a new career in show business as Willie D. Wadd, producer of several infamous porno movies. Since 1980, Wadd has lived as a retiree and registered sex offender in the Mojave Desert community of Blythe.

For three decades, San Francisco wrestled with its civic schizophrenia. Proud of the Manhattanization of its skyline, Ess Eff remained narcissistically deluded in its self-image as romantic Bagdad by the Bay, a fiction inhabited by local characters whose antics were chronicled by Sam's *Paean to the City*.

In retirement, the City's most famous transvestite, Paula DuBois, entertained at senior citizen communities. Graduating from night school, Rod Organ founded the Super Van Company, the nation's largest airport-to-city shuttle service.

In a moment of illogical weakness, Sam and E Lyn Chamberlin married in 1960 and divorced a year later, both realizing that Paean's true wife and mistress was The Column.

Sam continued to write *Paean to The City* until his death in 1998. At his memorial service, the University of California awarded Paean a posthumous honorary degree in Journalism. E Lyn Chamberlin Paean continued as Sam's trusty assistant for five years after their divorce. In 1968, she married a wealthy widower who became a popular Mayor of the City for most of the Decade of the Seventies. Because of her third husband's long term of office, E Lyn is known as "Mrs. San Francisco."

The early Sixties saw the end of the era when Greek affiliation was a guarantee of success and happiness, as Cal was no longer the private preserve of wealthy, white males.

T.A. Brewster, Casey's competitor in Frisbee, became a popular folk singer, then a popular movie actor, under the stage name of Geoff Geoffstopherson.

Monty Maitland, the penny pitching hustler, played minor league baseball before turning to sports officiating. He is

Executive Director of the Major League Umpires Association.

Among the P U's, only Chip Fist attained any sense of normalcy. Fist owns The Bitchin' Beer Co., California's largest distributor of Kerrs beer.

Chauncey Remington passed the Bar and, after practicing law in San Francisco, was appointed Dean of the Stanford University Law School. He died at age 35 from complications of AIDS.

After leading the Bears to an upset victory over Ohio State in the Rose Bowl - the last time Cal went to Pasadena - Joe L. Capp became Cal's football coach, and later Athletic Director for 25 frustrating years.

Former student body president, Ralph Van de Kamp, made and lost several fortunes in junk bonds. In retirement, he participated in a landmark medical study for a revolutionary new drug to treat male erectile dysfunction.

The Gamma Delta sorority motto, *Remember Who You Are and What You Represent* took on new meanings for members of the House of Beauty.

Joan Dildeaux married a young Swedish doctor who pioneered a plastic surgery technique that transformed her into a stunning beauty. The former, homely legacy enjoyed a brief modeling career and today is business manager of her husband's medical facility, *The Beverly Hills Before and After Body Sculpturing Clinic.*

After five failed marriages, Mergetroid (Muffy) Peachwick returned to Cal and earned a PhD in Human Sexuality. Today, Muffy is a recognized sex therapist and hosts a nationally syndicated radio talk show, *Sex and Stuff With Dr. Muff.*

Gee Dee housemother, Miss Willa Haversham, retired and moved to the Peaceful Valley Old Folks home where she was the bridge partner of Crazy Martha Howell. When Crazy Martha passed away, Willa Haversham buried her friend with a box of Martha's favorite rum soaked cigars.

Dandy Cane flunked out of Cal in her sophomore year and joined her sister Candy as a flight attendant for CAT Airlines. Dandy married an older wealthy, SC alum, the president of a condoms company, and the couple settled in Newport Beach where they raised their10 children.

For many of the Dooch Dormies, their Cal education was the start of life long adventures.

Bernard (Butch) Tanenbloom married a Jewish American

Princess (a Five Star General) and enjoyed a successful career as a prosecuting District Attorney in Manhattan before running for public office. He is serving his third-term as Mayor of New York City.

Ruppert (Ruby) Lips founded the *San Francisco Gay Men's Opera Company* that has performed to enthusiastic audiences throughout the world. He and his partner of 30 years live in a renovated San Francisco mansion along embassy row, overlooking the Golden Gate Bridge.

After earning an MBA degree, Mortimer (Mo) McCart became a wealthy, professional sports agent. In 1990, Mo was elected Commissioner of the *National Football League.*

Marty Silverstein (Super Sleuth) served as Director of the Secret Service for three U.S. presidents. Retired, he resides in Palm Springs where he enjoys daily strolls along *El Paseo*, ogling and appreciating the parade of stylish, women shoppers.

Some Dormies followed their natural instincts.

The All Pro received a PhD in Speech and established the University of California, Department of Media Studies. Rooster Face is the International President of the Eddie Fisher Fan Club.

Homer (Waz) Wazlewski is New Jersey State Director of Traffic Safety and rides his '56 Vespa to work.

Michael Hu manages the many dot com ventures of his worldwide conglomerate, Living Buddha HK Ltd.

Cable television's most popular show, *Wide World of Wrestling,* is owned by Oliver (Ollie) Punch's HA! HA! HA! Productions.

Julio (Hunch) Hitowski became a millionaire from his invention, a musical dial tone for phones and settled in Malibu with his wife, Lynda Svelter, a former Miss California.

Royal French founded a private security service for celebrities and married the noted California, contemporary artist, Marilyn Anglais. The couple raised their children, Mitch, Charles, and Julie at *Pickfair*, the former Hollywood home of Douglas Fairbanks and Mary Pickford.

A few Dormie lives took curious turns.

After serving 12 years as an Air Force pilot, Gerald Farthing married a belly dancer. The couple own *Fart-ing Enterprises*, a distributor of tofu products.

Robert B. Jean, gave up a promising art career and returned to the family clothing business. The Lizard is Chairman of the

Board of *Le Bleu Jean Company*, world's largest manufacturer of denim clothes.

After retiring from a career as a Kennedy Space Center Engineer, Dick Phuncque opened a popular fast food chain in South Florida called *Wienies 'R Us.*

Tommy Tubbins dropped out of Cal in his junior year to study in Nepal and Kathmandu before settling in Marin County where he and his wife breed pet llamas.

True Love Ways had twists and turns.

Anna Cappuccino married a Cal classmate and returned to Italy to teach at Milan University and raise her two children. After the assassination of Pablo Zarzana, Anna completed her step- father's term of office and continued a brilliant political career, culminating in her election in 1998 as the first female Prime Minister of Italy.

Ari Scott taught Medieval Philosophy and coached the Bear track team until 1974 when he retired to marry Anna's mother, Sophia Cappuccino, the widow of Pablo Zarzana. Now in their eighties, Ari and Sophia share their golden years along the shores of Lake Como in northern Italy, enjoying visits from their Italian and American grandchildren.

Dirk Krum III was admitted to the Napa Valley Institution for the Incurably Insane in 1965 after Kate Howell spurned his repeated marriage proposals. Krum spends his days watching a movie video of Grace Kelly singing "True Love," in *High Society.*

Casey Lee became a professional song writer. His musical *Dormie* displaced *Grease* as the longest running show on Broadway. He is married to the country western singer, Em Hanna. The couple live, with their adopted daughter, Katie, on Long Island, along the Atlantic Ocean.

Kate Howell never married.

During the '67 Summer of Love, the Golden Goddess had a brief romance with the son of an oil sheik. The affair produced twin boys who were kidnaped by their father and spirited to the Middle East. A year later, the children were rescued in a daring paramilitary operation by a squad of former Green Berets led by Royal French. With her inheritance from Crazy Martha's estate, Kate Howell moved to Big Sur where she raised her twins, Casey and Lee.

Silver haired, but still stunning, Kate Howell lives alone in a glass aerie on a rocky outcrop high above the pounding surf of the Pacific Ocean. Occasionally, during the burnished glow of sunset, the former Golden Goddess sips a *Jack Daniels* and meanders through the recesses of her memory, calling up the echo of that soothing voice, envisioning the indelible image of those exotic eyes, recalling her halcyon days as a member of the House of Beauty . . . and Cal.

* * *

At the Cleveland, Ohio Rock and Roll Museum, in a darkened corner of a floor dedicated to the legendary pioneers of rock and roll, a single beam of ethereal light illuminates a glass case sitting on a black marble pedestal. Tourists studying the exhibit, wear headphones attached to tour cassettes playing a soundtrack of "That'll Be The Day," "True Love Ways," "Maybe Baby," "Peggy Sue," "Every Day," and "Words of Love."
Nearby, a small, Sterling silver plaque reads:

Buddy Holly

Clear Lake, Iowa - February 3, 1959

Donated by Jonathan Aldon

Within the case, a pair of black hornrimmed glasses rest on a scarlet cushion turning slowly on a golden lazy susan.
As the hornrims rotate, visitors scrutinize the scuff marks on the frames, squint at the minute bubbling of the skull temples, and stare at the clear, unblemished lenses.
Unnoticed is a single thread that begins as a knot at the bridge, follows a crease of the cushion, then curls out of sight beneath. Unseen at end of the tether is the remnant of an ancient ice cream stick.
On the frayed shard of wood, in a faint, childlike scrawl, are penciled the words,

. . . Not Fade Away - Crunchy Munchy . . .

BIBLIOGRAPHY

Bender, Richard. *Building On The Past*: California Monthly, December 1980.

Campus Planning Study Group. *Campus Historic Resources Survey*: University of California 1978.

Charbonneau, Bob, Stephanie Kaza, and Vincent Rush. *Strawberry Creek-A Walking Tour of Campus Natural History*:University of California, June 1990.

Claremont Resort. *Elegant Lady With A Past-The Claremont Resort, Spa and Tennis Club.*

Delehanty, Randolph. *The Ultimate Guide-SF* Chronicle Books 1989.

Desruisseaux, Paul. *The Return Of The Repressed*: California Monthly, February 1979.

Dorson, Richard M. *American Folklore* 1959.

Dovey, Kim. *A Self-Guided Tour of the Berkeley Campus*: University of California 1987.

Fong-Torres, Ben.*Louie On Parade*:SF Chronicle, May20,1988

Garchick, Leah. *For Whom The Bells Toll? A Carillon Call Around The World*: SF Examiner August 1978

Hardy, M.J. *The Lockheed Constellation*: Arco Publishing Co.

Kantor, James. (Editor) *Centennial Record of the University of California*: University of California 1974.

Kidder, Lynn. *60 Years At International House*: University of California Public Information Office, March 1991.

Minneapolis-St. Paul International Airport: *Wold-Chamberlain Field History* 1987.

Partridge, Loren W. *John Galen Howard & The Berkeley Campus: Beaux-Arts Architecture In The "Athens Of The West"*: University of California.

Peri, Camille. *Ivory Tower*, SF Examiner, March 2, 1986.

Pfaff, Timothy. *Leaves Of Class*: California Monthly, May1982.

Rosenblatt, Roger. *Waiting For Mr. Shuttlecock*: *Time* February 15, 1982.

Williams, Monte, *Flight Attendants-The Good Old Days*: NY Daily News, August 12,1990.